# Becoming an Archaeologist

*Becoming an Archaeologist: A Guide to Professional Pathways* is an engaging handbook on career paths in archaeology. It outlines the process of getting a job in archaeology, including various career options, the training required, and how to get positions in the academic, commercial, government, and charity sectors. This new edition has been substantially revised and updated. The coverage has been expanded to include many more examples of archaeological lives and livelihoods from dozens of countries around the world. It also has more interviews, with in-depth analyses of the career paths of over twenty different archaeologists working around the world. Data on the demographics of archaeologists has also been updated, as have sections on access to and inclusion in archaeology. The volume also includes revised and updated appendices and a new bibliography. Written in an accessible style, the book is essential reading for anyone interested in a career in archaeology in the twenty-first century.

Joe Flatman is an Environmental Consultancy Manager at The National Trust.

# Becoming an Archaeologist

## A Guide to Professional Pathways

### Second Edition

Joe Flatman

CAMBRIDGE
UNIVERSITY PRESS

# CAMBRIDGE
## UNIVERSITY PRESS

University Printing House, Cambridge CB2 8BS, United Kingdom

One Liberty Plaza, 20th Floor, New York, NY 10006, USA

477 Williamstown Road, Port Melbourne, VIC 3207, Australia

314–321, 3rd Floor, Plot 3, Splendor Forum, Jasola District Centre, New Delhi – 110025, India

103 Penang Road, #05–06/07, Visioncrest Commercial, Singapore 238467

Cambridge University Press is part of the University of Cambridge.

It furthers the University's mission by disseminating knowledge in the pursuit of
education, learning, and research at the highest international levels of excellence.

www.cambridge.org
Information on this title: www.cambridge.org/9781108495608
DOI: 10.1017/9781108850490

First published 2022

*A catalogue record for this publication is available from the British Library.*

*Library of Congress Cataloging-in-Publication Data*
NAMES: Flatman, Joe, author.
TITLE: Becoming an archaeologist : a guide to professional pathways / Joe Flatman,
The National Trust, UK.
DESCRIPTION: Second edition. | Cambridge, United Kingdom ; New York, NY : Cambridge
University Press, 2022. | Includes bibliographical references and index.
IDENTIFIERS: LCCN 2022025420 (print) | LCCN 2022025421 (ebook) | ISBN 9781108495608
(hardback) | ISBN 9781108797092 (paperback) | ISBN 9781108850490 (epub)
SUBJECTS: LCSH: Archaeology–Vocational guidance. | BISAC: SOCIAL SCIENCE /
Archaeology
CLASSIFICATION: LCC CC107 .F53 2022 (print) | LCC CC107 (ebook) | DDC 930.1023–dc23/eng/
20220707
LC record available at https://lccn.loc.gov/2022025420
LC ebook record available at https://lccn.loc.gov/2022025421

ISBN 978-1-108-49560-8 Hardback
ISBN 978-1-108-79709-2 Paperback

*To my parents, Frances and Martin Flatman*
*With my love and thanks for providing a unique grounding in*
*the pleasures and perils of professional life*
*"Not all Greeks were Spartans"*

# Contents

# Contents

# Figures and Tables

## Figures

## Tables

# Preface and Acknowledgements
## for the First Edition

I wrote this book primarily to help prospective archaeologists (in particular, archaeology students) better plan their futures. However, this book is also borne of my frustration at the widespread misunderstanding of the practice of archaeology and lifestyle of archaeologists in the modern world. As a consequence, although I have tried to paint a balanced portrait of archaeology throughout the book, this is, inevitably and unashamedly, partly a personal perspective – one to which some readers may take exception. I make no apologies for that. One thing that I would emphasize in particular, however, is that although this book is about 'professional' archaeology, it is absolutely not a call for a solely paid archaeological sector in which all voluntary/amateur/avocational/community/independent involvement has been driven out of existence. As a long-standing member of the United Kingdom's Council for British Archaeology (dating back to my teenage membership in the Young Archaeologists Club), and later and very proudly serving on that organization's board of trustees, I would emphasize my belief in the key place of the independent individual or group in archaeology, and that archaeology and wider society are big enough places to see both paid and unpaid archaeologists working to the highest professional standards. I do not believe that these two ways of doing archaeology are mutually exclusive, as some commentators suggest. Nor do I believe that the improved living and working standards so many archaeologists urgently deserve can only and inevitably come through the loss of the volunteer. As I highlight repeatedly throughout this book, I sincerely believe that the single best thing that anyone can do to get involved in archaeology is to join their local archaeological or historical society.

In terms of acknowledgements, first and foremost I am extremely grateful to Beatrice Rehl at Cambridge University Press for seeing the potential of a book on this subject, commissioning it, and then editing it. The anonymous peer reviewers of this book's proposal and draft also made many exceptionally useful comments, for which they should be thanked.

Dozens of friends and colleagues around the world have – often unknowingly – contributed to this book through conversations, conference papers, emails, websites, and blogs. Many students whom I have taught in the United Kingdom and Australia also made passing comments that became the seeds of issues explored here. Consequently, a full list of contributors is impossible to provide – too many issues that eventually made it into this book began life as random comments and fleeting moments. To anyone who reads this book and thinks that they may have been the first to mention an issue or idea to me, my apologies for not formally acknowledging you here: next time we meet, remind me of my failure and I shall attempt to make amends. In particular, however, I wish to thank my former colleagues at Surrey County Council and University College London, especially Emily Brants, Giles Carey, Phil Cooper, Martin Higgins, Tony Howe, Gary Jackson, Sophie Unger, and David Williams at the former; and Cyprian Broodbank, Ian Carroll, Lisa Daniel, Charlotte Frearson, Andy Gardner, Kris Lockyear, Roger Matthews, Judy Medrington, Gustav Milne, Norah Moloney, Gabriel Moshenska, Kirsty Norman, Darryl Palmer, Dominic Perring, Matthew Pope, Andrew Reynolds, Bill Sillar, Kathryn Tubb, Sjoerd van der Linde, Tim Williams, and Sarah Wolferstan at the latter. There is simply no way that I could have written this book without the advice of such dedicated colleagues at these organizations.

Special thanks and acknowledgements should also be made in relation to the photos reproduced, including Jeremy Ashbee, Kath Buxton, Ian Carroll, Leanne Chorekdjian, Nathalie Cohen, English Heritage, Brendan Foley, Charlotte Frearson, Andrew Gardner, Elizabeth Graham, Tony Howe, David Jeffreys, Dominic Perring, Brett Seymour, Dean Sully, Chris Waite, and Lynley Wallis. In addition, thanks specifically to Archaeology South East, Nick Blows, Andres Diaz, Alice Gomer, Vanessa Saiz Gomez, Louise Holt, Amy Lindsay, the Marco Gonzalez Project, Danny Markey, the US National Park Service, the Petrie Museum, the Portable Antiquities Scheme, Stephen Quirk, Kyle Rice, Matt Russell, Elizabeth Saunders, Jane Siddell, Rachel Sparkes, the Thames Discovery Programme, UCL Institute of Archaeology, Jenny Walsh, Rachael Warren, and Andrew Wright.

An array of other individuals who have made a marked or formal contribution to this book must also then be thanked, including Jon Adams, Kenny Aitchison, Mark Beattie-Edwards, Paul Belford, Marc-André Bernier, Heather Burke, Dan Carsten, Martin Carver, Nathalie Cohen, Dave Conlin, Kara Cooney, Geoffrey Craig, Bethan Crockett, Steve Cross, Ian Cundy, Dominique de Moulins, Sarah Dhanjal, Amanda Evans, Robert Epstein, Paul Everill, Frances and Martin Flatman, Zoe Flatman, Hannah Fluck, Brendan Foley, David Gaimster, Joanne Gillis, Mark Gillis, Alice Gorman, Erica Gittins, Lizzie Glitheroe-West, David Graham, Paul Graves-Brown, Lisa Gray, Lalage Grundy, Abby Guinness, Jenny Haimes, Mary Harvey, Jon Henderson, Don Henson, Nigel Hetherington, Mike Heyworth, Carly Hilts, David Hinton, Peter Hinton, Fred Hocker, Tim Howard, Tom Irvin, Hilary Jackson, Peta Knott, Rebecca Lambert, Kyra Larkin, Chris Loveluck, Colin Martin, Paula Martin, Miriam Miller, Chris 'Bazooka' Morris, Tom Munnery, Ali Naftalin, Courtney Nimura, Matt O'Neill, Aidan O'Sullivan, Mike Page, Richard Perry, Cass Philippou, Julian Pooley, Rob Poulton, Patricia Reynolds, Nathan Richards, Isabel Rivera-Collazo, Marcy Rockman, Blake Sawicky, Claire Seaward, Barney Sloane, Amanda Smith, Claire Smith, Mark Staniforth, Lynley Wallis, Barbara Walthall, Gareth Watkins, Rebecca Weiss, Howard Williams, Michael Williams, Deborah Wenger, Elliot Wragg, and Jennifer Young.

# Preface to the Second Edition

I wrote the first edition of this book during the spring of 2010. At that time, I was an archaeologist working jointly in local government and as an academic in a university. Fast-forward ten years, and I am no longer formally employed as an archaeologist (I now lead an interdisciplinary environmental consultancy team within The National Trust), and I am working on the revised edition of this book in 2020 and 2021 during a global pandemic that has impacted upon everyone's lives and which none of us was prepared for. My circumstances may have evolved, but my enthusiasm for archaeology remains undimmed. In the last ten years, everything and yet nothing seems to have changed. To focus on the positives first: archaeology is still archaeology. It is even more relevant in our contemporary world than it was a decade ago. Archaeologists work on ever more sites across and even in orbit around the globe; they have embraced the last decade's worth of technologies; and they have reached out in time and space. Thanks to archaeologists, we know more about the human past, and more about our potential futures, than we did before. And crucially, archaeology in the past decade has become much more accessible. More people, from a greater diversity of backgrounds, are involved in archaeology, and it is easier than ever to become involved in the discipline. In other aspects, though, the field of archaeology, like our wider society, is a more fearful and fractured place than it was a decade ago. In terms of geopolitics and climate alone, archaeologists and archaeological sites alike have witnessed some horrifying changes. We have lost wonderful people and extraordinary places that can never be restored due to war and terrorism, flood and famine, melting ice and rising seas. Archaeology is not immune to wider social changes, either, and these changes bring their own challenges. The #MeToo movement has rightly impacted upon archaeology, highlighting historical and modern-day abuse and abusers alike in our community who have destroyed people's lives through their actions. The #BlackLivesMatter movement has similarly focused attention upon the horrors of many nations' colonial pasts and the challenges of the post-colonial present of our societies, in which archaeology has long been complicit and must play a role of ongoing cultural restitution. Our sector has had to face the grim reality that its veneer of friendly accessibility has in the past, and continues today, to hide in plain sight the abusers of many kinds who walk among us. Great challenges lie ahead if we are truly to make archaeology the safe, accessible, and diverse community that it can and ought to be.

## Preface to the Second Edition

This revised edition of *Becoming an Archaeologist* includes two major sets of changes. The first of these is a comprehensive updating of facts and figures, names and places, references and links – anything that has changed in the past decade that needed to be corrected to make this book as useful as possible, along with the removal of errors in the original text that slipped past the author. The second of these changes is more fundamental. The first edition of this book focused on those parts of the world where I had the most direct experience of working in – the United Kingdom, the United States, and Australia. In this revised edition, I have sought to include a much greater diversity of voices and experience from around the world. There are new and expanded interviews with practitioners from a broader range of backgrounds and locations, as well as new information about the realities of working in a more diverse array of locations and roles. The intention is that these additions better reflect the global community of archaeology, its places, and peoples. Archaeology belongs to us all, and anyone who wants to be involved in it ought to be able to – it is a fundamental birth right of humanity.

# Acknowledgements for the Second Edition

I offer particular thanks here to the interviewees who appear in this book, both old and new, and to those friends and colleagues who helped me identify these individuals, including Carlos Ausejo, Anna Brace, Stefano Campana, Madhumathy Chandrasekaran, Ethan Cochrane, Dave Conlin, Kate Dommett, Paul Everill, Niall Finneran, Hannah Fluck, Charlotte Frearson, Andy Gardner, Pablo Garrido González, Hsiao Mei Goh, Paul Graves-Brown, Brenna Hassett, Jorge Herrera, Nigel Hetherington, Tom Irvin, Gai Jorayev, Tiva Montalbano, Rui Pang, Shanti Pappu, Marcy Rockman, Isabel Rivera-Collazo, Randy Sasaki, Eleanor Scerri, Iain Shearer, Kristian Strutt, Suzie Thomas, Jess Thompson, Doortje Van Hove, Sofie Vanhoutte, Lynley Wallis, Sarah Ward, Tim Williams, Kevin Wooldridge, Rebecca Wragg-Sykes, and Haiming Yan.

Special thanks and acknowledgement are due to those who provided new photos for the second edition: Eduardo Castillo, Nathalie Cohen, *Current Archaeology*, Jorge Hererra, Carly Hilts, ICOMOS, Markus Milligan, Harvey Mills, The National Trust, Richard Osgood, Andrew Potts, Marcy Rockman, Suzie Thomas, and Jessica Thompson.

Thanks are also due here to my 'work family' since April 2019 at The National Trust, especially to my amazing, inspirational colleagues Kirstie Arnould, Jo Barnes, James Brown, Sarah Burr, Nathalie Cohen, Leo Constantinou, Tina Crawley, Sarah Davidson, Nick Dutton, Gordon Gardner, Mike Greenslade, Rob Haines, Rosie Harris, Natalia-Nana Lester-Bush, Katherine Mills, Jo Mirzoeff, Ruth Mitchell, Dan Morey, Maria Morris, Ian Prichard, Charles Pugh, George Roberts, Hugo van Maasakkers, Rebecca Wallis, and Paul White.

Between the writing and editing of the first and second editions of this book, two of the key mentors of my career in archaeology sadly passed away: Seán McGrail and Colin Platt. Without them I would never have had a career, and this book would never have been written. I honour and cherish their memories here. On a happier note, my daughter Zoe was born between the production of the first and second editions of this book. Her energy, enthusiasm, and thirst for new experiences and knowledge never ceases to inspire me.

## Acknowledgements for the Second Edition

The editorial and production teams at Cambridge University Press have been incredibly supportive and patient during the process of producing this book amid the midst of a pandemic. I am profoundly grateful to my editor Beatrice Rehl and to her assistant Edgar Mendez; to the book's project manager Indra Priyadarshini Siddharthan; and to the copy editor Stephanie Sakson. All errors, omissions and inaccuracies are and remain my fault alone.

# Introduction

One of the things that most archaeologists dislike about archaeology is how misunderstood it is. We meet people all the time who have never met an archaeologist, or who did not realize that one can have a career as an archaeologist, or who think that archaeologists spend their time digging up dinosaurs. Almost as bad, we meet people who have heard of archaeology and perhaps even have met real archaeologists, but who have a misconceived notion of the discipline and its practitioners.

The myth of archaeology runs from the adventure of tomb raiding at the one extreme to the tedium of unending work in dusty archives at the other. The reality is, of course, far more complex. Thus, this book is an introduction not to what archaeology *is*, but to what archaeologists *do*, and, therefore, to what the archaeological community is like. To that end, this book is about the profession of archaeology, because modern archaeology is a vocation akin to law or medicine; the various chapters of the book discuss the different jobs open to budding archaeologists.

Although the main users of this book are likely to be prospective archaeologists – archaeology students, in particular – the intention is that this book will be of interest and use to anyone who has ever wondered what archaeologists actually do on a daily basis. Friends and family of current archaeologists might thus find this book of use; so too should anyone in industry, business, government, or the non-profit sector who has contact with archaeologists, as well as colleagues in related disciplines and professions such as geography, geology, and history (who may identify some similarities in outlook and lifestyle). This is a potentially very large audience, which says something about how much archaeology has an impact on people's daily lives, whether they realize it or not.

1

## Why Archaeology Matters: Archaeology in the Real World

In a book about the profession of archaeology, it is as well to address early on the significance of archaeology: why archaeology matters in the real world. At the time of this writing, the world is embroiled in crises, both human and natural – wars, social and economic disorder, unexpected environmental disasters, and human-created incidents. It is thus a fair question to ask: Why does archaeology matter? Why should people spend their time studying archaeology, and why should society at large fund and support archaeology through various means? Should not this time and these resources be spent on something else, something potentially more 'useful' to society? As the archaeologists Fritz and Plog (1970: 412) once wrote: 'We suspect that unless archaeologists find ways to make their research increasingly relevant to the modern world, the modern world will find itself increasingly capable of getting along without archaeologists.' True in 1970 and equally true now, the following sections highlight the major reasons that archaeology is relevant to society and why archaeology is a justifiable thing on which to spend scarce time and resources. See especially Sabloff (2008) for a more detailed explanation of this.

*Studying, exploring, protecting, and managing the past for present and future generations is a moral obligation of any civilized society.* There is demonstrable evidence that humans have shown an interest in their past since the very origins of humanity itself – that such an interest is one of the defining features of humanity, a characteristic that makes us what we are. As a starting point, it is reasonable to suggest that a society with no respect for its past is no society at all. Imagine, not a world, but just a single country, without any heritage – no books or TV shows; no historic sites to visit; no imagination, thoughts, or cares about the past. This imaginary world is dystopian – close to that depicted by George Orwell in his novel *1984*. An appreciation of the past, of history – of *archaeology* – is integral to civilized society. And even the most dystopian of real or imaginary worlds tend to have some historical narrative at work within them, even if that narrative is false. Particularly as pertains to archaeology, the study of the past in the present through surviving material culture is an especially appealing part of the wider social sciences, because humans are a tactile species – we like objects that we make and manufacture, touch and see, collect and curate, lose and destroy. Given all this, it is fair to propose that archaeology is part of the fabric of society – not a desirable extra, but a quintessential part. It is in the interests of archaeologists, and society in general, to better acknowledge this reality.

As regards the subject of social justice in society, there is the related issue of individuals and communities recognizing not just the past itself, but specifically past bad behaviours, actions, and outcomes. This is part of what has become known as 'contested heritage'. As the national heritage agency Historic England puts it: 'The historic environment is one of the reasons people visit England, and why our oldest places are often our most treasured. Sometimes it brings us face-to-face with parts of our history that are painful, or shameful by today's standards.' A morally engaged society, one committed to improving social justice and equity, recognizes, debates, and engages with *all* of its past, not just those aspects of the past that we pick and choose for politically motivated reasons, or that make us feel good. The study of the past can be a painful experience for us as communities and individuals. Humans are complex creatures, and we have reached great highs and great lows. To name but three examples, it is important for society – and so for archaeology – to meaningfully engage in debate and discussion about the forcible, usually violent colonization of large parts of the globe by European nations in the sixteenth to nineteenth centuries; about the related, forced transportation, and subsequent inter-generational enslavement of people from Africa to Central and North America; and about the displacement of other peoples and the diminishment of their cultural identity and rights through forced land transfers and the denial of civil rights as experienced by many Indigenous communities, such as those of Australia, the modern-day United States, and Canada. Some critics call this recognition 'political correctness' or 'wokeness'. Such critics imply in this branding that the recognition and analysis of the past in such ways is at best a pointless flagellation of contemporary society for past sins that we are not personally responsible for and, at worst, a politically driven rewriting of historical narratives that recognizes only the failures of the past and none of the successes. Some critics go even further. Driven by their own ideologies, they attempt to turn such debates into 'culture wars', frequently citing pseudo-science and pseudo-archaeology (see more on this in Chapter 1) to demonstrate the alleged 'superiority' of certain cultural groups or societies over others, in order to justify the actions of colonization and enslavement mentioned above. Such misinterpretation is blatantly false, and it ought to be vociferously challenged. If we return to the core issue at stake here, that of social justice, then we can only progress as individuals and societies through the recognition of the complexity of our collective pasts, be these good, bad, or indifferent. Through such recognition we learn, adapt, and evolve. We cannot change the past, but we can change the present and the future through such self-awareness.

*Archaeology tells us about the past, and the past tells us about both our present and possible future worlds.* If archaeology tells us about our ancestors and ourselves, it follows that it can also be used to help us shape the future in ways that we want, including trying to avoid the worst aspects of the past. As Sabloff (2008: 17) writes:

> Archaeology can play helpful roles in broad, critical issues facing the world today. Archaeological research not only can inform us in general about lessons to be learned from the successes and failures of past cultures and provide policy makers with useful contexts for future decision-making, but it really can make an immediate difference in the world today and directly affect the lives of people at this very moment.

There is, for example, a large body of work on archaeological lessons of climate change – how human adaptation to past climate change can be used to inform modern decisions about responses to climate change in our and future worlds. This is the type of 'critical issue' identified by Sabloff. Archaeology demonstrates, time and again, that humans are resourceful, inventive, and above all adaptive: as a species, we are good at dealing with change. Archaeology helps give both 'broad brush' and 'little picture' examples of how humans can adapt to climate change, from entire civilizations down to individuals – for example, how we can live in a more sustainable manner in more energy-efficient buildings. The problem is that archaeology is rather bad at highlighting this supremely practical use of its knowledge. The global community of archaeologists needs to work much harder at demonstrating this use to decision makers in government and industry alike.

Archaeology, of all the sociohistorical disciplines, is uniquely good at connecting with people, because it deals with things – with real, tangible objects. Telling a story with images and objects; learning through handling and especially doing things; having a physical connection with a place, culture, and past by exploring an ancient site are demonstrably some of the best ways to engage with both the past and the present. Such types of active learning are also among the best types of learning in terms of engagement and data retention by humans, those types of learning most recommended by educational psychologists. Thus, if archaeology can contribute to planning for critical issues such as climate change, it can do so in ways that really connect with people. For example, climate change is an issue that can seem insurmountable – a problem too big and too complex for any community, let alone individual people, to deal with. However, one of the key lessons of archaeology – and one of its unique advantages – is the human scale. Archaeology can be used to humanize responses to climate change; to take responses down to a personal, individual level; to show how we as individuals and small groups such as families can make changes in our own lives that matter collectively – things such as energy efficiency, recycling, and so on that were done in the past and need to be done more now and in the future.

*Archaeology contributes more to any economy than it takes from any economy: archaeology is a net contributor to many national economies.* This is the ultimate, market-led reality of archaeology, and in the brutal economic circumstances of mid-twenty-first-century globalized capitalism, it sometimes appears to be the only argument that holds much sway with the public and with politicians alike. The following is an indicative example of the purely economic value of broader heritage in contemporary society, which comes from England alone for the year 2018 (see Historic England 2019, 2020) (similar data exist for other countries as well; see Chapter 1):

- Heritage attracts millions of domestic and international tourists each year: in 2018 alone, 218.4m visitors spent £17.0bn at heritage sites.
- The heritage sector is an important source of economic prosperity and growth, with a total Gross Value Added (GVA) of £31.0bn, equivalent to 1.9% of national GVA. In 2018, England's heritage sector alone generated a larger GVA than the security industry, defence industry, aerospace industry and the arts and culture industries combined in the whole of the UK.
- £7.1bn in GVA was generated by heritage-related construction activities in England in 2018. 6,000 people were employed as archaeologists on such sites; 24,000 architects, building and civil engineers and chartered surveyors were involved in heritage-related activities; and 100,000 construction workers were involved in heritage related activities.
- Heritage is an important employer: in England alone, it directly accounts for over 464,000 jobs, and for every direct job created, an additional 1.34 jobs are supported in the wider economy through associated industries and supply chains.

The historic environment is intrinsically linked to economic activity, with a wide range of economic activities occurring within, dependent upon, or attracted to it. Historic sites are a key driver of international tourism: there were 17.5 million heritage-related international visits to England in 2018, and more inbound tourists plan to visit historic sites than to visit the theatre, museums and galleries, or sporting events. Six out of the top ten of the most visited paid attractions in England in 2018 were heritage attractions (number one was the Tower of London, with 2.8 million visitors).

Crucially, heritage has a value beyond economic value. Heritage has cultural, social, and environmental values as well as economic value. As the 2019 Historic England report 'Heritage and the Economy' emphasizes:

> Many of the benefits obtained from heritage are not supplied (or only partially supplied) in private markets and therefore do not have a market value. Economists have developed the concept of Total Economic Value (TEV) to categorize the different ways in which individuals value goods and services which are not (fully) traded in markets based on use values and non-use values. Non-use values are economic values assigned by individuals to goods/services unrelated to their current or future uses. For unique assets such as heritage, the non-use values can in fact outweigh use values.

*Archaeology is fun – and fun is too important a thing not to be taken seriously.* Countless studies have demonstrated that a society that has adequate leisure time is healthier in both mind and body. Moreover, people want to be involved in the study and protection of the past. As an example, more than ten times as many people belong to heritage organizations than belong to all political parties *combined* in the UK. In the spring of 2020, just before the outbreak of Covid-19, member-ship of the National Trust (a key charity sector heritage body in the UK) was 5.8 million people. The allied organization the National Trust for Scotland had in addition over 333,000 members. In total, some 66 per cent of the historic environ-ment of the UK is supported, managed, or owned privately or by civic heritage bodies, and there are more than 2,000 community archaeology groups with more than 200,000 members. The National Trust alone has over 65,000 volunteers: in 2018–19 their efforts equated to almost 4.8 million hours of voluntary time caring for cultural and natural heritage. People lead busy lives, and they usually volunteer to do things that help make them happy and fulfilled: it is a fair estimation to suggest that the bulk of those 65,000 individuals volunteered because it made them *happy* to do so. And being happy, simply joyful and content, is something that we all ought to have time for and strive collectively to achieve.

Beyond simply making us happy, there is also extensive evidence that archae-ology – more broadly, heritage – makes us healthy too. As an example, a report published in 2018 on well-being and the historic environment demonstrated the links between access to historic sites/activities and improved health by addressing issues of health inequality and aiding social cohesion. Such a focus on well-being reflects a shift away from an exclusively economic valuation model based on gross domestic product (GDP) to one that shows that physical and mental well-being have a significant impact on life quality, and that there are extensive routes to well-being using the historic environment. Put simply, the past not only *makes* society money; it also *saves* society money. People who live in communities with access to historic sites live longer, healthier lives: they place less burden on medical and social services, and live more cohesive, community-focused lives (see Reilly et al. 2018). Another recent study reinforces these points, including the following observations and data (see Heritage Alliance 2020: 10–12):

- Visiting heritage sites saves the National Health Service (NHS) over £193.2 million each year through reductions in GP and psychotherapy appointments, with a further contribution of £105.1 million each year from visits to museums.
- Heritage's offer is varied, and provides opportunities for all five of NEF's [New Economic Foundation's] wellbeing actions – connection, mindfulness, activity, learning, and contributing to the community – and often several at once.
- Heritage volunteering, which accounts for 5.5% of all voluntary work undertaken in England, generates distinct benefits as regards wellbeing. Interest in heritage unites people, and heritage sites offer volunteers opportunities to develop new skills, connect with new people and places, access enjoyable physical activity, and give back to the community.
- Heritage can provide healing spaces and activities for people living with specific health conditions such as dementia and post-traumatic stress disorder (PTSD). Heritage also helps individuals who would otherwise be at risk of exclusion from mainstream society.

Archaeology matters for all these reasons. It is worth doing and it is worth studying. It is worth paying for, and it is worth protecting. It is worth fighting for when placed under threat.

## What Is This Book About?

This book provides a guide to the profession of archaeology in, primarily, Britain, North America, and Australia. In this second edition, I have sought to widen the book's international coverage, including more examples of archaeological lives and livelihoods around the globe. The following chapters outline, in as straightforward a fashion as possible, the entire archaeological career process in these nations – the various job options, the training that is required, and how one gets positions in the academic, commercial, and government worlds (see Figure 1). Focused on archaeological employment (i.e., work connected directly to the understanding of past societies through the recovery and study of material culture), the book also includes discussion of careers in related heritage professions such as museums and conservation sciences – although it does not go into detail about these, which are too specialized not to be the subject of an entirely different book.

As discussed in Chapter 1, there are archaeologists at work in almost every nation of the world, and this is an ever-expanding profession. There are, for example, more archaeologists now at work in nations such as India and China alone than in much of

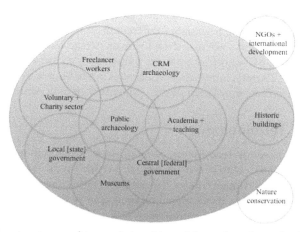

Figure 1. The structure and interrelationships of the archaeological job market and related disciplines.

the rest of the world combined, due to the sheer scale of those countries. A third version of this book published in ten years' time will tell an ever-changing story of the experiences of this growing global community of archaeologists; so too would a version of this book written, for example, by a Chinese or Indian archaeologist at work today, or a book written by an Indigenous archaeologist living and working in the US or Australia.[1] The amazing work of archaeologists across the many different nations of Africa, to name but one continent, for example, is almost entirely unknown outside a small circle of practitioners – and although the results of their fieldwork are well published, the experiences of undertaking this fieldwork are not (although see, for example, the many contributions in Philips' (2005) *Writing African History*, and the work of Walz (2009) for a frank example of fieldwork in Tanzania).

Closer to home, only a few hours away from the author's base in Hampshire in which this book was written, a French archaeologist writing in their home in Normandy would tell a very different story, for the archaeological community and career structure of France is profoundly different from that of the UK. And even just within Europe, the communities and career structures vary considerably – the hypothetical French archaeologist works in a very different cultural environment from that of potential research collaborators elsewhere in Europe, far more so than the differences in experience and career structure among archaeologists working in different parts of the US, UK, and Australia. But one of the sad facts of present life

---

[1] See Bruchac et al. (2010), Gould (2020) and Ucko et al. (2007) for evidence of the former in various nations around the world; Smith and Burke (2007, chapter 6) for a discussion of working with Indigenous Australians; Silliman (2008) and Watkins (2000) for an example of the Indigenous archaeology of the US; Gnecco and Ayala (2012) for an example of the role of Indigenous Peoples in the archaeology of Latin America; and Nicholas (2010) and Smith and Wobst (2005) for examples of people being and becoming Indigenous archaeologists around the world. See also White (2016) for broader observations on careers in archaeology.

is that the professional community and public alike grossly underappreciate the stories and experiences of these archaeologists' different lifestyles. There is shockingly little written about the lives of modern archaeologists anywhere in the world: as discussed elsewhere in this book, we do not even know how many archaeologists are currently at work globally. Therefore, one of the wider aims of this book is to encourage more archaeologists out there to tell their stories – to write their own versions of this book.

## A Note on Terminology

To make this book as readable as possible, it is structured into some broad overarching chapters on the main sectors of archaeological employment. These chapters' titles use the same terms for the different sectors discussed in the text. But archaeology is a complex international business, and not everyone uses the same terms, which can easily lead to confusion.

To try to keep things clear and simple, I outline below what is meant by the terms used throughout the rest of the book for the different sectors of archaeological employment:

- *Cultural resource management (CRM) archaeology*: archaeological employment undertaken because of various 'polluter pays' laws, policies of different countries, and/or legal requirements for archaeological work to be undertaken in advance of developments such as housing, industry, or transport. This is sometimes also referred to as *cultural heritage management (CHM)*, especially in a broader context of work on historic sites beyond archaeology.
- *Academic archaeology*: archaeological employment undertaken within the setting of a university, college, or other place of higher education, and generally connected with teaching and research.
- *Local government archaeology*: archaeological employment undertaken within the setting of a state (in federal systems such as the US and Australia), county, borough, district, unitary, or other local authority settings, usually in relation to the provision of information to people and the enforcement of local heritage laws within a defined geographic area.
- *Central government archaeology*: archaeological employment undertaken within the setting of regional or national government (the federal-government level in those countries that have such systems), usually in relation to provision of information to people and the enforcement of national heritage laws.
- *Public and community archaeology*: archaeological employment undertaken within the setting of interaction with the public. In truth, it is not a distinctive sector comparable with the preceding sectors, which all involve (or should involve) public and community archaeology. There are specialist skills relating to these practices, however, which is why these are considered in a separate chapter of this book.

# Chapter 1

# What Is – and Isn't – Archaeology?

## What Is Archaeology?

Archaeology is usually defined along the lines of 'the study of past cultures through the analysis of surviving material remains'. If a historian is someone who studies surviving *documents* to understand the past, so an archaeologist is someone who studies surviving *objects* (the formal term is 'material culture'). Digging deeper, this means that an archaeologist might study, at the large scale, an entire landscape to look at traces of, say, ancient agriculture, and, at the small scale, the microscopic remains of plant pollen from a particular site in that same landscape to understand the species of plants propagated by the people who once lived there. Along the way, the archaeologist of this imaginary landscape is likely to look at a mass of other evidence, too, down to the broken pots dumped in a disused well by way of the outline of the houses in an abandoned village. It is likely, too, that the imaginary archaeologist will find evidence of trade and exchange – perhaps some worked beads made of a stone that is foreign to the study area and in fact come from only a few specific locations hundreds of miles away, perhaps even from across the sea.

In this brief portrait, a host of different aspects of archaeology as a discipline, and archaeologists as a community, are touched on. Archaeology studies tangible, material things that one can pick up, touch, and feel; it also studies, through these surviving things, far more ephemeral concepts about people and places, cultures and communities. The aforementioned stone beads were worked by someone who had some artistic scheme for them in mind; the stones had been appealing enough for someone else to trade them, perhaps multiple times, over a long distance until they ended up in their final location. The archaeologists who found the beads then did so after a series of other processes that took them to that one site, in that one landscape. They will have planned to visit that site after a long period of research and planning; or they may have been led to it because of development or industry in the area; or even because of its chance discovery. The archaeologists had to have the training to be able to identify the beads and to excavate them in a controlled fashion, so the beads' exact location was recorded in relation to hundreds, perhaps thousands, of other materials found on site; they also had to have equipment and resources to get to the site in the landscape, along with permission from various government and/or private authorities to be there in the first place. Having completed their fieldwork, the archaeologists then had to take the beads away and analyze their structure in a laboratory to realize that the beads came from far away; they also had to compare their data with those of other archaeologists to understand the significance of the find. Having realized the significance of the discovery – or equally, having realized that the find is mundane and insignificant, because identical beads have been found on many similar sites both near and far away – the archaeologists will have written up the results of their exploration and discovery and published these results in a book or journal, as well as online in different formats. They may also have presented their findings in a lecture or at a conference, or even on a TV or radio show, podcast, or online video. The beads, meanwhile, will have remained in a laboratory to be conserved before being put on display or stored in a museum or archive.

This outline gives a sense of the different components of an archaeologist's life: project planning and management in advance of any work; fieldwork, exploring, and excavating an archaeological site; lab work, analyzing remains; and desk work, thinking about the meaning of a discovery before writing, speaking, and other forms of public engagement – both in person and online. A formalized understanding of all these skills can be gained from the UK *National Occupational Standards for Archaeology* (ISGAP 2012), which gives some idea of the diverse array of skills put into play by a modern archaeologist. There can be no doubt that it is this mix of practical and theoretical, physical and intellectual activities that represents one of the strongest appeals of archaeology to its practitioners.

So much for the basic truth of archaeology and archaeologists; what of the myth? Depending on whom you ask, archaeology is either incredibly lucky or utterly damned by being an eternally stereotyped profession – adventurous, perhaps even glamorous, and above all popular, considering the viewing figures for archaeology-themed TV shows and book sales: millions of people around the world are interested in archaeology. The profession has endlessly debated the rights and wrongs of this public perception of archaeology. This subject has even been tackled in a formal way by the über-archaeologist of archaeologists, Cornelius Holtorf (2005, 2007a). In 1999, the US-based Society for American Archaeology was so concerned about this issue that it commissioned a report exploring public perceptions and attitudes about archaeology, an exercise that was repeated in 2018 (see Ramos and Duganne 2000; SAA 2018). It is not the purpose of this book to debate the rights and wrongs of the mass representation of archaeology. However, a few pop-culture characteristics can usefully be noted that are of significance to the public understanding of what archaeology is and thus what archaeologists actually do.

Key within this is simply the fact that people *do* care about archaeology and, by default, about archaeologists – many people are interested in both the process and people. Secondary to this is the fact that this interest is overwhelmingly positive. Archaeology is a field that enjoys a special place of enduring, affectionate popular myth: we are the 'good guys', at least in European-influenced society (although the populations of many other countries do not always feel the same way, where the history of European colonial oppression means that archaeologists are often viewed with suspicion at best, and open hostility at worst). Not too many other professions have such an unequivocally positive place in popular culture; for every good TV cop or lawyer there is a bad one, for example. Even in comparable academic settings, archaeology has an enviable position – there are plenty of historians who would kill for the kind of media attention that archaeology regularly commands. On a slow news day, it is often an archaeological project or discovery that will be used to fill pages or airwaves, and major discoveries of new sites or finds consistently make headline news around the world.

Archaeology, truth be told, is generally seen as a distinct and even glamorous field; its practitioners are fortunate that people are rarely cynical about archaeology and archaeologists. To use a political analogy, this makes archaeology a tiny country that 'punches above its weight' on the global stage and enjoys a special relationship with many other nations. But this is an incredibly small community. Globally, there are no total recorded figures for professional archaeologists, because the sector is too small for government statisticians to track the industry (although specific albeit partial figures for some nations do exist, as discussed later), but a fair guess would be no more than 40,000 people globally employed in archaeology, with perhaps another 40,000 students of various types. To this should be added, however, hundreds of thousands of active volunteer archaeologists at work around the world, and many millions more consumers of archaeology through books, TV shows, and site visits.

## Focus on: Eleanor Scerri (Germany)

I am Eleanor Scerri, and I am Head of the Pan-African Evolution Research Group at the Max Planck Institute for the Science of Human History in Jena, Germany. My Group is focused on understanding the emergence of our species and its major evolutionary stages up to the inception and spread of agriculture. I started this position in 2019 and since that time I have been building up my Group and its associated projects. The position is extremely varied. I do everything from budgeting, administration, and team management to networking, establishing new research cooperations and consortia, writing grants, planning fieldwork and conducting research, as well as supervising PhD students and, when time affords, teaching at the universities that I am affiliated with.

I grew up in Malta, which has a high density of spectacular archaeological sites. I was inspired by these from early childhood, which drove me to study archaeology at the University of Malta. I took courses on human evolution, which crystallized my interest in this area. I received support to travel to the Natural History Museum in London in my final year, which turned into a career inflection point. On advice received there, I did an MA at the University of Southampton, where I stayed on to do a PhD. I worked part time in management through most of this, which really helped me to learn about budgeting, administration, and team leading. Along with the research skills I learned, these other experiences really helped me in my career.

I held three independent postdoctoral fellowships after my PhD, one in the United Kingdom, one in France, and one in Germany. Besides aiding scholarly independence, these positions gave me exposure to different labs and research cultures that really helped my professional growth. These experiences also allowed me to build a large research network that crossed different disciplines. Ultimately, this led to the development of my own research agenda, which I was able to translate into a successful bid for my own research group in 2019. One of the best parts of this new role means that I can help other promising young researchers.

My time is divided between working on my own research, my team's research projects (including supervising graduate students), and administration, which includes setting up/maintaining collaborations, writing grants, budgets, and planning fieldwork/research projects. I also set as much time as I can afford for collegial activities such as reviewing papers and grants. Finally, I participate in management and research school meetings at my institute as well. The best part of my role is being able to pursue the research that I love with the input of so many inspiring and talented young researchers and colleagues.

My top tip for pursuing a career in archaeology is a mixture of persistence, ensuring that you do not keep all your eggs in one basket, and being open to opportunities that you may not have initially envisaged taking. My career led me from Malta to the United Kingdom, to France, and finally to Germany, a pathway I never could have foreseen. Maintaining a diverse mixture of ideas, projects, and skills is also important. Maintaining a sense of humour and being able to step back is also critical. As with any strongly vocational career, working in archaeology can be wonderful, but it is important not to confuse your career with who you are as person.

Malta gained its independence the decade before I was born, and I grew up in the shadow of post-colonialism. Maltese scholars still face many challenges, and many end up accepting positions overseas due to a lack of funding and opportunities at home. The University of Malta has a research trust – every donation helps towards building a national science and humanities programme: https://researchtrustmalta.eu/. Together with my colleague Prof. Nicholas Vella in the Department of Classics and Archaeology at the University of Malta, I am also trying to help by building a major programme of archaeological research in Malta, providing key opportunities for young Maltese students and early career scholars.

# The History and Development of Archaeology as a Career

Until the early 1960s it was relatively simple to define what archaeology was and who archaeologists were. Archaeology, from its antiquarian origins in the eighteenth century onwards, involved a tiny group of people, all of them white, all of them middle or upper class, and virtually all of them men, working on the surviving evidence of past cultures, both excavated physical remains and surviving documents. A few of these people were paid to be archaeologists, but most had private incomes of one sort or another to support their research. And the majority of these people were based in universities and museums in affluent early industrialized nations, particularly Britain and the United States but also in other European colonial powers such as France and Germany, with a few permanent offices of these nations (historically referred to as 'schools', e.g., the British School of Archaeology in Iraq, now known as the British Institute for the Study of Iraq) scattered adjacent to the archaeology that these people were most interested in excavating, especially in major urban centres such as Rome, Athens, Jerusalem, and Baghdad. In the United States there was also dedicated research into the prehistoric civilizations of the Southwest – locations equally remote, both physically and conceptually in that period at least, from the urban centres of academia and government, where most researchers were based (see Figure 2).

Around these lucky few individuals circulated a far larger band of semi-professional archaeologists of much more varied background and ability, ranging from genuinely dedicated and able scholars to liars, charlatans, and thieves who saw in the burgeoning scientific discipline of archaeology a chance to get rich, get famous, or simply to have a good time (see Hudson 1981 for a sample discussion of this in the United Kingdom; Patterson 1994 or Neumann and Sanford 2001: 3–23 for a discussion of this in the United States). This period was, by all accounts, a hedonistic age enjoyed by a fortunate few, and it is the archaeological world depicted by people such as the novelist Agatha Christie, whose second husband, Max Mallowan, was one of the archaeologists in question (see Trümpler 2001). This is also the world that has inspired many modern depictions of archaeology, from the *Indiana Jones* and *Mummy* movies to the *Lara Croft/Tomb Raider* video games and movies, amid countless others.

Hesitantly at first in the 1950s and 1960s, then speeding up in the 1970s and 1980s, a series of occurrences changed the world of archaeology forever. Some of these changes came about from within the discipline of archaeology; others came from outside the community and were the result of much larger changes to society. Undoubtedly, the biggest impact came from the rise of the 'ownership debate', linked to the domestic reform of civil liberties, on the one hand, and the formalization of the legal protection of heritage sites, on the other. A major external driver of this process was also the wider decolonization process following the break-up of European colonial rule around the world following World War II, where many newly self-governing nations saw the protection and promotion of their distinctive cultural heritage to be a key part of their nation building.

Until the mid-1960s there was, effectively, no legal protection for antiquities in almost any country of the world – with precious few exceptions, the owners of

13

Figure 2. The development of archaeology as a career: British archaeologist Mortimer Wheeler visiting an excavation while working as Director-General of the Archaeological Survey of India in the late 1940s. Wheeler was one of the first 'professional' archaeologists and also one of the first ever 'television archaeologists', appearing regularly on TV shows from the 1950s onwards (copyright UCL Institute of Archaeology 2010, courtesy of Ian Carroll).

land could pretty much do what they liked with historic materials on their property, and, as long as they had permission from the landowner to be there and thus did not break broader laws of trespass and theft, so could anyone visiting a property. Although, technically, many nations had some basic laws to prevent the movement of historic materials outside their home country (in the United Kingdom, for example, the Ancient Monuments Protection Act of 1882; in the United States, the Antiquities Act of 1906), in reality these laws were regularly flouted; in many cases a 'scientific' justification of 'research' was used for the removal of materials. As a result of a series of important sites being destroyed, however, there was increasing pressure to better protect historic sites, both above and below ground. This lobbying coincided with a far louder, larger, and fundamentally more important lobby for civil liberties, particularly for comprehensive legal (including property and voting) rights. A part of that battle included a fight, still shamefully not yet won in many corners of the world, for the control of cultural sites and remains by descendant, Indigenous communities – particularly the Indigenous communities of the Americas, Australasia, and elsewhere. This process includes battling for control of entire landscapes and seascapes covering hundreds of thousands of square miles and for the repatriation of stolen material items and even human remains. The latter, held in their thousands in major Western museums and archives since their 'collection' by various colonial powers in the nineteenth and early twentieth centuries on the basis of, at best, pseudoscientific study, is one of the great historic crimes of archaeology, and remains an extremely emotive issue for descendant communities (see Atalay 2006b; Bruchac et al. 2010; Colwell-Chanthaphonh and Ferguson 2008; Gnecco and Ayala 2012; Gould 2020). This is now a topic of intense debate that has become actively political on a public scale, especially in relation to the museums of former colonial powers such as the United Kingdom. Millions of objects still reside in such museums with direct links to nations around the world, and those museums are facing growing calls for the repatriation of such materials – this is one of the most hotly debated topics in the early twenty-first-century cultural heritage community (see Hicks 2020; Procter 2020; Turnbull and Pickering 2010; Weiss and Springer 2020).

In terms of the practice of archaeology as discussed in this book, the reform of the legal system had a greater impact in a different way. Until the 1960s, people practicing archaeology usually worked outside their home countries. Although funding and facilities might be based in, say, the United States or United Kingdom (and although materials might be shipped back to those locations), the majority of actual fieldwork was being done in other nations, particularly in the Middle East but also in Central and South America, the Indian subcontinent, Africa, and Australia. In this work, these individuals were simply following the established principles of their respective colonial empires. Following (and in some cases as a result of) the destruction, rebuilding, and colonial collapse of World War II and its aftermath, however, more and more archaeological sites began to be discovered in 'home' nations such as the United Kingdom and the United States. Some of these sites were discovered as a result of research, but an increasing number of discoveries came about as a result of accident, during new road or building construction or in the course of major landscape works such as dam construction and even new farming techniques, such as the introduction of mechanized deep ploughing in Britain, which led to countless sites being discovered in the post-war period. The rebuilding of many historic cities of Europe following the aerial bombardment and ground conflict of the war also led to such discoveries, as ruins were pulled down and new buildings, requiring deeper foundations, constructed in their place; our understanding of the ancient origins and layout of cities such as London was transformed as a result of such discoveries.

Meanwhile, post-war urban planners were also taking their toll on such heritage, as new road schemes, grids, and even entire new urban landscapes were laid out. The 1960s' focus on domestic archaeology also saw new approaches to the different types of sites being discovered, an expansion of what society as a whole understood as 'archaeology'. The dominance of classical archaeology began to wane under these circumstances, and new approaches and schools of thought emerged. On one hand, the detailed study of prehistoric civilizations became a key issue; on the other hand, 'historical archaeology' began to drive a very different approach to both classical and prehistoric archaeology. The differences in philosophy and approach of these three strands of archaeology created a theoretical divide that remains, to some extent, in the present day, and is discussed in more detail later.

By the late 1960s, the needless destruction of historic sites led to the rise of what became known as 'rescue archaeology' in the United Kingdom and 'salvage' archaeology in the United States and elsewhere. At the forefront of this movement in the United Kingdom at least were two organizations: RESCUE – the British Archaeological Trust (founded in 1971) and Save Britain's Heritage (founded in 1975). Philip Rahtz's famous book *Rescue Archaeology* (1974) brought the plight of archaeological sites under threat to a wider audience, and poet John Betjeman's involvement in the campaigns to save the architecturally significant Euston Arch and St Pancras Railway Station in central London similarly brought to light threats to historic buildings, especially those of more recent construction, such as those from the Victorian period (see Delafons 1997; Jones 1984). Central to this process was lobbying to enhance the legal protection of historic sites, particularly to create legal instruments specifically associated with the protection and preservation of historic materials. In the United States, a cornerstone of this process was – and remains to this day – the National Historic Preservation Act (1966), which established several key institutions: the Advisory Council on Historic Preservation, the State Historic Preservation Office, the National Register of Historic Places, and the Section 106 review process, a series of organizations and policies further strengthened by the enactment, three years later, of the National Environmental Policy Act (1969) (see King 2002, 2009, 2012; Neumann and Sanford 2001). Similarly, in the United Kingdom, a series of Historic Buildings Councils (one each for England, Scotland, and Wales) was created via the Historic Buildings and Ancient Monuments Act (1953), the forerunners of the modern national heritage bodies in the United Kingdom of Historic England, Historic Environment Scotland, and Cadw, which were established under the terms of the National Heritage Act (1983) and responsible, in particular, for key nationally important historic sites protected under the Ancient Monuments and Archaeological Areas Act (1979) (for archaeological sites and monuments) and the Planning (Listed Buildings and Conservation Areas) Act (1990) (for listed buildings) (see Hunter and Ralston 2006).

Even given such new legal protection, however, archaeology in this context remained woefully under-protected and under-funded for the next twenty years, until the formal rise of the 'polluter pays' principle in the late 1980s and early 1990s – the principle that the activities and organizations adversely affecting a historic site should pay for its monitoring, study, protection, and preservation whether in situ (being left in place) or by record (destroying the site but creating an extensive documentary archive of what was previously there) (see King 2016b: 60–62). Such a principle had its origins in much earlier, similar statutory protection for significant natural rather than historic environment sites and features such as parks and gardens, 'green belt' sections of countryside on the fringes of cities and important woodlands, and coastal and other major landscape features. In the United States, the drivers for such practices are laws such as the National Historic Preservation Act (1966, amended 1980 and 1992), the National Environmental Policy Act (1969), the Archaeological Resources and Historic Preservation Act (1974), and the Archaeological Resources Protection Act (1979) – at least, primarily when projects have an impact on federally managed lands and seas (also on projects in which there is some kind of federal involvement, in the form of federal funding or licensing arrangements). On private land in the United States, however, state laws and regulations (as well as Tribal and other local laws) that protect heritage vary widely from state to state, and a similar situation is in place in many other federal systems, such as in Australia and Canada. For example, in Canada there is little legislation at the federal (i.e., national government) level for the protection and preservation of historic sites and objects. Most heritage protection and preservation legislation here is enacted by the ten different provincial and three different territorial governments, each of which has its own legislation and policies to protect and preserve cultural heritage, including that of Canada's Indigenous communities (often referred to as First Nations) (see examples in Ferris 2003). Other nations around the world function in a very different manner. In India, for example, the overriding heritage legislation is that enacted and enforced at the national level, with the Ancient Monuments and Archaeological Sites and Remains Act of 1958 (AMASR) protecting sites and monuments of national importance and regulating archaeological excavations. This Act also regulates the functions of the Archaeological Survey of India – the government agency responsible for archaeological research and the conservation and preservation of cultural monuments in the country. China has a broadly similar, nationally led approach to that of India, with its Law on the Protection of Cultural Relics first enacted in 1982 and updated in 1992 and again in 2002 (see Underhill 2013: see also Yingying Jing (2019) on particular steps taken in China at the national level to protect its underwater cultural heritage).

In the United Kingdom, the arrival of dedicated protection for historic sites came about only in the 1990s thanks to a series of related pieces of government policy, Planning Policy Guidance (PPG) Notes No. 15 (*Planning and the Historic Environment*) (1994) and No. 16 (*Archaeology and Planning*) (1990) in England and Wales, Planning Advice Note (PAN) No. 42 (*Archaeology*) (1994) and National Planning Policy Guideline (NPPG) No. 5 (*Archaeology and Planning*) (1998) in Scotland, and Planning Policy Statement No. 6 (*Planning, Archaeology and the Built Heritage*) (1999) in Northern Ireland. These policies finally enshrined the principle of statutory payment for work on historic sites in advance of development – in the United Kingdom's case, on all land, irrespective of government, private, or other ownership – and led to the formalization of the cultural resource management (CRM) archaeology environment of the present, alongside its corollary, the curatorial archaeological community charged with monitoring such work. In 2010, PPGs 15 and 16 in England and Wales were replaced with one overarching but essentially similar piece of guidance covering the entire 'historic environment' (i.e., archaeological sites, historic buildings, and historic parks, gardens, and landscapes): Planning Policy Statement (PPS) 5: *Planning for the Historic Environment*. This policy in turn was replaced in 2012 (and updated in 2018 and again in 2019) with the *National Planning Policy Framework* (NPPF), and at the time of writing in 2020, this policy framework is again under review by the government.

Similarly, in 2010 in Scotland, PAN 42 and NPPG 5 were replaced with Scottish Planning Policy, an overarching planning framework in which heritage is one component (as advised by the *Scottish Historic Environment Policy* [SHEP] of 2009). This policy was in turn updated and replaced in 2019 with the *Historic Environment Policy for Scotland* (HEPS). Similar laws, policies, and processes to those described previously for the United States and United Kingdom exist in many other nations around the world, covering both terrestrial and maritime archaeology. There are also particularly strong laws protecting Indigenous archaeology in many nations, most famously the Commonwealth Aboriginal and Torres Strait Islander Heritage Protection Act (1984) and the Commonwealth Native Title Act (1993) in Australia, and the Native American Graves Protection and Repatriation Act (1990) in the United States.

Archaeology also began to undergo change from the 1960s onwards as a result of broader social factors. Central to this was the rise of the 'new' universities – linked to new social mobility, itself the result of the baby boomer population explosion of post–World War II – and within these a vast increase in the number of university departments of, and courses on, archaeology. Until the 1960s there were both very few courses on, as well as jobs in, archaeology; after the 1960s there were more of both. Although this process was most visible in countries such as the United Kingdom, United States, and Australia, it was taking place in many other countries around the world.

Particularly in the United Kingdom, United States, and Australia – and, to a more varied extent, in other countries – the changes discussed previously also created a greater need for professional CRM archaeologists to advise on work in relation to development; the new demand for university courses similarly created a greater need for professional academic archaeologists based in universities to teach and undertake research. Although this was at first a mutually agreeable situation, the realities of the different pay, working conditions, and social status of these different types of archaeologists soon began to lead to a literal split, reflecting the existing split in conditions and locations, of the practice, methods, and theories of archaeology. The uneasy relationship between CRM archaeologists, on one hand, and academic archaeologists, on the other, is something that is returned to later in this chapter and has its origins in this period. Although all within the discipline agree that archaeology is, broadly, a social science tasked with studying the surviving physical remains of past societies, there can be no doubt that for certain sectors of the archaeological community, the primary focus is on research into these materials and the understanding these provide of their parent societies, whereas for other sectors of the archaeological community the primary focus is on managing and maintaining these historic materials (sometimes referred to as historic resources) in situ or by record. In truth, all archaeologists are involved, or at least should be involved, in all these different processes.

Archaeology, as a broader whole, has enjoyed an unprecedented intellectual, as well as technical, growth from the 1960s onwards, a process that has further sped up in the past decade thanks to the incredible recent advances in computer technology. The archaeologist of today benefits from a wealth of different theories, methods, practices, tools, and techniques developed over the past fifty years. Some of these advances have come from within the community and are of immense practical benefit. For example, the resistivity meter, which uses variations in an electric current passed through the soil to reveal evidence of buried features and structures, is really of use only to archaeologists and has been developed and refined largely within the discipline. In comparison, other advances have been developed by archaeologists in conjunction with other disciplines that have use for a particular technology – such as different forms of scientific dating technique, from the commonplace, such as dendrochronology and carbon-14 dating, to the rare and specialized, such as thermoluminescence, electron spin, and potassium-argon dating. Archaeology has also been unafraid to benefit from techniques and technologies developed entirely independent of it, one of the most useful recent examples being LiDAR (light detection and ranging), a form of ground-based and aerial laser-scanning survey. More recently, wider advances in data management, storage, and processing have transformed the nature of analytical work in archaeology, with reduced costs alongside enhanced miniaturization, mobility, and portability. The average archaeologist at work in 2020 has, just like the average citizen, access to an extraordinary array of digital tools for recording, storing, manipulating, and presenting data through commonly available mobile devices, computers, and 'cloud' access. The transformation in the past decade alone between the first and second editions of this book is startling, driven entirely by advances made outside the sector. For example, the improved capacity and versatility of the average mobile phone in 2020 versus 2010 is dramatic. Delving more deeply, within archaeology itself, advances have been as transformative, albeit less publicly visible. With exponentially improved digital data storage matched to advanced computing power have come dramatic advances in synthetic 'big data' analyses (including the use of machine learning) in archaeology, transforming our ability to compare data sets, to model landscapes, and so to predict patterns of human behaviour in the past and thus possible site locations and layouts. Put simply, archaeologists are undertaking more complicated analyses, utilizing more data, more quickly than ever before. And the pace of change in this field is remarkable, as it is in the wider technological landscape. If there is one crucial 'top tip' that I would emphasize between the first and second editions of this book, it is to focus on the use and manipulation of data in archaeology, including the use of Geographic Information Systems (GIS), which are a crucial tool of the discipline. An archaeologist with experience in digital data collection, management, and manipulation is always going to be welcome on any project, and they are unlikely to struggle to find work. And a third edition of this book published in 2031 is likely to point to even more dramatic changes in this field than seen between the first and second editions in 2011 and 2022.

Alongside such refinements to the ways in which archaeologists can find, identify, and interpret sites, there has been a great theoretical development in archaeology – how archaeologists think about the ways people lived their lives in the past. Archaeological theory often has a bad name, accused of being a self-serving, overly complex, and wilfully confusing process designed to obscure, rather than interpret, the past. A detailed discussion of theory is outside the scope of this book, but at heart archaeological theory is a tool – just like the other, more immediately practical, tools discussed earlier – designed to help us better understand the past. Just as a practical technique such as a resistivity survey helps identify *where* walls or ditches once ran, so good archaeological theory can help give an insight into *why* people felt it necessary to construct those same walls or ditches. People's lives – and, particularly, motivations – are complex things at the best of times in present circumstances, where we share similar values, beliefs, and lifestyles; people's lives in the past, even the relatively recent past of only a few generations ago, are far harder to understand, and their motivations are incredibly difficult to identify. Archaeologists use theory to help explain at least some small part of the thoughts that lie behind the physical evidence of particular materials, places, or activities. An excellent introduction to theoretical archaeology comes in the form of two mystery novels written by the archaeologist Adrian Praetzellis, *Death by Theory* (2000) and *Dug to Death* (2003). A more conventional but easy-to-read introduction is Johnson's (2019) *Archaeological Theory: An Introduction.*

## World Archaeology

Archaeology in the twenty-first century is a global profession. Virtually every nation on earth has some professional archaeologists at work, although as discussed earlier, no one knows how many there are in total. The focus of this book, as discussed in the Introduction, is primarily the United Kingdom, United States, and Australia, but this focus should not discourage any budding archaeologists reading this book anywhere in the world. If you want to become an archaeologist, then although some of the circumstances described in this book may not fit your particular country, the basic principles of why and how we do archaeology remain the same. Moreover, archaeology is an international, inclusive discipline. Within this, it acknowledges its past mistakes – and the behaviour of many European colonial archaeologists working in other countries in the nineteenth and twentieth centuries was disgraceful – and strives for a better future for all. No one, of any age, origin, or background, should ever feel discouraged from becoming involved in archaeology. No one should ever be told – at least not by an archaeologist – 'you cannot be involved'. The future of archaeology clearly lies in more and more archaeologists learning and working in their home nations around the world, rather than the current European-US-Australian dominance of practice and theory. The global growth areas for archaeology are the same as wider socio-economic growth and leadership areas: Asia (especially China), the Indian subcontinent, Africa, and South and Central America. All these regions already have well-established archaeological communities, but there is no doubt that it is these communities that will experience distinctively greater growth, come to relatively greater prominence, and become leaders in both archaeological practice and theory in the future, more so than the longer established European-US-Australian archaeological communities. Although the practice of archaeology will undoubtedly continue in such locations, the future of archaeological leadership lies beyond these traditional centres of power of the discipline.

## Focus on: Suzie Thomas (Finland)

I am Suzie Thomas, and I am an Associate Professor of Cultural Heritage Studies at the University of Helsinki, Finland. I moved to Helsinki in 2014, initially to take up a lectureship in Museum Studies, but I have since moved over to Cultural Heritage Studies and a tenure-track position. I am based right in the city centre, and I do fieldwork most years in Finnish Lapland. I teach Cultural Heritage Studies at the MA level, and I supervise PhD students on topics related to Cultural Heritage Studies and Museum Studies. I am also learning Finnish!

I loved history at school, and as I was not sure if I would like archaeology, I applied for a joint degree in Archaeology, Prehistory and Medieval History at the University of Sheffield, thinking that I could change courses if I wanted to once I had begun my studies. In the end archaeology won out, and I dropped the medieval history part of my BA. During my degree, I discovered that I was most interested (and got the best grades) in heritage-related courses, and so for my MA I decided to move to Newcastle University to study heritage education and interpretation. I stayed on for my PhD, which initially I did part-time due to lack of funding. This allowed me to get a part-time museum job, the experience from which proved invaluable. Since that time, I have had training through work in topics such as writing grant applications, teaching in higher education, and so on.

I had different museum jobs, first in the year between ending my BA and starting my MA and then later on, on a part-time basis while doing my PhD. My first full-time job post-PhD was as Community Archaeology Support Officer at the Council for British Archaeology in York. I stayed there for three years, gaining an incredible grounding in the issues and challenges around community participation in archaeology in Britain. Then I returned to academia with a research associate role in a project at the University of Glasgow, studying the illicit trade in antiquities. Returning to academic research was a steep learning curve, but I figured out the differences in the work culture and tried to adapt as well as I could. Two years later, I was lucky to be offered a permanent position at the University of Helsinki. In my search for a more stable position, I had to look outside the United Kingdom, and I had also applied for positions in the United States and Belgium. I have no regrets about moving. Now I am in a tenure-track post, which is a bit of a gamble after a permanent lectureship, but if all goes well I will have a fully tenured professorship in the end.

I am not sure that there is such a thing as an average working week for me. Sometimes I have courses to teach, which currently (2020) are entirely online due to the Covid-19 pandemic, but this is not always the case. In Finland, there are also certain pinch-points when the major national research funders have their deadlines, so September and October tend to be filled with grant-application writing. In August most years I am in Lapland for at least a couple of weeks with fieldwork; I have an ongoing interest with several colleagues in the material remains of the Second World War in the far north, and their impact on local communities (see Figure 3). I also have a project running until next year in which we are developing a prototype portal and reporter for a Finnish version of the UK Portable Antiquities Scheme. My PhD looked at metal detecting and archaeology, so it is nice to continue with this theme in my new country.

My top tip for pursuing a career in archaeology is that you should not be afraid of taking an unusual path. I am not in the country where I started out in archaeology, and I not only transitioned from the third sector to academia, but also moved from my first degree in archaeology and prehistory to a much more heritage-focused career path. Speaking as someone who always wanted to work in academia and is grateful to be doing it now, I would say: expect it to be challenging. There are always more people than there are jobs, unfortunately. I think it is also sensible to have alternative plans in case your first dream does not quite come true. I was happy also working in museums and charities, but in my case, I got very lucky and got an opportunity to work in academia.

I am very excited about the two projects I have been most involved with in Finland. These are Lapland's Dark Heritage, https://blogs.helsinki.fi/lapland-dark-heritage/, and FindSampo: https://blogs.helsinki.fi/sualt-project/.

Figure 3. The realities of fieldwork, part 1: Volunteers at the public excavation of the Second World War military hospital site in Inari, Finnish Lapland, in 2016 (copyright Suzie Thomas 2021).

# Thematic Routes in Archaeology

The thousands of archaeologists at work today around the world comprise myriad different approaches to, and training in, archaeology. The particular issues of the different types of training involved are discussed in Chapter 2. However, it is worth briefly outlining the major different approaches – sometimes called schools or disciplines – of archaeology, how these approaches interrelate, and what the differences between these approaches mean for the employability of archaeologists (see Figure 4). Although it is possible to work within more than one of these approaches, the reality is that most professional archaeologists end up fairly firmly fixed within one from an early stage – usually when they decide for which university courses to apply or, at the latest, when they choose to go on to specialize as postgraduate students. Archaeology is such a broad field that to thrive, people inevitably must specialize. These different approaches are also, however, theoretical – concerned with variations in the differing conceptual approaches involved in interpreting the physical remains of the past – and so at times are also ideological/political: some members of these different groups have fundamental disagreements with the philosophies and physical approaches to the past of other groups, in the same manner as other people have fundamental disagreements over political or religious outlooks and beliefs. This can be a deadly serious issue – very occasionally, people have come to physical blows over such disagreements, but much more often there is formalized confrontation at academic symposia and through specialized books and media. However, it should also be noted that partly this is an issue of geography – these approaches or schools of archaeological approach are at least partly drawn along

Figure 4. The major thematic groupings in archaeology and related disciplines.

national lines and are also partly a question of regional environmental specialty – such as African, American, Asian, Australian, Chinese, European, or Indian archaeology.

## Anthropological Archaeology

Anthropological archaeology is the study of the physical evidence of the human past before records began – an incredibly long span from millions (in terms of the general evolution of humans) and hundreds of thousands (in terms of the specific development of biologically modern humans) of years ago to, depending on where you look in the world, only thousands of years ago. In this sense, it is sometimes seen as the root of all other archaeological approaches – and it is certainly as influential (and contentious) as this implies. There are also marked differences in theoretical and practical approaches within anthropological archaeology and among the anthropological approaches of different countries. In the United States, where the term originates, this always has been the dominant force in academic archaeology and, indeed, the theoretical worldview of many other professional archaeologists, the focus of the majority of university departments and museums, a driving force of much theory and debate, and so the dominant influence on the majority of students. This is so much so that 'anthropological archaeology' is virtually synonymous with simply 'archaeology' in much of the United States, as well as in other countries with strong ties to the United States. In comparison, in the United Kingdom (and, to a lesser extent, in Australia and elsewhere), the term 'anthropological archaeology' is not commonly used; in these locations, the related disciplines of archaeology and anthropology are more clearly delineated, and the term 'anthropology' is usually used specifically for what, in the United States, is often termed 'cultural/social anthropology' (the study of living cultures through anthropological techniques). However, many of the theoretical and practical approaches of anthropological archaeology are shared with what is commonly known as prehistoric archaeology in the United Kingdom and Australia. Akin to the United States, prehistoric archaeology in these countries is the focus of many university departments and museums. This is also true of many other locations in the world – many nations of Europe and Asia, as well as parts of the Americas and Africa, for example, have an extremely strong focus on the study of prehistory.

The incredibly long time span of anthropological archaeology means that it is a focus of much development of both theory and practice – hence, its driving influence of much of the rest of wider archaeology. In terms of theory, the absence of written evidence, on one hand, and the complex, fragmentary, and ambiguous nature of the limited physical evidence, on the other, drives debate about how people lived and thought thousands or even hundreds of thousands of years ago. This same relative scarcity of evidence also drives much conflict about different theoretical approaches to the past.

In terms of practice, anthropological archaeology works closely with many related subjects and disciplines. These including geology, biology, physics, and chemistry in the study of ancient remains. A particular thematic focus in relation to biology is the study of biological or physical anthropology, for example, the study of human evolution and genetic/physical variations. A similar focus in relation to physics is then the study of the accurate dating of the past through different 'absolute' techniques of radiometric dating (based on the constant rate of decay of radioactive isotopes). Anthropological archaeologists also work with social science and humanities subjects, such as linguistics, in the study of ancient languages, and with art history in the study of ancient arts.

The diverse range of skills associated with anthropological archaeology, combined with its dominance of the university sector, means that anthropological archaeologists are employed in all the different career sectors of archaeology described in the following chapters. The dominance of this approach in the university sector also means that many different pre-university backgrounds are considered suitable for study in this field: newly arrived undergraduate students will come from a diverse array of backgrounds – some from the liberal arts and humanities, others from the sciences. Students of the latter in particular find anthropological archaeology, with its focus on applied science, especially appealing.

## Historical Archaeology

If anthropological archaeology is the study of the physical evidence of the human past before records began, then historical archaeology is its natural partner – the study of cultures with some form of self-created documentary record. This makes historical archaeology hard to define (the date of first appearance of such documents varies enormously around the world) and also politically problematic: for example, what is the exact definition of 'writing' – the most commonly accepted form of documentary record – and how does this relate to other types of documentary evidence, such as art or even oral history? By seeking to define itself, historical archaeology runs the risk of making pejorative assumptions about different cultures and civilizations, of being biased towards documentary cultures and assuming that any culture without a written record is somehow lesser than others that possess such records. Historical archaeology also runs the risk of being biased towards Eurocentric approaches to the past in terms of documentary chronology – not a perception of the past in relation to the present shared by all civilizations and cultures. These are certainly the accusations that many Indigenous communities in the United States and Australia make against historical archaeology, and with good reason: the study of their civilizations by non-Indigenous, colonial archaeologists making such biased assumptions was a major contributor to the destruction of these same cultures in the past, as the 'findings' of archaeologists about these communities' lack of what, at the time, was accepted as documentary evidence – and so these communities' implicit primitiveness – was used to justify their destruction. Only more recently has the astounding evidence of oral, art historical, and other records of these cultures and their ways of perceiving the relationship of the past and the present begun to be appreciated. Modern historical archaeology works hard not to be biased in these ways, but the scars of past harm and the distrust this produces remain strong in many places around the world. Historical archaeology remains a complicated theoretical approach, combining theories and approaches of both anthropological and classical archaeology (and arguably a part of broader historical archaeology) alongside some of its own special skills.

'Modern' historical archaeology emerged in the United States in the late nineteenth and early twentieth century, through the study of the physical evidence of European colonization of the Americas (meaning within the post-1492 European impact across South, Central, and North America). At first, historical archaeology focused more on the earlier periods of historical archaeology – of the evidence of fifteenth-, sixteenth-, and seventeenth-century colonization and settlement. More recently, historical archaeology has expanded to encompass the study of the remains from the eighteenth, nineteenth, and even twentieth and twenty-first centuries, including sites of 'living memory' such as remains and documents of World War II and Cold War structures (even space debris), as well as twenty-first-century sites such as Ground Zero in New York. Historical archaeology is also strong in other former locations of European colonization, in particular, Australia, with the study of pre- and, in particular, post-1788 European arrival on the continent, as well as in some nations of Africa – in particular, South Africa, with its long history of Portuguese, Dutch, and later British colonization. Historical archaeology is also now a major focus of British archaeology (and, to a much lesser extent, elsewhere in Europe), with the study of the physical remains of the industrialization of that country and even its post-industrial world of the twentieth and twenty-first centuries on and even off-Earth. A growing field of study, for example, is that associated to the 'space race', including objects on, in orbit around, and off-Earth (see Gorman 2019). Contemporary historical archaeology has also become increasingly politicized of late. The connection of archaeological evidence to the study of, and responses to, climate change fall into this subject field, as do the studies of contested heritage mentioned in the Introduction. Such work blurs the traditional lines between archaeology and anthropology, between archaeology and history, and ultimately between the past, present, and future in its consideration of the archaeology of contemporary societies.

Central to historical archaeology is an inclusive approach to evidence. Although led by archaeology – by the study of physical remains – historical archaeology also uses documents of all kinds (e.g., texts and photos), oral and art histories, and anthropological sources – everything produced in some format by past societies. The physically rich remains of these more recent pasts make for incredible, in-depth understanding of wider civilizations as well as smaller communities and even groups or individuals of a type rare in prehistoric archaeology. Historical archaeology also uses many of the techniques – in particular, types of radiometric dating techniques – first developed by anthropological archaeology. And historical archaeology includes a number of subdisciplines and relationships with other disciplines: of the former, some historical archaeologists are specialists in particular types of surviving physical evidence such as historic buildings or ships; of the latter, there is a particularly close working relationship between historical archaeologists and many historians and art historians.

Once seen as very much the 'poor cousin' of anthropological archaeology, historical archaeology is now a significant focus of university departments and museums, a driving force of much theory and debate, and thus a significant influence on many students. The sheer mass of historical archaeology that surrounds us in many countries – from historic buildings to parks, gardens, and landscapes, to shipwrecks and even historic aircraft – also means that this approach to archaeology has growing political influence, as well as a growing part of the archaeological job market, with historical archaeologists employed in all the different career sectors of archaeology described in the following chapters. In some cases, anthropological archaeologists and historical archaeologists work together in the same university departments and other organizations (particularly true in the United Kingdom); in other cases, these groups work separately – for instance, in the United States, many historical archaeologists work not in anthropology departments but in combined historical archaeology and history departments.

Prospective students of historical archaeology, just as prospective anthropological archaeologists, tend to come from a diverse array of backgrounds. However, there can be no doubt that this approach attracts particularly those with an existing interest in history and art history – more students from a liberal arts background than the more science-oriented approaches of anthropological archaeology.

## Classical Archaeology, Ancient History, and Egyptology

As mentioned above, classical archaeology and Egyptology – the study of the physical remains of the civilizations of ancient Egypt, Greece, and Rome – are the origin of 'professional' archaeology: this is where people were first paid a living to work as archaeologists. Since that heyday, and in particular in the last generation or so, the disciplines of classical archaeology and Egyptology have seen something of a decline of influence – falling student numbers, closing university departments, and a drop of interest in key related skills, such as ancient languages. Alongside this, however, has been a somewhat confusing trend towards greater popular interest in these subjects in terms of TV shows – turn on the Discovery Channel almost anywhere in the world and at any time of day and the likelihood is that you will find a show titled something such as 'Secrets of the Mummy'.

Classical archaeology remains a major force in global archaeology, in particular, within museum archaeology, where collections of classical-era materials remain a key component of many major international museums, such as the British Museum in London and the Louvre in Paris. The same is also true of Egyptology, discussed here with its sister discipline, classical archaeology, for reasons of clarity and brevity, but in truth a distinct subject of its own. There are, however, relatively few jobs in these fields in comparison with anthropological and historical archaeology. Although it may seem unfair, the truth is that even though graduating university students with a degree in classical archaeology or Egyptology are just as well trained as their classmates in these other specialties, they face a genuine problem of employability within the archaeological community, at least – CRM archaeology firms and local and national government offices of the types discussed in the following chapters generally prefer what they see as the more directly transferable skills of anthropological and historical archaeology. The irony is that, as noted earlier, many of the approaches and skills of historical archaeology are also those of classical archaeology and Egyptology, with an inclusive approach to all kinds of physical evidence. In addition to this, students of classical archaeology and Egyptology also have additional language skills in one or more ancient and modern languages. Altogether, the package of skills presented by a classical archaeologist or Egyptologist should be extremely attractive to any prospective employer, archaeological or otherwise. But the fact remains that this is a – albeit gently – declining subject, for reasons no one quite understands. Either a cause or a consequence of this is that it also tends to be much more self-selecting than either anthropological or historical archaeology: those who choose to enter this field tend to have an existing interest in it, fed by specialist skills such as the language competency highlighted earlier.

## Indigenous Archaeology

Nicholas (2008: 1660) defines Indigenous archaeology as 'an expression of archaeological theory and practice in which the discipline intersects with Indigenous values, knowledge, practices, ethics, and sensibilities'. In this sense, it arguably encompasses both non-Indigenous archaeologists who work with Indigenous communities and Indigenous archaeologists themselves, although this itself is an emotive issue: some archaeologists and Indigenous peoples alike might disagree with this definition. Indigenous archaeology emerged out of the broader civil rights movement among the Indigenous peoples of the world that is still actively being fought to this day. The longest histories of Indigenous archaeology are in the United States and Australia, although in various forms its fight continues in many nations of the world, and not just in commonly expected places such as former European colonies or in environmentally threatened locations such as the Arctic. For instance, some members of European groups such as Gypsy-Roma-Traveller communities certainly define themselves as Indigenous (and their distinctive cultures are under threat in similar ways); to a different extent, there is also a move towards 'Indigenous archaeologies' of more modern communities such as the modern 'traveller' groups of the 1960s onwards (distinct from the Gypsy-Roma-Travellers).

In terms of professional pathways in archaeology, it is the Indigenous archaeology, and Indigenous archaeologists, of the United States and Australia that are the focus of this book. This is not meant to be exclusive – it is simply recognition of the distinctive history of Indigenous archaeology among these communities, including a long history of political activism as well as academic study and self-definition (see, e.g., Nicholas 2010; Watkins 2000). Even though advances have been made, Indigenous archaeology is likely to – and needs to – advance still further. There are relatively few Indigenous archaeologists at work around the world, and few dedicated university departments, museums, or government offices. The laws to protect such communities and their cultural heritage around the world also remain relatively weak (especially in comparison with other types of cultural and natural heritage protection). Thus, there is still something of a self-denying process at work here: few Indigenous people become archaeologists, not because they are not interested in archaeology but because the opportunities for study and employment are too few. Meanwhile, in general, Indigenous people also remain underrepresented among university students because of glaring disparities in wealth and pre-university education, and thus access to university. The solution to this imbalance is, simply, additional investment by the public and private sectors alike – in schools, in university courses, and in jobs in and open to Indigenous archaeologists, an investment that, with luck, will make the twenty-first century the century of Indigenous archaeologies. In the meantime, the few Indigenous archaeologists who do work in this field often have a background in broader anthropological or historical archaeology. To this they bring unique additional skills of use to all archaeologists at work everywhere in the world regarding Nicholas' aforementioned 'values, knowledge, practices, ethics, and sensibilities'. All archaeologists at all levels should thus be aware of at least the basics of Indigenous archaeology – take courses in, read books about, and ideally work alongside Indigenous archaeologists. This includes, crucially, learning – and committing to – the terms of engagement which Indigenous communities rightfully expect from those outside their communities who wish to work with them. Working with such communities is a privilege, not a right. It comes with obligations on the part of outsiders, and ought to be approached with sincerity and humility. Specific advice on such approaches is provided elsewhere in this book.

## Cultural Resource Management

Given the preceding discussion of anthropological, historical, classical, and Indigenous archaeologies, this subsection on CRM might seem superfluous. As outlined earlier, all the aforementioned approaches to archaeology provide a broad-based university training that is sufficient for most professional archaeologists – including those employed in the field of CRM itself. Nonetheless, this is a major – arguably, now *the* major – field of employment in archaeology, and as such there are a growing number of archaeology departments that offer specialized training in CRM skills, both theory and practice, as well as a growing number of dedicated CRM departments and other organizations in their own right. There is also, most crucially, a clear theoretical, philosophical basis for this approach to archaeology – allied to, but distinctive within, the broader archaeological mindset and certainly as self-aware (the academic term is *reflexive*) as these anthropological, historical, classical, and Indigenous archaeologies.

The origins of CRM were discussed earlier; what is increasingly in question is the place of CRM within archaeology – not whether CRM should or should not occur, but, rather, whether CRM is a part of archaeology, something with its own intellectual focus, traditions, and concerns (see, e.g., the writings of Smith 2001, 2006). This book is not the place to discuss this complex topic. It is an issue worth bearing in mind, however, not least in terms of professional pathways in archaeology, because of its impact on the training of archaeologists. Most archaeologists around the world gain a mixed array of training that covers, to a greater or lesser extent, anthropological, historical, classical, and Indigenous archaeologies. Included within these is usually some training in, or at least awareness of, CRM, without

CRM being the primary focus of study. The question is whether, as some in the industry attest, the balance should be switched: that professional archaeologists, at least those intending to work in certain sectors of archaeology, should rather take training primarily focused on practical and theoretical applications of CRM as understood through anthropological, historical, classical, and Indigenous archaeologies. This is a subtle but key distinction, and the argument is made based on employability – that too many university students graduate with a degree in archaeology but limited practical application suitable for a career in the world of CRM. The argument is that such students would be better off studying these other specialized approaches to archaeology within the more defined practical sphere of their application in real-world CRM circumstances, and included within this a theoretical/philosophical understanding of the uses of heritage in the past, present, and future worlds – a philosophical stance for CRM as clear-cut as that of the longer-established specialties of archaeology. Within this are major questions of not only the relationship of archaeology to related disciplines, such as history and anthropology, but, more broadly, the relationship of archaeology to the study and management of the natural environment, and thus how, in an increasingly uncertain and unstable world, we manage the environment in a sustainable and, above all, holistic (all-encompassing) manner. This is one of the major battlegrounds of the twenty-first-century archaeological community.

## Maritime and Underwater Archaeology

Of all the different specialties of archaeology, maritime and underwater archaeology is one that is as well established in the public imagination as it is misunderstood by amateurs and professionals alike. For this reason, to clear up these misunderstandings, it is worth discussing here as a separate section, although in reality it is a part of the anthropological, historical, classical, and Indigenous approaches to archaeology explored earlier, with archaeologists from across these specialties using the tools and techniques described later.

Defining what this specialty is, the best description is one of the earliest (Bass 1966: 15):

> Archaeology under water, of course, should be called simply *archaeology* [original emphasis]. We do not speak of those working on the top of Nimrud Dagh in Turkey as mountain archaeologists, nor those at Tikal in Guatemala as jungle archaeologists. They are all people who are trying to answer questions regarding [hu]man's past, and they are adaptable in being able to excavate and interpret ancient buildings, tombs, and even entire cities with the artefacts they contain.... The basic aim of all these cases is the same. It is all archaeology.

This quote comes from George Bass, author of what is arguably the first and still one of the best books on the subject, *Archaeology under Water* (1966). Bass goes on to explain that 'the problems presented ... should be considered only as an extension of those already met and solved for dry land archaeology' (Bass 1966: 20).

Figure 5. The Greek national research vessel *Aegaeo* (operated by the Hellenic Centre for Marine Research) demonstrates the high-tech realities of modern-day maritime archaeology. Shown here are the human-occupied vehicle *Thetis* and the autonomous underwater vehicle *Seabed*. At the time, the *Aegaeo* was working off the coast of Milos in the Aegean, undertaking archaeological fieldwork (copyright Brendan Foley 2010).

Archaeology under water, therefore, is the subspecialty related to the technical practicalities of working in the marine zone – making sure one has the right planning, training, equipment, logistics, and backup to work safely and effectively in the marine environment (from the waterfront to the depths of the ocean), doing good archaeology with the right people, and bringing those people safely home at the end of the day (see Figure 5). Related to this, however, is the specialty of maritime archaeology. This is not a practical or technical concern, but rather a theoretical concern: the rationale for excavating different types of sites relating to the marine zone, including sites on dry land that ostensibly have nothing to do with the sea. Another of the key names in this specialty, Keith Muckelroy (1978: 4), defined it thus: 'Maritime archaeology ... can be defined as the scientific study of the material remains of [hu]mans and [their] activities on the sea.'

Maritime archaeologists and underwater archaeologists often work together, and often have the same skills, but need not – these two specialties are not indivisible. It is possible to do maritime archaeology on dry land (an example is Scandinavian Viking Age boat graves); it is equally possibly to do non-maritime archaeology under water (an example is the now-submerged remains of prehistoric settlements that were formerly on dry land but that became submerged owing to long-term sea level rise after the end of the last Ice Age). These definitions also help make clear what is *not* underwater or maritime archaeology: treasure hunting or looting. If any project – in any environment – involves as a primary objective the recovery of objects for sale or irretrievable dispersal, then, as discussed below in the section on ethics, this is not archaeology. Archaeology is a scientific discipline that undertakes systematic research into the human past for the common good of humanity. Randomly diving into the ocean to find things to sell does not meet these broad disciplinary aims.

In terms of professional pathways towards becoming a maritime or underwater archaeologist, therefore, it should be clear that prospective specialists in these fields need exactly the same skills as every other archaeologist – good schooling in a broad array of subjects allowing them to move on to at least a first, if not multiple, university degree in archaeology, anthropology, and related disciplines. Most undergraduate archaeology/anthropology degrees now include classes, in some cases optional courses, in underwater and/or maritime archaeology; there are also specialist MA/MSc programs around the world, and many active underwater/ maritime archaeologists also have PhDs in related topics.

The only things that can, in truth, be seen to distinguish underwater and maritime archaeologists from all other archaeologists are the following:

- *Conservation training*: Archaeological materials recovered from marine zone sites are often very fragile; certain types of 'wet' sites (on land as much as underwater) also contain substances such as the remains of organic materials not commonly found on archaeological sites. The excavation, recovery, stabilization, and conservation of such materials is complex, can be expensive, and requires highly specialized training (see Robinson 1998).
- *Diving training*: Those wishing to become underwater archaeologists need to learn how to dive. Initially, and for many practitioners (such as most academics), this can be the same training as for sports divers. There are numerous well-known international organizations that provide the qualifications to dive in most corners of the world – perhaps the best known of these is the Professional Association of Diving Instructors (PADI). However, for those wishing to work as CRM archaeologists in the marine zone, much more complex commercial dive training is necessary, required under various national laws, and the same as that for any other marine zone professional, from an offshore oil industry diver to a marine conservation officer. Such training can take weeks or months, is expensive (costing thousands), and includes learning how to use surface supply rather than SCUBA diving equipment. In the United Kingdom, such training

must be certified by the Health and Safety Executive, in the United States by the Occupational Safety and Health Administration, and in Australia by the National Offshore Petroleum Safety Authority.

- *Excavation training*: Archaeology under water involves the use of specialized equipment that necessitates training. This is distinct from diver training. Such archaeologists use tools such as water or air dredges to help remove silt and sand from around archaeological sites; they also learn how to handle tools such as tape measures, drawing boards, and pencils in the weightless marine environment. Many of the skills that we take for granted on a land excavation, such as simply drawing a sketch of a site or taking some notes and measurements, must be relearned for the underwater environment (see Bowens 2009).

- *Legal training*: Various distinctive laws govern the marine zone around the world. Some of these are generic and international – the most notable example is the United Nations Convention on the Law of the Sea (1982) that agrees to what the national marine boundary limits are and the rights of free passage through these areas. Other laws are national but generic – different laws on marine zone safety, environmental protection, and industrial regulation. Finally, many countries also have laws specific to marine zone heritage. In the United Kingdom, for example, there is the Protection of Wrecks Act (1973); in the United States, the Abandoned Shipwrecks Act (1988); in Australia, the (Commonwealth) Historic Shipwrecks Act (1976). In addition, many separate federal states/territories of the United States and Australia have their own similar laws. There are also distinctive government organizations involved in the management and monitoring of the marine zone, including its heritage – for example, in the United Kingdom, the Maritime and Coastguard Agency and the Marine Management Organization; in the United States, the Bureau of Ocean Energy Management, Regulation and Enforcement and the National Oceanographic and Atmospheric Administration; and in Australia, the Australian Maritime Safety Authority. There are also voluntary international agreements on maritime heritage – most notably, the UN Convention on the Protection of the Underwater Cultural Heritage (2001) (see Dromgoole 1999, 2013).

- *Marine zone safety training*: Working in the marine zone – anything from the edge of a river or lake, by way of the foreshore, right out to the middle of the ocean – requires an awareness of particular risks, and thus particular safety precautions, that need to be taken into consideration. At the most basic level, this might mean making sure that mobile phones work at the destination and that they are kept in a waterproof pouch alongside the phone number of the Coast Guard; at the upper end, this involves all the logistics of taking a suitably sized and equipped vessel into the deep ocean.

- *Survey training*: Marine geophysics – the science and technology of marine zone remote sensing and survey – is a distinctive, multibillion-dollar, high-tech industry. Underwater and maritime archaeologists do not necessarily need to be specialists in this field, but they do need to have a sound working knowledge of the basic technologies and techniques that can be used to identify and survey archaeological sites in the marine zone.

- *Technical training*: One of the major focuses of maritime archaeology is the study of ancient watercraft. Humans have been building different types of rafts, boats, and ships for thousands of years: the oldest remains of such vessels date back only a few thousand years to around 6000 BCE, but there is circumstantial evidence for prehistoric sea crossings in locations such as Australasia as long ago as 60,000–100,000 years ago. Archaeologists who choose to study the remains of ancient vessels need extensive training in the technical minutiae of such craft – the tools and techniques needed to construct such vessels, the names of different components, and so on (see McGrail 2001).
- *Vessel-handling training*: Some underwater and maritime archaeologists also have vessel-handling training. As with diving training, this is the same type of training as for other marine zone users and falls into amateur and commercial sectors. The amateur sector includes various yacht and powerboat handling/ratings and training, as managed by organizations such as the Royal Yachting Association in the United Kingdom, the US Sailing Association, or the Australian Sail Training Association. The professional sector includes a comprehensive array of larger vessel handling skills overseen by organizations such as the UK Merchant Navy Training Board, the US Merchant Marine Academy, and the Australian Maritime College.

In terms of who works as an underwater or maritime archaeologist, all the chapter-based job sectors that follow in this book employ individuals with these specialist skills. Because these specialties are all part of broader archaeology (and because a great deal of the globe is covered by or adjacent to water in some manner), it would be odd for such jobs not to be. CRM archaeologists specializing in the marine zone work all over the world in relation to marine zone industries such as the oil, gas, and minerals industries, as well as for shipping and dredging companies, and increasingly for energy companies, working in relation to offshore wind farms and tidal energy barrages (this is a distinctive growth area of marine zone CRM archaeology); academic underwater/maritime archaeologists research and teach these subjects; government underwater/maritime archaeologists advise developers and related sectors on maritime archaeology public policy and law and monitor the activities of other archaeologists; and public underwater/maritime archaeologists explain this subject to the wider community as well as involve people in fieldwork. Because of the latter group, there are active avocational underwater/maritime archaeology groups around the world that anyone interested in these specialties can join. To name but three examples, in the United Kingdom there is the Nautical Archaeology Society, in Australia the Australasian Institute of Maritime Archaeology, and in the United States, a host of regional societies, including the Advisory Council on Underwater Archaeology. Most other nations of the world have their own groups as well.

## Focus on: Carlos Ausejo (Peru)

I am Carlos Ausejo, and I am a maritime archaeologist, heritage specialist, and history professor who lives and works in Peru. Currently, I work at the Peruvian Centre for Maritime and Underwater Archaeology (CPAMS) as a board member and researcher. I also provide private consultancy on heritage and culture issues to companies interested in the protection and promotion of cultural heritage, and I work teaching history to the public.

I spent my childhood living very close to an archaeological complex. I always wondered what it was and what was done in that place, where it was forbidden as a child to explore. That did not stop my curiosity, and with my friends we would sneak in and walk around it. Those memories marked me deeply and guided my interest in archaeology. When I enrolled at university, I also developed my interest in photography, and I studied this subject professionally. When I finished my undergraduate degree, I devoted myself in parallel to photography and archaeology, which combined perfectly. Later on, my interest in maritime and underwater subjects awakened, and thus, I trained as a diver and followed some courses available in Latin America. Finally, I studied for my MA in maritime archaeology at UCL in London.

When I finished university for the first time after my BA in 1997, the possibilities of finding permanent work in archaeology in Peru were limited, so I participated in research projects while also working in photography. My experience led me to work for a large government archaeological project photographing Inca trails and sites. This is how my interest in cultural heritage management began. After returning to university for my MA, I continued developing my own private heritage company, teaching at the university, and together with some colleagues I formed an institution dedicated to maritime and underwater archaeology. Throughout my professional life I had three 'tours' in the now Ministry of Culture, the last being as General Director of Archaeological Heritage. My experience in the arts, academia, and abroad led me to understand that everything is connected, and the importance of making history in its broadest sense available to the public.

Currently, I am dedicated to CPAMS, to the private teaching of history, and to current affairs. I spend half of my time reading, researching, and reviewing the news, so that I can prepare the contents of my classes and my own research. The remaining half of my time I dedicate to teaching archaeology classes, to meeting different people, and to resolving people's queries in relation to heritage. What I enjoy most is talking to people of different background and age. This allows me to enrich my ideas, to be able to see other points of view, and to realize that you can always continue learning.

My top tip for pursuing a career in archaeology is that it is important to keep an open mind and to think outside the box; in that sense an archaeologist must be able to develop a great diversity of skills, for example, both to know how to lead groups of people and to have administrative skills. You must be able to communicate both to specialists and to the public, and in that line, to have a great capacity for empathy. Finally, you must be aware that heritage is not yours; it belongs to everyone, to all people, in very different ways.

Currently, together with my partner, we have an idea to develop a large repository of traditional oral stories from Peru so they can be heard by children and adults. The stories will be narrated in their original language (Quechua, Aymara, Spanish, and Amazonian languages) and will also be translated into other languages of our country. In this way the stories will be able to last, and everyone will have the possibility to hear them in their own language. We don't yet have a website or social media pages, but you can write to us at cause-jo@yahoo.com if you want to know more about the project.

## Archaeology as a Career: The Contemporary Archaeology Job Market

Ask the average person in the street whom they think employs most of the archaeologists at work today and the answer is likely to be universities and museums. Follow up that question with the query, 'And do you think that industry is a major employer of archaeologists?' and the answer is likely to be, 'I don't imagine that many archaeologists are employed by industry.' In reality, almost the exact opposite is true, with, broadly, from most to least numbers of archaeologists employed, the running order being industry (by which I mean CRM archaeology – undertaking work in advance of new developments such as roads, houses, or pipelines), academia, local government, central government, professional and charitable (including educational and lobbying) organizations, and finally museums.

The most recent survey of archaeological employment in the UK was conducted in 2018 and 2019 on behalf of the Chartered Institute for Archaeologists (CIFA), the Federation of Archaeological Managers and Employers (FAME), and Historic England (Aitchison 2019; Aitchison and Rocks-Macqueen 2020). At the time of writing, there is no more recent data, but the assumption must be that the global economic crisis precipitated by the Covid-19 outbreak of early 2020 onwards has, and will continue, to impact severely upon the sector for many years. While unquestionably now out of date, the 2018 data still provides a useful snapshot of the sector at that time, and it can also be usefully contrasted with the data presented in the first edition of this book from a decade earlier (2008), to show changes to the sector over time. This is shown in Table 1.

Care must be taken in any comparison of this data. The survey types and sizes vary significantly between 2008 and 2018, so an absolute correlation of the two datasets is not possible. But anecdotally, this overall balance of employment types and of changes between 2008 and 2018 would seem accurate. This was a period of significant economic volatility following the global economic crash of 2007–8 onwards (see Schlanger and Aitchison 2010), with a sustained drop in the total numbers of archaeologists employed. CRM archaeology grew and diversified in this period while local government significantly cut back, and academia evolved its

TABLE 1. Primary archaeological employment sectors in the United Kingdom, 2008 and 2018

|  | CRM + Freelance | Local government | Academia | Public, charity + other | Central government |
|---|---|---|---|---|---|
| 2008 | 46% | 31% | 10% | 8% | 5% |
| 2018 | 52% | 16% | 4% | 18% | 10% |
| % change 2008–18 | up 6% | down 15% | down 6% | up 10% | up 5% |

*Sources:* Aitchison 2019; Aitchison and Richards 2008.

free-market operating model, reducing its number of permanent staff but increasing the number of individuals on temporary or part-time contracts. These patterns are all broadly reflected in this data comparison. Of these different sectors, in the past decade industry continually employed the majority of archaeologists, and it also controlled the largest amount of money spent on archaeology, both directly – in terms of payment for archaeological services – and indirectly, in terms of government grants and awards. Fine-grained data on the funding for archaeology in any country are hard to find, but as a survey for England only in 2018 demonstrated, £7.1 billion in gross value added (GVA) was generated by heritage-related construction activities in England in 2018, with 6,000 people directly employed as archaeologists on such sites, together with an additional 24,000 architects, building and civil engineers, and chartered surveyors and a further 100,000 construction workers involved in heritage-related activities (see Historic England 2019). Another survey undertaken on behalf of the Association of Local Government Archaeological Officers (ALGAO) (see Rocks-Macqueen and Lewis 2019) revealed similar data: in 2018 commercial archaeology made a £218 million direct contribution to the economy, with 74 per cent (over 5,000 individuals) of all archaeologists in the United Kingdom at that time employed on sites connected to commercial archaeology. Broadly similar data are recorded from the Republic of Ireland, where CRM archaeology accounted for 89 per cent of jobs in 2007 (McDermott and La Piscopia 2008) and 63 per cent of jobs in 2012–14, the last such survey point (Cleary and McCullagh 2014: 42).[1] A similar pattern of such dominance is also visible in Australia, where CRM archaeology accounted for 49 per cent of jobs in 2004–5 (Ulm et al. 2005), for 52 per cent of jobs in 2012 (Ulm et al. 2013), and, most recently, for 55 per cent of jobs in 2015 (Mate and Ulm 2016). And this pattern continues in the United States, with 50 per cent of all archaeological jobs in CRM in 2004 (ARI 2005). It is worth noting, however, that this evidence from the United States is the oldest data compared in this book's

---

[1] Those seeking detailed comparisons of European archaeology will be interested in the project funded by the European Commission between 2012 and 2014 'Discovering the Archaeologists of Europe', although sadly, there are no such data for the period after 2014 (see York Archaeological Trust 2014).

second edition, since in comparison to the other nations here, there have not been comparable surveys of US archaeology in the mid-2010s. Anecdotally, all informal feedback the author receives indicates that the true figure of the CRM community in the United States is now likely to be much higher, accounting for around 60 per cent of all archaeological jobs, in line with other nations.

Exact figures on any aspect of archaeological employment are few and far between; both the best and virtually the only reliable data come from the surveys periodically sponsored by different professional organizations, such as the Chartered Institute for Archaeologists in the United Kingdom; the American Cultural Resources Association, Register of Professional Archaeologists, Society for American Archaeology, and Society for Historical Archaeology in the United States; and the Australian Archaeological Association and Australian Association of Consulting Archaeologists in Australia. These published surveys are for very specific locations, and no such comparable surveys have ever been undertaken for many nations of the world where thousands, if not tens of thousands, of archaeologists are at work. The closest that anyone has come to such a global analysis has been the work of the World Archaeological Congress, as reported in a special issue of *Archaeologies: Journal of the World Archaeological Congress* (vol. 10, no. 3) (see Aitchison 2014). A fascinating and unusual recent study is the book *Why Those Who Shovel Are Silent: A History of Local Archaeological Knowledge and Labor* (Mickel, 2021), which is based on six years of in-depth ethnographic work with current and former site workers at two major Middle Eastern archaeological sites – Petra in Jordan and Çatalhöyük in Turkey. And any survey of archaeologists at work in individual nations such as India or China, or at work in specific continents such as Africa or South America, would undoubtedly reveal many different patterns. Budding archaeologists in such locations should not be put off or misled by these very partial figures for specific places. The most recent, easily available of these sources are the following:

- Australia: *Another Snapshot for the Album: a Decade of Australian Archaeology in Profile Survey Data* (Mate and Ulm 2016). See also Smith and du Cros (1991) for wider contextual evidence.
- United Kingdom: *Discovering the Archaeologists of the United Kingdom 2012–2014* (Aitchison and Rocks-Macqueen 2014). See also Aitchison (2012, 2019), Aitchison and Rocks-Macqueen (2020), Cobb and Croucher (2020), and Everill (2012) for wider contextual evidence.
- Republic of Ireland: *Discovering the Archaeologists of Ireland 2012–2014* (Cleary and McCullagh 2014)
- United States: the Society for American Archaeology and Society for Historical Archaeology Salary Survey (ARI 2005) and the Register of Professional Archaeologists Needs Assessment (ARI 2006). See also Rocks-Macqueen (2014a) and Zeder (2000) for wider contextual evidence.

Drawing the data from these surveys together, it becomes clear that the following broad picture of the archaeological community (with a bias towards the CRM community in the data) may be drawn from these surveys but *not* about the world as a whole (see Table 2):

TABLE 2. Comparison of the 2015 Australian, 2013 British, 2013 Irish, and 2004 US surveys of archaeologists

| | Australia | United Kingdom | Republic of Ireland | United States |
|---|---|---|---|---|
| **Survey period** | 2015 | 2013 | 2013 | 2004 |
| **Surveys size** | 355 | 234 | 362 | 2143 |
| **% of responses** | 48% | 31% | 50% | 52% |
| **Top two age groups** | 26–35, 14% 36–45, 17% (67% below 45) | 30–39, 16% 40–49, 14.5% (average 42 years) | 30–39, 49% 40–49, 26% (83% below 49) | below 40, 25% 40–49, 26% (average 47 years) |
| **Top sector** | 55% CRM | 59% CRM | 63% CRM | 50% CRM |
| **Gender split** | 51% F 49% M | 46% F 54% M | 49% F 51% M | 40% F 60% M |
| **Average salary** | A$96,171 (UK£53,444) | UK£27,814 | €36,450 (UK£32,644) | No comparable data |
| **Core qualification** | 97% BA/BSc | 94% BA/BSc | 98% BA/BSc | 99.6% BA/MSc |

*Sources*: Australia: Mate and Ulm (2016); Britain: Aitchison and Rocks-Macqueen (2014); Ireland: Cleary and McCullagh (2014); United States: ARI (2005).

*Age*: Most working archaeologists are aged between twenty-five and fifty years old (although there are much younger and much older archaeologists hard at work out there). The average age of survey respondents is the early to mid-forties, which says more about the profiles of those willing and able to respond to surveys than it does about the sector itself – from personal experience, particularly in CRM archaeology, the author meets far more twenty and thirty-year-olds, with older age profiles more common in academia and government. Closer examination of such data also reveals marked patterns that reflect wider demographics. Younger age groups are generally in more junior, more physically active roles in archaeology, and more often identify as women. As the age demographic ages, so does seniority of role, and alas the gender balance shifts in favour of people who identify as men, although over time this seniority/gender balance has been improving.

*Ethnicity*: In the surveys analysed, some 99 per cent of archaeologists define themselves as ethnically 'white' (i.e., of European origin), bearing in mind the previous qualifier that these data are gleaned from surveys in a few very specific Eurocentric counties and do not represent the global situation, where many people of widely different ethnic origins practice as professional archaeologists. Nonetheless, to put this in context, for the United Kingdom alone this is significantly at odds with the overall demographic make-up of the nation, the most recent 2011 census data reporting that Asian ethnic groups formed 7.5 per cent of the population, Black ethnic groups 3.3 per cent, mixed/multiple ethnic groups 2.2 per cent, and other ethnic groups 1.0 per cent – a total of 14 per cent 'non-white' groups. The lack of diversity in archaeology has been recognized for decades now in countries such as the UK, and attempts to improve this situation have made only limited success (see Benjamin 2003, 2004; Cobb 2015; Council for British Archaeology 2012). Surveys from Australia and the United States include wider demographics for Indigenous archaeologists from those nations. For example, in Australia in 2015, 2.8 per cent of respondents identified as Indigenous.

*Gender*: The split is roughly equal, with a gradually increasing number of people who identify as women over time in archaeology that, assuming the trend continues, will lead to more women overall working in the sector than men. However, as noted above, there are biases both between and within sectors of archaeology – CRM archaeology tends to have slightly more men, public archaeology slightly more women, and academia slightly more women (although anecdotal reports suggest that this is imbalanced internally, with more women in younger, junior positions and more men in older, more senior positions). Cobb and Croucher (2020: 95) also highlight considerable differences in gender balance per country: 'in some countries such as Greece, Italy, and Portugal, more than 70 percent of the workforce are women, whilst in others, women make up less than 40 percent of the workforce (e.g. Romania, Poland, Bosnia, and Herzegovina, Slovakia)'. Cobb and Croucher also note that 'where data is available, it is apparent that there is a global lack of women in senior, managerial, and professorial posts' (ibid.). There are also issues of gender recognition/identification here: all the surveys included in this comparison provided only a binary female/male choice. At the time of writing in mid-2020, the author is not aware of any comparable surveys that consider broader and/or fluid identities. One of the only published works to consider such issues is Cobb and Croucher (2016). Cobb and Croucher (2020: 96) also note that 'the "Digging Diversity 2017" study included an option to self-identify gender, which revealed that just under 2.5 percent of students and 0.7 percent of professionals in the study identified with a non-binary gender identity'.

*Sexual Identity:* Cobb and Croucher (2020: 96) note that 'sexuality has rarely been a parameter in labour market profiling. Consequently, little is currently known about this important area of identity within the profession globally'. One study that has examined this is Cobb's *Digging Diversity* work (Cobb 2015; Cobb and Croucher 2016). In the 2011 study, just under one in five respondents (professional and student) did not self-identify as heterosexual. This is considerably more diverse than the national picture in the United Kingdom. At the time of writing the second edition of this book in 2020, the author is not aware of any additional data on sexual identities in archaeology. It is important to flag here the related issue of specifically queer archaeology, a field that has challenged heteronormative approaches in archaeology (see, e.g., Dowson 2000, 2005). As Cobb and Croucher (2020: 108) note, 'Dowson (2000) is clear that a queer archaeology is not simply about researching different sexualities in the past; rather, it is about challenging methods and processes which are inherently heteronormative.' Given the lack of tangible data on sexual identities in global archaeology it is difficult to draw direct links between the demography of the archaeological community and the interpretation of the past, but simply put: there were clearly multiple different sexual identities in the past just as there are in the present. Given this, it is crucial that a multiplicity of such voices and perspectives is represented and indeed celebrated both in our community and through our work. Anything less is unacceptable – not on the grounds of political correctness but on the grounds of accuracy and authenticity.

*(Dis)Ability:* When I researched the first edition of this book in 2010, issues of dis(ability) were starting to enter the wider archaeological consciousness, and I included discussion of this issue in chapter 2, which I have expanded upon in the second edition. In 2020, thanks to the work of several individuals and organizations, most crucially the Enabled Archaeology Foundation, there is now a much wider and open consideration of how everyone can be involved in archaeology. In terms of the evidence base for (dis)abled archaeologists, this remains modest: Aitchison and Rocks-Macqueen (2014) and Cleary and McCullagh (2014) both reported that just over 2 per cent of surveyed archae-ologists in the United Kingdom and the Republic of Ireland identified as having some (dis)ability (without fine-grained data on the different types of this (dis)ability), as compared with approximately 7 per cent of the entire UK

workforce. For discussion of such issues in archaeology, see Cobb and Croucher (2020: 97–99), O'Mahony (2015, 2018), Phillips and Creighton (2012), and Rocks-Macqueen (2014b).

*Pay*: Drawing on the data from Australia, Britain, and the Republic of Ireland only, the bottom 10 per cent of archaeologists are paid under UK£17,500 per year, and a significant, worrisome minority even less, earning around £11,000. The average annual wage for archaeologists in these countries lies somewhere between UK£27,814 (UK average) and UK£43,956 (Australian average) (a median salary range of A$80,000–90,000 (UK£43,956–49,474) (Mate and Ulm 2016), with the average wage for archaeologists in the Republic of Ireland sitting between these two poles at UK£33,667 (€37,680; Cleary and McCullagh 2014). This can be usefully compared with the average for all UK full-time workers of UK£32,700 – so, overall, in 2014 the average archaeologist earned 85 per cent of the UK average (Aitchison and Rocks-Macqueen 2014). The highest earnings reported were up to between UK£92,095 and UK£104,490 (€103,000 in Ireland and A$190,000 in Australia). Detail on the highest-paid archaeologists in Britain is not available, but Aitchison and Rocks-Macqueen (2014) report only the highest 10 per cent earning over UK£40,000. Cleary and McCullagh (2014) also add a crucial qualifying note that applies in all these circumstances: 'most of the workforce were earning less than even the average, the average salary being pushed up by a small number of well-paid senior positions'.

*Sector employment*: CRM archaeology is consistently the largest sector, amounting for more than 50 per cent of all careers, with academia and government following up as the second and third largest sectors (Cleary and McCullagh 2014).

*Training and education*: The majority of archaeologists, around 98 per cent, have a BA/BSc in archaeology or anthropology, and approximately 30–40 per cent also have an MA/MSc in a related specialty; a growing number – between 1 and 15 per cent of those surveyed – have a PhD.

Overall, a picture can be built of a young, dedicated, well-trained, and talented archaeological community that works very hard but for limited reward, with pay, benefits, and working conditions all lower than usual for university graduates (for virtually all are) of this calibre. However, job satisfaction, quality of life, and all other indicators of general happiness seem high for archaeologists (see Everill 2012). This is the crux of the issue: ask most archaeologists why they first became involved in archaeology and later got jobs within the discipline, and almost all will respond along the lines that they 'love' or are 'fascinated by' archaeology, have been since childhood, and rarely imagined doing anything else – a long-held dream made real. If asked about the pay or conditions, most will readily admit that these are at best a constant worry and at worse a genuine problem, particularly for those with family with whom they share financial responsibilities. The conclusion seems to be that most archaeologists are poor but happy, love but are frustrated by their jobs, and are surrounded by friends and family who are pleased that their loved ones are so committed to their chosen career but sad that this career does not respect or reward them better.

In terms of the prospective archaeologist considering a career in the discipline, the conclusion is then clearer-cut – archaeology is a vocation and, like all vocations, will involve sacrifice. But being a vocation, if you genuinely feel that this is your calling, then there is probably very little that will stop you from pursuing it, so the thing to do is to get the right mix of qualifications and experience possible to maximize your employability. The only people who should hesitate about pursuing a career in archaeology are thus those people already hesitating for a variety of reasons – if the vocational pull is not strong enough, or is not present at all, then no matter how exciting the subject, then ultimately those long hours, that poor pay, and that job insecurity are going to wear you down and you should know when to cut your losses and quit.

Within this, however, should come the qualifier of the un-surveyed minority, those former professional archaeologists who left the discipline to pursue careers elsewhere. There has never, to the author's knowledge, been a formal survey of such former archaeologists (especially as many continue on with archaeology in some informal capacity even after they leave paid archaeological employment), but anecdotal evidence suggests that the poor pay and job security are usually the driving forces in people leaving the profession but that no one had a particularly difficult struggle to find work in a different area after this, moving either directly or after retraining into employment that perhaps offers lower job satisfaction but provides at least much greater security and stability, and often much greater pay as well.

## The Archaeological Mindset: The Pleasures of Archaeology

The archaeologists Trent de Boer (2004) and Paul Everill (2012) have provided an excellent and detailed overview of, respectively, UK and US CRM archaeologists (whom de Boer calls 'shovelbums' and Everill 'diggers'). Similarly, Smith and Burke (2007) sum up many of the characteristics of the Australian archaeological community (see also Baxter 2002; Holtorf 2005, 2007a, 2007b; Membury 2002; Russell 2002a, 2002b; Talalay, 2004; Zarmati 1995). De Boer and Everill, in particular, however, are focused on the specifics of the CRM archaeology community – the least known but undoubtedly most distinctive sector of the community rather than the wider whole.

Two things that archaeologists often get asked are, first, 'Why do you do archaeology?' and second, in relation to this, 'What is it like to do archaeology?' Although this entire book is broadly dedicated to answering the latter question, these questions are considered here briefly by making a few observations about the archaeological mindset and so the pleasures of archaeology – those things that keep people coming into the profession and going to work each day.

Dealing with the pleasures of archaeology – for these are the more tangible of the two motivations behind being an archaeologist – one of the most cited pleasures is the combination of mental and physical exercise that archaeology offers. The ability to, sometimes simultaneously, be involved in a deeply cerebral activity that also puts one out in the fresh air undertaking physical exertion is hugely addictive and is one of the great attractions of archaeological fieldwork. Within this is also the flexibility of working that archaeology often offers: get the right position, and not only does one get that balance of metal and physical exercise, but one also gets to choose where, and most importantly when, to exercise brain, brawn, or both together, which usually translates into picking the places one would most like to visit in the most pleasant seasonal weather those places offer.

Moving on, another commonly cited appeal of archaeology is one that everyone has experienced first-hand at some point: the thrill of discovery. For some people, that thrill comes from collecting clothes, books, or music – stumbling across that rare record or volume in a store somewhere. For others, the thrill comes perhaps from visiting new places, being the first to explore undiscovered or little-known locations, or spotting a rare animal – this is certainly what drives many cavers and divers to probe ever deeper into the depths of the earth and the oceans, or birdwatchers to spend days waiting in a blind. All these and many more examples can be drawn in comparison with archaeology.

Going back to the first point about the appealing mixture of the mental and physical in archaeology in relation to the thrill of discovery moves this discussion into the other, somewhat intangible, question of the archaeological mindset. Here, two sometimes-contradictory motivations are at play. First, as Mortimer Wheeler (1954: 13) famously noted, 'the archaeologist is digging up, not things, but people'. Archaeologists have an inherent interest in people – all people, people now, but particularly people in the past, what they were up to, what they were thinking, and how those materials or physical marks in the landscape that survive reflect behaviour and cognition. Politely, interest such as this can be called curiosity; impolitely, nosiness. This means that the archaeologist is always 'at work' – every person met, and every place visited, has the potential to offer archaeological inspiration. This, in turn, is related to the generally outgoing character of most archaeologists, who like nothing more than to chat over a drink, to ponder at length on human nature. What makes the archaeological mindset so contradictory, however, is the other side of archaeological practice that seems so at odds with this person-driven, outgoing perspective: successful archaeologists combine with the above an equal love of complexity – of puzzle and problem solving, of sifting and sorting data from many different sources in a gigantic, multispectral matrix. A love of detail for detail's sake plays a part in this, especially in fieldwork, in which accuracy of recording and repetition of a prearranged, systematized, routine approach is necessary if an archaeological site is to be recorded accurately and systematically. This focus on detail and repetition at times makes for what borders on obsessive-compulsive behaviour among archaeologists, when rituals of repetition, collection, and characterization can begin to look like a low-level disorder – a sort of occupational anal-retentiveness – that under other circumstances might be treated by medical practitioners. Such disorders, however, are commonly associated with *asocial* behaviour. Thus, the archaeological mindset is a contradiction – at once outgoing and human-oriented, inward-looking and object-fixated. There is space within the community for all sorts – from the quiet and introspective to the loud and extroverted.

All the above, then, gives some sense of what it is like to do archaeology. The good days balance the mental and the physical, the social and asocial, the micro and macro perspectives at an interesting site in good weather, where the archaeologist works alongside responsive, enthusiastic colleagues to uncover new information. Under such circumstances, an archaeological project enjoys a unique and seductive rhythm of passing days, weeks, or even months or years, as the three-dimensional jigsaw of the site (or sites) being studied becomes daily more complex and the archaeologists have to daily respond to this – a real-time game infinitely more complex that any ever dreamed up by a computer-game designer, but with the same sense of quest, in some cases narrative, but above all an addictive lure. Into such a world are drawn the archaeologists at work around the world today (see Figure 6).

Figure 6. The archaeological mindset: The pleasures of archaeology are clearly visible here, where a CRM archaeologist uses an upended wheelbarrow as an improvised seat while updating site records on a sunny day in southeast England. Note, however, the amount of dried mud on the archaeologist's clothing – it had not been sunny all the time (copyright Archaeology South East UCL 2010, courtesy of Dominic Perring).

## What Isn't Archaeology? Archaeology and Ethics, Professional Standards, and Codes of Conduct

To conclude this chapter, it is worth defining what archaeology is *not*. The sad truth remains that archaeology is one of those fields of study, as well as forms of employment, that is surrounded by a fog of simply wrong- or at least muddle-headed thinking, pseudoscientific half-truths and outright lies, snake-oil merchants and con artists. Much of this is harmless and amusing: archaeologists should be no more worried about the latest TV show or film that misrepresents them than lawyers, doctors, or police officers should be concerned about comparable representations of their respective vocations. But there is a fringe, often a vociferous one, that is more harmful and is, frankly, a real worry.

On the one hand, such fringe activity involves the misrepresentation of archaeological (as well as broader scientific) data in support of a variety of myths and fables, some of these very ancient, such as various creation myths to do with a rich spread of gods, monsters, and aliens alike being responsible for the origins and antiquity of Earth and/or humankind. Material such as this sells amazingly well in the popular press and is irritating to archaeologists, although rarely directly harmful to actual archaeological sites (see Fagan 2006; Lovata 2007). Most people who write such junk thankfully seem to like to do so from the comfort of their homes rather than from the rigor of the field, office, or lab, and rarely if ever are willing to go out and check data to verify their misguided hypotheses.

On the other hand, there is a small but influential fringe involved in actual physical activity on archaeological sites that is by varying degrees damaging, destructive, and, frankly, disastrous. Some of this is state sanctioned (such as the Taliban destruction of the two statues of the Buddha carved into the cliffside at Bamiyan in Afghanistan in 2001) or even government licensed (Florida, for example, is burdened by a relic law of the 1960s that licenses treasure hunting off its coastline, to the immense frustration of its archaeological community), but much is the result of private enterprise driven by the pursuit of short-term financial profit – looting and treasure hunting. At one end of a sliding scale, this can comprise lone individuals or small groups looting on single sites or across small areas (see King 2016b: 120–22). At the opposite end of the scale is well-financed and formalized looting of archaeological sites by commercial organizations. Often working under the guise of what they would term legally legitimate salvage – increasingly and erroneously phrased as 'commercial archaeology' – these organizations feed the international trade in illicit antiquities, and some items eventually pass hands a sufficient number of times for them to become 'clean', entering the legitimate antiques trade in a similar way to money laundered by international crime and terror organizations. Such salvage occurs all over the world, above, across, and below water, and has of late spread into the deepest abysses of the oceans; there is no location or time period that is free from this scourge.

What is interesting is that in their own activities, and especially in their publicity, many such salvage organizations demonstrate that they do, in fact, know right from wrong and recognize that what they are doing is harmful and damaging. Numerous treasure-hunting organizations go to great ends to justify their activities by insisting that their work is necessary to protect heritage because such sites are already under threat from either human or natural processes, such as low-level looting, storm damage, and erosion – in other words, they argue that 'it is better that we pull this stuff out of the earth and sell it, since if we do not it is going to get destroyed anyway'. Such organizations also frequently attempt to give at least a veneer of archaeological respectability to their work, either employing archaeologists (or, at least, people with a range of real, as well as spurious, archaeological qualifications) or working with what, in passing, appear to be archaeological techniques, such as using site grids or recording finds in situ prior to recovery. When attacked by real archaeologists in the media or in other outlets such as government inquiries, such groups are also prone to vociferously claim persecution from an elite intellectual cabal bent on controlling sites in the protection of their own self-interests, a claim that collapses in the face of the overwhelming evidence discussed elsewhere in this book that most archaeologists are woefully under-paid and insecure in their jobs (if there was an international archaeological 'mafia' that decides who is in and who is out, would we not have sorted the labour laws in our favour ages ago?).

Thankfully, it is relatively easy to judge whether an individual or an organiza-tion is undertaking genuine archaeological work. There exists a wide variety of domestic, as well as international, codes of ethics and conduct, professional standards, treaties, conventions, and statutes for archaeologists. Choosing to undertake work that meets the terms of such standards costs an individual nothing – one does not have to pay a fee or join any organization to personally abide by such standards of ethics or codes of practice, although one can choose to formally join such groups – and adherence to such good practice can usually be demonstrated easily. For individuals and organizations, these standards are defined by the codes of conduct of various professional organizations that regulate archaeologists and their work. Examples of these include the Australian Archaeological Association's Code of Ethics, the UK Chartered Institute for Archaeologists Code of Conduct, the American Anthropological Association's Statements on Ethics: Principles of Professional Responsibility, the US Register of Professional Archaeologists Code of Conduct, the Society for American Archaeology's Principles of Archaeological Ethics, and the US Society for Historical Archaeology's Ethical Principles. There is also increasing recogni-tion of the impact of what has become known as 'heritage crime' on commu-nities. Police and justice systems are much better now at recognizing that the theft of materials from archaeological sites, far beyond the financial value of any objects looted, concerns a more profound theft of knowledge about our com-munal pasts. An object stolen from a site may sell for a precise sum of money on the black market, but the theft of the knowledge that surrounds that object were it to be left in situ, of the loss of long-term communal knowledge that its theft represents, is priceless. Courts increasingly take such cultural heritage losses into account when sentencing those who loot historic sites.[2]

For entire nations, the situation is far less clear-cut, mainly because international law runs more on precedent than enforced statute – that is, nations tend to pick and choose what laws and treaties they sign on the basis of a variety of interests, and even if they do sign a treaty, ensuring – especially enforcing – and even simply monitoring good practice can be extremely difficult. However, some of the better-known and wider-ranging examples include, in chronological order:

- International Council on Monuments and Sites (ICOMOS) (1964) International Charter for the Conservation and Restoration of Monuments and Sites.
- United Nations Educational, Scientific and Cultural Organization (UNESCO) (1970) Convention on the Means of Prohibiting and Preventing the Illicit Import, Export and Transfer of Cultural Property.
- UNESCO (1972) Convention Concerning the Protection of the World Cultural and Natural Heritage.
- Council of Europe (1985) Convention for the Protection of the Architectural Heritage of Europe (the Grenada Convention).
- Council of Europe (1992) Convention on the Protection of the Archaeological Heritage (the Valetta Convention).
- United Nations Economic Commission for Europe (UNECE) (1998) Convention on Access to Information, Public Participation in Decision-making and Access to Justice in Environmental Matters (the Aarhus Convention).
- UNESCO (1999) Convention for the Protection of Cultural Property in the Event of Armed Conflict.
- Council of Europe (2000) European Landscape Convention.
- UNESCO (2001) Convention on the Protection of the Underwater Cultural Heritage.
- UNESCO (2003) Convention for the Safeguarding of the Intangible Cultural Heritage.
- Council of Europe (2005) Framework Convention on the Value of Cultural Heritage for Society (the Faro Convention).

Real archaeology, in fact, comes down to a relatively simple range of good practice and personal ethics. Although much argued about, none of these is a particularly radical suggestion. Not unlike all other forms of good behaviour in any community, it comes down to people choosing to act in a thoughtful and responsible manner, to respect one another and the environment, and to endeavour to make as small a physical impact as possible, so that there is something left for future generations. This is no different from the basic 'campsite rule' taught to many of us as children – to leave a site as good as, or ideally better than, we found it. What this means for professional archaeologists is the following, paraphrased from the CIfA *Code of Conduct* (2019).

---

[2] See https://historicengland.org.uk/advice/caring-for-heritage/heritage-crime/tackling/ for case studies from England.

***Maintain, develop, and promote the highest standards of professional practice***: Archaeologists try to be well informed, preparing for projects in advance by reading relevant literature. Throughout their career, this means that they will keep up to date on advances in archaeological ideas and techniques (a process known as 'continuing professional development', or CPD), and they will not agree to undertake archaeological work for which they are not adequately qualified. Once on a project, they will try their utmost to present archaeology to one another, as well as to the public, in a responsible and timely manner. They will tell people about their work quickly and in a clear and straightforward manner, keep a detailed and thorough record of their work, store materials and records appropriately, and reference as well as give appropriate credit for work done by others in final publications, which they will seek to publish quickly and make easily available in different formats.

*This means that it should be easy for anyone to find out more about any archaeological project's location, aims, objectives, team members, funding sources, fieldwork, outcomes, conclusion, and the final site of deposit of the project archives. Any project for which this is not possible is, frankly, suspect.*

***Actively discourage and combat the trade in illicit antiquities***: Archaeologists know and comply with all laws applicable to their professional activities. They do not engage in illicit or unethical dealings in antiquities, so they will not buy or sell artifacts recovered during either their own or others' fieldwork. More broadly, this means that they will be cautious about the financial benefits resulting from their work, especially if this seems to relate, in any way, to the recovery or sale of objects or materials recovered during archaeological fieldwork. But this does not mean, for instance, that they cannot or will not be paid to work on an archaeological site. So long as the primary intention of any project is to analyse a site, rather than recover materials for their own sake or to sell them to make a profit, then such paid work is legitimate.

*This means that anyone involved in selling or buying materials recovered from an archaeological site, whether named or unnamed, is not an archaeologist. This also means that if an individual or project sets out with a primary motive to recover materials for sale, then that project is not an archaeological project and that person is not an archaeologist.*

***Work to preserve the scientific integrity of a total site***: Archaeologists strive to conserve archaeological sites and material as a resource for study and enjoyment now and in the future and encourage others to do the same.

*This means that when it is not possible to leave a site untouched or materials in place, archaeologists will seek to ensure the creation and maintenance of an adequate record through appropriate forms of research, recording, and dissemination of results. It also means that when destructive investigation is undertaken, those involved will endeavour to ensure that this destruction has the smallest possible impact on the archaeological site or remains.*

***Recognize the rights of communities to control access to and information on their cultural heritage***: Archaeologists will take account of the legitimate concerns of groups whose material past may be the subject of archaeological investigation.

*This means that archaeologists will work with communities that are involved in an area — be these communities near or far away — to plan any project, and that they will work with such communities to ensure that materials recovered from a site or other archives that result*

49

*from a project will be placed in the best possible location for community access in the future. This means involving descendant communities from the outset and acquiescing to their cultural expectations, even if this runs against common archaeological practice (for example, agreeing not to undertake analyses of human remains where such communities object to this practice). Communities, not archaeologists, own their cultural heritage, and real archaeologists recognize the overarching right of descendant and Indigenous communities to control remains as they see fit.*

## Personal Conduct in Archaeology

Above all else, archaeologists have a personal responsibility to behave in a manner that respects places and especially peoples – communities and individuals alike. As stated at the start of this chapter, archaeology is 'the study of past cultures through the analysis of surviving material remains'. Given this, just as medical doctors ascribe to the Hippocratic Oath, so too archaeologists ought to commit with similar seriousness to care for people and places alike. There are wide-ranging codes of conduct in archaeology available, and most organizations will ask anyone working with them, in either a voluntary or professional capacity, to commit to following such codes. The UK Chartered Institute for Archaeologists has some excellent examples available online (see CIfA 2017, 2018, 2019b); see also the work of DigVentures and British Women Archaeologists. The archaeologist Sarah Perry (2019) also has excellent advice on this subject, as do Kayt Hawkins and Cat Rees (2018). For those readers interested in, or about to work with Indigenous communities, there are also specific codes of conduct and ethics associated to such circumstances, such as those of the Canadian Archaeological Association (2020) or the Australian Archaeological Association (2020).

We study the past for the benefit of present and future generations – within this, we ought to seek proactively not to harm any people or places in the process of our discovery. Some of this means committing to the points raised above regarding the ethics of professional practice in relation to the sites, materials (including data), and communities with which we interact. For individuals, this definition can be usefully expanded to encompass a wider sensibility, including what can loosely be termed 'research ethics'. This means committing to the highest standards as practitioners of undertaking our work with integrity, sharing ideas and data freely, trusting others and being trusted – not stealing or plagiarizing others work or ideas. A different perspective on this is committing to invest as much in others as we invest in ourselves, through supporting people in a myriad of ways, both formal and informal – being collegiate, helping others, mentoring and advising one another, and being supported in return. There is a rich ecosystem in archaeology of mutual, non-pecuniary benefits. Any archaeologist worthy of the name constantly helps and supports others' lives and careers by giving advice, sharing contacts and networks, reviewing and critiquing people's writing or grant applications, and so on. Such a network is central to the lives of us all, the author included: it was only possible to write this book through the support of hundreds of different contacts built up by the author over the past quarter-century. Favours were given by others to help write this book; favours will be returned in due course.

This is the best of archaeology – but what of the worst? There are dark corners of archaeology that lie like shadows close to the brightest sunlight. Where there is friendship there is also enmity; where there is support there is also abuse. One of the most marked changes between the first and second editions of this book is the much greater public recognition that archaeology as a community has systematic-ally denied, and in some cases systematically sought to hide abuse by organizations and individuals. Such abuse has been perpetrated upon individuals in the past and, shamefully, still occurs in the present. This is part of the wider, ongoing cultural recognition around the world faced by countless organizations and groups – faith and community groups, military and scientific units and organizations, charities and businesses, single families, and multi-billion corporations. Archaeology continues to harbour abusers of the worst kind – those who use their power and influence to bully others on the basis of their background, ethnicity, gender, race, sexuality, and other characteristics, and those who abuse others for their own selfish desires, up to and including the most serious crimes of mental and physical, including sexual, abuse. Lives have been lost to suicide through such abuse; livelihoods and families destroyed through it.

Slowly, painfully, archaeology is undergoing its own #MeToo transition. This is a process, not an event, and within it we all have a personal responsibility to recognize the seriousness of the situation at hand and to proactively help deal with it. It is not enough to be a passive observer in this: passivity is tacit consent for abuse to continue. Each of us must be the change that we wish to see in our community. Our personal responsibilities can loosely be collated under the following three headings; see also the additional guidance on fieldwork codes of ethics in the appendices at the end of this book.

*Personal behaviours*: This means thinking seriously about how our personal behaviours, including our often unacknowledged, implicit biases, impact upon others. In part this means being self-reflective and questioning, striving to learn about others and to consider how we interact with them through empathy and respect. But this also means taking practical steps to put others at ease and to avoid putting them in situations that might compromise or jeopardize them, for example, choosing to meet new people in public, socially neutral environments where they can feel safe – a cafe in the middle of a town during the daytime rather than a bar at night. It may seem strange to non-archaeologists that such an obvious step of safeguarding even needs suggesting, but, alas, it does. The off-hours, deals-struck-over-drinks culture of archaeology is deep rooted, one of the historic characteristics of the profession that needs challenging.

*Operational environments*: This means the practical steps that we all ought to put in place when in charge of a working environment ourselves, or that we ought to expect to be put into place by others where we are not in charge. Everyone has a right to work in a non-threatening, safe, and secure environment. Much of this ought to (and often does) fall under the guise of 'health and safety': a workplace where the risks of being physically injured have been minimized, and where we have access to the basic human rights of water, food, and shelter. But to take this health and safety analogy further, there is much more that *can* be put into place but sadly often isn't: gender-neutral toilets; private spaces and facilities for religious observance, medical, or other personal needs (e.g., spaces for nursing mothers or easy access to menstrual health products on site[3]); and simply ensuring a non-threatening environment that has zero tolerance for the bullying of others on the basis of their background, ethnicity, gender, race, sexual orientation, or other characteristics. And some of this *is* down to personal responsibility – for example, publicly challenging non-inclusive language, jokes, and similar 'banter' when faced with it by colleagues.

*Organizational frameworks*: This means having frameworks, codes of conduct, reporting mechanisms, and other safety processes clearly in place, so that if an incident of abuse does arise it is handled as quickly, fairly, and transparently as possible. For those new to archaeology, this above all else ought to be the litmus test of appropriateness: if you are considering becoming involved in archaeological work, of any sort, then very early on you ought to be given a formal induction by those in authority on these safety processes, how these processes apply to you, and how you can put their measures into action – for example, having explained to you who is in charge, how to complain to them, and, crucially, how to complain *about* them if they compromise, threaten, or abuse you. If such processes are not explained to you, or if you feel that these processes are insufficient and/or cannot be challenged, then leave, and when in a safe mental/physical space, complain. No archaeology is more important than your personal safety and well-being.

---

[3] See www.archaeologists.net/sites/default/files/Seeing_Red_Guide_FinalV1%20%282%29.pdf.

# Chapter 2

# Skills and Training in Archaeology

## Introduction

The archaeological job market, as can be inferred from the discussion in Chapter 1, is akin to a small island on a geologic fault line: community-based with a nice lifestyle and amazing opportunities, but also volatile, owing largely to factors outside the population's control. One consistent outcome of all the different professional surveys of archaeologists, though, is that of training and education. The modern archaeologist is exceptionally well trained, with at least one (and often several) qualifications in archaeology or a related subject, backed up by a raft of wide-ranging experience.

Until relatively recently it was possible to get a job in archaeology with a lot of experience but only a little formal education. The opposite is now true, however – statistically, a lot of education and a little experience are the defining characteristics of the present-day professional archaeologist. Many would argue that this is a bad thing, that archaeologists with well-honed field experience are in shorter and shorter supply, and that this skills gap is harming the practice of archaeology at a fundamental level. This is certainly a recurrent theme of meetings and conferences of CRM archaeologists, who feel that the university sector is letting them down, churning out ever more graduates from the academic "sausage factory" who simply do not have the skills required for the posts that need to be filled. Such a debate is not within the scope of this book. Here, all that can be stated are the facts as presented by various professional surveys; these surveys demonstrate that more and more professional archaeologists hold multiple degrees in the subject or its related specialties.

It appears that if one wants to get ahead in archaeology, with a degree but not much field experience, there is at least a chance of getting a job, but with a lot of field experience but no degree the chance of finding a job is minimal.

## Why Study Archaeology?

Many students come to formal archaeological study with a burning passion for the subject. To them, the answer to the question 'Why study archaeology?' is simple: *because they want to*, and in many cases, they have done so from an early age. Such individuals may well go on to take multiple university degrees in archaeology and become professional archaeologists themselves. But for others, the situation may be less clear-cut, be this at school, college, or university. Many people may be uncertain about studying a subject with what seems, at first glance, limited wider applicability. This section is for these people in doubt.

Archaeology is worth studying, from the school level right up to and even beyond a bachelor's degree, because it offers an unrivalled array of transferable skills that can be used in virtually any corner of the world and in all job sectors. This is made clear in various governmental reviews of the discipline; see also Cobb and Croucher (2020) for a consideration of teaching and learning in the discipline. For example, the UK Quality Assurance Agency for Higher Education (QAA)'s 2014 *Subject Benchmark Statement: Archaeology* comments:

> The broad-based nature of the subject and the skills it gives graduates provides a strong grounding for a wide range of career paths. The archaeology graduate is extremely well equipped with transferable skills, from the mix of humanities and science training, engagement with theory and practice, and individual and team-based learning, together with the intellectual curiosity to continue learning, and the skills to benefit from challenging work environments. Archaeology also offers much non-professional involvement, via continuing education courses, local societies, museums, heritage groups and so on, so graduates not employed within archaeology have many opportunities for lifelong learning and to share their expertise within the community.

With its feet spanning the arts and the sciences and with its mind engaged in both high-level thinking and ground-level practicalities, an archaeological training provides a host of transferable skills. Archaeologists regularly:

- Apply scholarly, theoretical, and scientific principles and concepts to specific problems.
- Use diverse sources of evidence to formulate an argument.
- Appreciate the importance of recovering primary data through practical experience.
- Critically apply methodologies for quantifying, analyzing, and interpreting primary data.
- Understand the concepts and application of scientific methods used in collecting, analyzing, and interpreting data.

- Interpret spatial data.
- Select and apply appropriate statistical and numerical techniques.
- Marshal and critically appraise other people's arguments.
- Produce logical and structured arguments supported by evidence.
- Communicate effectively orally, visually, and in writing to diverse audiences.
- Use IT, information retrieval, and presentation skills effectively in a variety of graphical media.
- Execute research, working independently.
- Collaborate effectively in a team.
- Act with sensitivity to different cultures and deal with unfamiliar situations.
- Critically but empathetically evaluate their own and others' opinions.

It is also notable that archaeology scores highly across the different types of learning styles that have been modelled. To take one example, the VARK neurolinguistic model breaks learning styles down into (1) visual (learning through seeing), (2) auditory (learning through listening), (3) reading/writing, and (4) kinaesthetic/tactile (learning through doing) styles of learning. Archaeologists, and thus archaeology students, get to use all these different learning styles in their training and professional development, which makes archaeology an extremely engaging subject to study. Archaeologists attain and then maintain a diverse array of useful, transferable skills, and they get to practice these skills on a regular basis.

Archaeology is obviously worth studying because of a love for the subject, but even if you are only a little bit in love with it, studying it is *not* going to harm your future career prospects in a wide array of roles outside the profession – indeed, the opposite may be true. Archaeology courses provide skills that can set up someone for life in a diverse range of occupations. And archaeology, lest we forget, is also simply cool. How many people at a party do not want to meet an archaeologist? And how many CVs will an employer sift through, looking for something that marks one candidate out from another – something like an archaeology degree?

It is worth emphasizing here how interconnected archaeology is within all science, technology, engineering, and mathematics (STEM) subjects. There is sometimes a misconception that archaeology is a purely "humanities" subject that does not connect into these core curriculum elements of most educational systems. This misconception needs to be challenged – although it is not helped by archaeology not being formally classed as a STEM subject by most governments. The special value of archaeology lies in its interconnection of the humanities, social, and "hard" sciences as both a culture and a practical discipline. Archaeologists constantly integrate a philosophical consideration of past behaviours derived from the humanities with a practical, in many cases a hands-on, application of the latest techniques in STEM subjects. This runs a gamut of approaches, from the use of cutting-edge dating techniques based on physics to chemical analyses of ancient materials, biological testing of ancient plant and animal DNA, technological analyses of ancient approaches to engineering, and the use of advanced mathematics and computing tools such as machine learning to sample and analyse datasets better and more effectively. Some of the most exciting uses of remote-sensing and data visualization come from archaeology; and some of the most remarkable discoveries of new technologies such as aerial and underwater drones too. Show an archaeologist an advance in a STEM subject, and they will show you a direct application of that advance that can be, and in many cases already is being, applied in archaeology. This is a point well made in a 2017 report by the British Academy in the United Kingdom,[1] as well as by many other archaeological organizations. The UK Young Archaeologists' Club, for example, has STEM-focused activities for people to engage with that are ideal for school and community groups,[2] and many of the CRM firms whose activities are flagged in Chapter 3 have exceptional examples of STEM in an applied archaeological context – see, for example, the work of Wessex Archaeology in the United Kingdom[3].

The following sub-disciplines of archaeology are of special relevance in this regard:

- Archaeological science (sometimes known as archaeometry): the application of scientific techniques or methodologies to archaeology, such as radiocarbon dating, statistics and remote sensing.
- Archaeozoology (sometimes known as bio-archaeology): the study of animal remains in human settlements, and the linked sub-discipline of palaeopathology, the study of ancient disease among animals and humans.
- Archaeobotany (sometimes known as palaeoethnobotany): the study of human-plant interactions in the archaeological record.
- Computational archaeology: the application of computers, particularly geographic information systems (GIS) to archaeology, and the linked sub-discipline of digital archaeology, the application of information technologies and digital media to archaeological questions.
- Forensic archaeology: the application of archaeological techniques to criminal investigations (this has become particularly prominent in the investigation of mass killings associated with war crimes).
- Osteology (sometimes known as osteoarchaeology or palaeo-osteology): the scientific study of human remains from archaeological sites, and the linked sub-discipline of palaeopathology – the study of ancient disease among animals and humans.

## Accessibility and Equality in Archaeology

As noted in Chapter 1, when I researched and wrote the first edition of this book in 2010, issues of dis(ability) were just starting to enter the wider archaeological consciousness, and I included discussion of this issue in this section, at that time entitled 'Archaeology and Disabilities'. For this second edition, I have comprehensively rewritten this section, retitling it 'Accessibility and Equality in Archaeology',

---

[1] See www.thebritishacademy.ac.uk/publications/reflections-archaeology/.
[2] See www.stem.org.uk/resources/collection/3165/young-archaeologists-club.
[3] See www.wessexarch.co.uk/our-work/stem-wessex-archaeology.

for if there is one key lesson that I have been taught by a wonderful array of archaeologists over the past decade, it is that no one is *dis*abled and that everyone can be *en*abled – as in the name of the Enabled Archaeology Foundation, set up by an incredible group of archaeologists to lead to inclusive archaeologies for all, and led by a truly inspirational archaeologist, Theresa O'Mahony, who sadly died in 2019. For discussion of such issues in archaeology, see Cobb and Croucher (2020), O'Mahony (2015, 2018), Phillips and Creighton (2012), and Rocks-Macqueen (2014b).

Around the world, various laws and policies enshrine the rights of us all not to be discriminated against, based on what are sometimes referred to as 'protected characteristics' in relation to employment, the provision of goods and services, education, and transport. For example, the UK Equality Act (2010) enshrines in law that it is illegal to discriminate against someone on the grounds of the following:

- Age.
- (Dis)ability.
- Gender reassignment.
- Marriage and civil partnership.
- Pregnancy and maternity.
- Race.
- Religion or belief.
- Sex.
- Sexual orientation.

Specifically as regards (dis)ability, there have been limited surveys of the number of (dis)abled archaeologists, primarily in the United Kingdom, together with a growing body of work on how to minimize barriers to entry into the profession. The archaeologists Hannah Cobb and Karina Croucher (2020: 97–99) discuss this in detail in their book *Assembling Archaeology*, and they also led one of the first such projects to actively consider such issues (see Cobb 2015; Cobb and Croucher 2016). For those seeking advice on how to maximize accessibility to archaeological projects, there is also excellent guidance available – see Phillips and Creighton (2012), Phillips and Gilchrist (2005), and Philips et al. (2007).

Even without laws in place to protect people, archaeology has, overall, a relatively good track record of inclusivity in all respects, and archaeology at its best provides a supportive and adaptable environment. The key thing is to make clear from the outset that no one, for any reason, should ever feel excluded from archaeology. While, for example, the physical demands of archaeological fieldwork might be *perceived* by some people as a barrier to full involvement, any such challenge that a person can think about has likely been overcome in the past. It is simply a matter of appropriate planning and preparation, beginning with a full and frank discussion with any individuals who may feel themselves in need of modifications to their working environments in advance of such work. Flexibility during a project, by both planners and participants, is also necessary, as is 'a recognition that ability is an attribute that will change and develop with experience and time' (Philips et al. 2007: 19) and also that 'simple, common sense solutions are usually the most successful' (ibid.). To take one very common example of a (dis) ability, many prospective archaeologists with dyslexia or dyspraxia might be worried that this prevents a career in a subject for which a university degree is a virtual necessity. Reading and writing long essays and reports can seem like an insurmountable barrier to such individuals. But there are plenty of archaeologists with dyslexia and dyspraxia, and nothing that cannot be supported in this regard through various practical adaptations. In a different vein, people with mobility issues may be worried about being excluded from undertaking archaeological fieldwork. But this issue is rarely a problem – or at least, it is not for any project (and project director) who cares and who plans. Plenty of people with mobility issues have worked on a diverse array of archaeological sites – on land as well as under water – and have enjoyed long and successful careers as archaeologists. The secret, as for everyone in archaeology, is dedication. Those who want to succeed will do so; potential barriers can and will be overcome; and no one who genuinely cares about and commits to our global community will ever use a (dis)ability as an excuse to bar involvement.

## Focus on: Madhumathy Chandrasekaran (India)

I am Madhumathy Chandrasekaran. I have been working as a maritime archaeologist and as an Adjunct Research Associate for an NGO called the Maritime History Society (MHS) in Mumbai, India, since October 2020. The Society, an academic initiative of the Western Indian Naval Command, is endeavouring to evolve into an eminent organization that will nurture and develop interest in India's maritime history and heritage. My primary responsibility is to identify potential archaeological sites, develop projects, conduct fieldwork, and publish the findings of our research.

I gained an interest in archaeology and history from my childhood visits to museums, temples, and other places of cultural heritage. I did not receive any formal training in archaeology until I began an MA in Maritime Archaeology at Flinders University in Australia. My attraction towards maritime archaeology comes from my love for the ocean, my curiosity to learn how the oceans were utilized in the past, and my deep-rooted love for ships and boats, which I find peculiar and beautiful. I grew up in the south-eastern coast city of Chennai in India, and I lived very close to the beaches there. I have always been fascinated by the sea, which led me to become a scuba diving instructor. I first received a BA in English Literature in 2016, and I enrolled in the MA programme in maritime archaeology in 2017. Currently, I am seeking PhD opportunities across the world. During my master's course I participated in several internships and fieldwork to gain experience and knowledge.

My first paid archaeological job was at the Tamil University, Tanjavur, India, for two weeks in February 2010 where I was asked to document artefacts. I also presented lectures and conducted tutorials in maritime archaeology. The position I hold at MHS is my second ever job in archaeology. The demand for maritime archaeologists in India is very low, hence I have had to create employment opportunities by myself. I got both jobs based on my experience back in Australia and other places where I have interned, which included both desk and site-based experience.

In an average week, I spend a lot of time surveying literature to propose projects, as well as writing reports. As I also teach scuba diving, I divide my time between archaeology and diving. At MHS, we have a designated archaeology team that I get to help with occasionally and find ways to collaborate with.

My top tip for pursuing a career in archaeology is to be open to learning different skills and to be multidisciplinary. Archaeology is constantly evolving, which means that a basic cognizance of many related fields is necessary. It is important to show enthusiasm and to always learn and acquire more knowledge in order to effectively decipher the stories of the past. It is also crucial to recognize the areas that you personally lag in and to try to improve your knowledge and understanding. For instance, I am in no way interested in photography, nor am I particularly well versed in technology or drawing, but I understand that these skills are important to stay up-to-date on, so I make the effort to get better at them.

While I do not have a particular organization or project or an initiative to share apart from the NGO that I work for, I try to conduct public outreach programmes to raise awareness about Indian maritime heritage and archaeology. I talk on public platforms, and I answer queries of any interested parties on my social media. Basically, I do my part in developing the field in India.

## Going on Your First Archaeological Project

Irrespective of the circumstances – school or college, local society, university or other – the following general advice is useful for all those individuals embarking on their first archaeological project (see Figures 7–9). *It is worth reading this section if you are unsure about going on archaeological fieldwork – if the following does not sound like it appeals, then are you sure that archaeology is the way forward for you?*

Prior to any project there will usually be a meeting of all the participants that gives a detailed briefing on the project, its aims and objectives, methodologies, and the logistics and practicalities of the project, including what equipment each participant is expected to bring and how they are expected to get to the project site. Assuming that a student's first field experience is to be on a traditional university-led survey/excavation project (sometimes referred to as a 'field school'), a few commonalities of all projects can be highlighted here (in alphabetical order) that may be of use:

- *Accommodations*: These can vary from the luxurious to the basic. At the top end it might mean hotel rooms with en suite washing and toilet facilities (usually

Figure 7. Fieldwork training in action: Field training takes place in many different environments around the world. Here, students record stone platform terraces at the Marco Gonzalez site, Ambergris Caye, Belize, in July 2010. The students in the background are excavating stone risers of another structure, and are also digging down in front of the risers in the hope of discovering a preserved plaza floor – which they ultimately did (copyright Elizabeth Graham 2010, courtesy of the Marco Gonzalez Project).

shared, occasionally solo-occupied). The sliding scale of quality then runs down through rather less amazing motels, dorms, and bunkhouses to tents – although a well-pitched modern tent in the middle of a lush green field beats a sketchy motel in a rundown neighbourhood any day of the week.

- *Activities*: A good project director will move participants around a site, so they learn both general principles of excavation and specific skills such as surveying, section drawing, photography, and the like. Such a director will also challenge students to apply their classroom thinking to the site's interpretation, under-standing, and presentation: Why is the site structured the way it is? What might

Figure 8. The realities of fieldwork, part 2: Field training often means novel travel arrangements. Here, students travel to the Marco Gonzalez site, Ambergris Caye, Belize, in July 2010 via their normal mode of transport: the back of a truck. They have just been picked up from their hotel and are passing the dig house and lab (behind the white fence on the right). It is about five and a half miles from the site of the photo to the excavation – the concrete road soon ends, replaced by a sand road (copyright Elizabeth Graham 2010, courtesy of Leanne Chorekdjian and the Marco Gonzalez Project).

the differential scatters of find types around the site say about social structures? How can we best present this site and its data to the public? Once in the field, if you do not feel that you are getting this kind of support, then do not be afraid to politely say so. On a training project you need to experience a variety of different roles and skills; you will learn very little if you end up digging the same section of a trench for three weeks straight.

- *Catering*: This is usually organized communally, often on a rotation basis, and arranged by the project team itself; the quality depends on the project's finances, on one hand, and the ability of the cooks, on the other. If the food you are being given is awful and you think that you can do better, then offer to take a turn shopping and cooking – it beats doing the washing up, another regular chore. Do not be afraid to challenge social expectations here: all too often, even in the 2020s, women often find themselves being asked (or not-so-subtly edged) into taking the lead on such 'household' responsibilities. As the archaeologist Sally Schanfield/Binford famously said, 'I'm not here to cook; I'm here to dig.' As

61

Figure 9. The realities of fieldwork, part 3: Field training can mean simple working environments. Here, students from the Marco Gonzalez site, Ambergris Caye, Belize, in July 2010 work in the project 'lab', a large area under the dig house in San Pedro Town. The students are cleaning the bones from a burial of c. 800–850 CE that they had previously excavated (copyright Elizabeth Graham 2010, courtesy of the Marco Gonzalez Project).

mentioned in Chapter 1, we all need to be the change we want to experience, so do challenge gender bias expectations in such circumstances. Given that fieldwork is usually physically demanding, expect hearty food. Do not be afraid to eat it even if you are officially on a diet – if you are not used to sustained physical labour (most people these days are not), then your body is going to need this fuel to prevent collapse. Vegetarians and vegans are usually well provided for – increasing numbers of digs are totally vegetarian or vegan on health and sustainability grounds. Picky eaters have a harder time of it, although if you have a genuine food allergy, this ought always to be respected. Food will usually be purchased for you, but additional snacks such candy will be up to you to provide. Remember to drink lots – and lots – of water when doing fieldwork, even in cool/wet weather; there should be extensive supplies of potable water provided on site.

- *Alcohol and drugs*: Social mores vary from country to country. Plenty of excavations (as, indeed, people and nations) around the world have a zero-tolerance approach to all and any drugs, including alcohol, and you will get into major trouble if you sneak drugs or alcohol onto such sites. Put simply – illegal substances and fieldwork do not mix and can lead to your being thrown out of the project, at best, or arrested, tried, and ending up with a criminal record and resultant sentence, at worst. Such a crime could jeopardize the entire project and the work of hundreds of other people. In terms of legal drugs, especially alcohol, project directors will make clear the rules for consumption. If you cannot abide by those rules, then you should not come on the project. Increasing numbers of projects are designated alcohol-free zones. That said, many archaeologists enjoy an alcoholic drink *after* a hard day's work (never on site). If you do not like alcohol, or if your health or belief prohibit its consumption, then do not worry – no one ought to hassle you to partake, but you should at least be comfortable sitting alongside others who do, matching a soft drink to their hard drink to be sociable – plenty of 'eureka' moments have been had in the bar at the end of the day that transform the understanding of a site.

- *Equipment*: Major project equipment will usually be provided for you, but every archaeologist should have their own basic field kit, together with clothing appropriate to the climate and weather (see the discussion that follows – especially regarding waterproof and sun-proof kits). A full list of such suggested equipment is included in Appendix B of this book. If nothing else, you need to own your own trowel. (In the United Kingdom the four-inch solid-forged WHS pointing trowel is preferred; in the United States, the standard is the legendary Marshalltown trowel. Paeans have been written extolling trowels, and they are the most beloved and protectively held of all archaeological equipment – see Flannery 1982.) Dig clothing tends to be informal, of the jeans and T-shirt type; most people wear solid boots of some sort, often steel-toecap safety boots (sometimes required; some sites may also require archaeologists to utilize additional safety equipment such as high-visibility jackets and hard hats). It is worth keeping a set of nicer, cleaner clothes to one side for when you head out into the general population – if nothing else, restaurants tend to take a poor view of archaeologists covered in dirt arriving at their premises. Three key tips are (1) avoid any clothes with political slogans or crude jokes on them; (2) be aware of local sensitivities – for example, in many countries, avoid clothes that expose a lot of skin and be cautious of wearing too much 'military' gear in others – that is, make yourself look as harmless and inconspicuous as possible; and (3) avoid clothes that, once wet, are uncomfortable and take an age to dry – especially jeans or other cotton clothing. On some projects you may also be required to provide other accommodation equipment, such as sleeping bags, ground mats, tents, and cooking and other camping equipment – you should be told in advance if you do.
- *Health and safety*: These issues are taken very seriously. You will be given a briefing on this subject prior to, as well as on arrival at, the project site. There will always be a dedicated, trained first aider on site, a first aid kit, and a list of emergency services contact details and locations. Many people also bring their own personal first aid kit for minor cuts and grazes. People with health issues such as allergies should let the project director know well in advance and discuss solutions, such as carrying an EpiPen. Specific health hazards and risks will be

identified and planned for well in advance, so do not worry unduly about these risks. Bear in mind that the climate and weather can have a serious impact when you spend all day outside – even on an apparently cool but sunny day, sunburn, heatstroke, and dehydration are a risk, especially for people unused to doing hard physical labour outside. Plan accordingly and remember: tools are just that – tools, not toys – so do not play around with them.

- *Leisure*: Most projects will usually have one regular day off per week. Sometimes it is entirely up to participants to decide what to do on those days; other times, a trip to a local town or historic site might be arranged. There can be no doubt that projects based anywhere near the coast tend to see people heading to the beach whenever possible. Above all else, though, remember that projects have clear objectives. So you should not expect much free time – this is work, not a vacation. Hours will be long – 6 a.m. or even earlier starts are not uncommon, with hard labour all day and additional tasks in the evening. There may also be evening lectures and other training events. Get used to those dawn starts, or risk facing the wrath of the project directors; *your* tardiness is slowing down *their* project, on which their careers may depend.

- *Washing*: Cleaning facilities, for both yourself and your equipment, can vary considerably – toilet facilities, in particular, especially if your project accommodation is a campsite. If you are squeamish about such things, then archaeology really may *not* be the career for you. Having said that, because accommodations can sometimes be in hotels, motels, and dorms, washing facilities can be pretty good, and if nothing else, someone will eventually make a dash to a laundry. Wet-wipes and antibacterial no-water hand-wash/sanitizers are the archaeologist's friend on site.

- *Weather*: Obviously, weather affects your life on site in a manner to which you may never have been accustomed. Except in exceptional circumstances, fieldwork will usually go on no matter what the conditions. Be prepared – the project director will brief you well beforehand on what to expect. If the project director tells you that it will be cold and wet, then bring lots of good warm and waterproof clothes and a stout pair of waterproof boots; if, similarly, they say it is going to be incredibly dry and hot, bring along loose, light clothing that covers all your skin – sunburn is no joke. Remember that you may be sitting and/or crouching and thus exposing bits of your skin that do not normally see much sun. Even on cloudy days it is possible to get badly sunburned, be the weather hot or cold – the key is to cover up, and especially to wear a hat of some sort as the prevailing weather necessitates, as well as to wear lots of high-SPF sunscreen.

## Pre-university Education and Training

As little as a decade ago, most students studying in an undergraduate degree program in archaeology would have had some previous experience in the discipline. This experience was gained either through their school or college or through membership in an archaeological society. Such students would have had at least some limited experience of work on an archaeological site that prompted the urge to undertake a formal qualification, some basic appreciation of fundamental archaeological principles, and perhaps even an understanding of the realities of life working as an archaeologist. A smaller number of students would then have had considerably more experience. Numerous now-senior archaeologists received their grounding in the subject as energetic teenage fieldworkers in the 1970s and 1980s, and by the time they arrived at university they were frequently highly skilled field archaeologists in their own right.

The reality now is very different, owing to the tightening of the national school curriculum (particularly in the United Kingdom), the relative decline of 'local society' field archaeology (especially that involving minors, because child protection and health and safety concerns have made the involvement of children in such fieldwork much harder), and the changes to the nature and public availability of archaeological fieldwork. Because of these changes, it is now far harder for volunteers to become involved in fieldwork. Most undergraduate archaeology students arriving for their first year of study have little, if any, experience of the subject beyond that gleaned from TV shows and the Internet (this was the case of the author and the majority of his peers when they first arrived at university to study archaeology in the early 1990s too). Whether this shift in experience is a good or bad thing is not an issue that requires discussion here; what does matter is the implication of such a shift for anyone, of any age, who wants to get experiences, and possibly qualifications, in archaeology that are not at the university level.

Some people may want non-university experience of archaeology so they can go on into the university sector and gain a degree in the subject; others may simply wish to formalize a long-held interest in the subject but not spend precious time and money on gaining what may be, for them, a superfluous formal qualification. It is important that people considering trying to get experience in archaeology have at least a vague sense of where they see themselves a few years from now – studying archaeology somewhere, or simply enjoying the practice and experience of archaeology from a better-informed position than before? The former group of individuals could be well served by taking a non-university continuing education course in archaeology, be this at school or college; the latter group of individuals might include this option, but could alternatively be better served through membership of one of the many local, regional, or national archaeological societies that provide an array of opportunities in return for a modest annual subscription. Membership in such organizations brings many benefits, most importantly, access to events such as lectures and seminars, as well as fieldwork opportunities, and many of these events are geared towards people who work, being held in evenings, weekends, and during holiday periods (see Figure 10). Many local archaeology societies also have specialist subgroups based around a period (e.g., Roman, medieval), subject specialty (e.g., industrial archaeology), or even an individual town, village, district, or neighbourhood. Other specialist groups also exist, such as the Nautical Archaeology Society for those interested in maritime and underwater archaeology.

It is relatively easy, and relatively cheap, to get directly involved in archaeology via organizations like these – to get away from the TV or computer and go and learn about archaeology, undertake fieldwork, and/or get specialized training. Few people today live more than a short journey away from the base of one or other archaeological organization. This is the best possible way to become directly involved in archaeology – it is cost-effective, gets you in the field in the shortest possible time, introduces you to like-minded people, and is flexible – it can lead to an entire career in archaeology for some, a lifelong interest and history of involvement for others. Voluntary archaeology is also still an ideal way for children and teenagers (with or without their families) to become involved in archaeology, because any excavations will be well planned as regards both health and safety and child protection concerns. And above all, local community archaeology of this sort is fun – and archaeology ought always to be fun.

## Archaeology in the School Curriculum

The constraints of different nations' school curriculums make it extremely hard to study archaeology in school – up until the ages of between sixteen and eighteen, depending on your location – in virtually all countries around the world. These curriculums give little room for innovation to teachers in the classroom, and they do not include specific archaeological courses. Keen teachers are the only possibility for such content to be integrated into the curriculum. For example, there is sometimes a focus in US and Australian high schools around ancient history, or a primary school focus on social studies, but this is not common, and it is generally up to the individual teacher rather than part of the curriculum (see Figure 10). In the United Kingdom, for example, the National Curriculum dictates to a large extent what can and cannot be taught in history lessons, the only format for archaeological data and materials until the age of sixteen. As Moshenska (2009: 56) notes, this situation is exacerbated by the lack of archaeological training of schoolteachers: 'Archaeology graduates usually find it difficult if not impossible to get accepted on to teacher training courses, as archaeology is not a curriculum subject and is generally not taught in schools. The paucity of archaeological knowledge amongst schoolteachers thereby becomes a self-perpetuating problem.' This is a similar situation to that in the United States and Australia. The easiest way to become involved in archaeology up to the age of sixteen in the United Kingdom, and up to the age of eighteen in the United States, is, therefore, to join an archaeological society and learn about archaeology in your spare time rather than as part of everyday schooling. In the United Kingdom, the obvious choice is the Young Archaeologists' Club (for eight- to sixteen-year-olds) run by the UK national body for archaeology, the Council for British Archaeology. Similar events are run in the United States through the National Park Service's Federal Archaeology Program (as well as by individual state- or county-level organizations), and by various state-level organizations in Australia.

In the United Kingdom at least, things improve after the age of sixteen, because archaeology can be studied in post-sixteen education through a variety of qualifications:

Figure 10. Archaeology in the school curriculum: Most children love to be taught about archaeology in a practical format, which appeals to their natural sense of fun, and archaeology can be used to help teach many different school subjects. Here, schoolchildren are taught to identify finds discovered in the course of a nearby CRM excavation (copyright Archaeology South East UCL 2010, courtesy of Dominic Perring).

- AS and A levels in Archaeology (England and Wales only).
- Scottish Highers in Classical Studies (Scotland only).
- Business and Technology Education Council qualifications (BTECs) in Countryside Management and Construction and the Built Environment.
- City and Guilds certificates and diplomas in Countryside and Environmental Studies.

For those who are no longer in school, there is also the National Vocational Qualification (NVQ) in Archaeological Practice. The qualification is offered at levels 3 (entry level) and 4 (experienced professional), with level 5 (strategic management) in development. Each level consists of core units and a range of options.

It should be noted in closing that AS and A levels – and equivalent high school qualifications – in archaeology are relatively uncommon. By no means all schools or colleges offer such courses, and it may simply prove impossible to find a course offered nearby, even as an optional evening class. The reality is that although experience of archaeology prior to university is no bad thing to gain, such skills are not essential if one hopes to eventually work as an archaeologist. An embryonic career will not be destroyed without such experience, nor will it be ensured with it. And no university entry tutor will hold it against someone who did not study archaeology at the pre-university level.

## Academic Pathways in Archaeology

The varied higher educational systems around the world make it impossible to sum up all possible academic pathways into archaeology prior to university. And even once at university, durations and structures of degrees vary markedly even within single nations. It certainly should be noted at the outset that around the world, and at all levels, part-time study is usually possible, although this normally doubles – at the least – the total duration of study. Such a program is thus worth considering by anyone who must work to pay for their studies and/or who has other financial or family commitments.

At the BA/BSc level, many institutions around the world also offer diplomas and certificates of higher education that are not degree level and are awarded to students who have successfully completed part of a degree course. Similarly, between the BA/BSc and MA/MSc levels, many universities offer graduate diplomas or graduate certificates that are not degree level and are awarded to students who have successfully completed part of a graduate degree course.

### Focus on: Sarah Ward (China)

I am Sarah Ward, and I am a Visiting Professor in Maritime Archaeology at Dalian Maritime University (DMU)'s Centre for Maritime History and Culture Research. I am based in the port city of Dalian on north-eastern China's Yellow Sea coast. Founded in 1909, DMU is China's cradle of navigators, a 211 'National Key University', and an International Maritime Organization Centre of Excellence. I principally work on two national and two international research projects related to Sino-foreign maritime exchange and inland water transport, which supported Chinese seafaring activity. I undertake desk-based, archival, and field research, and I disseminate that research through media and conference presentations, written papers, and publications.

As a child, I was fascinated with the sea and what lies beneath. I grew up on the water, and I learned to scuba dive as a child. However, it was not until after I had achieved a Bachelor of Commerce and an MBA that I turned my attention to archaeology. I have since completed diploma, master's, and doctoral degrees in maritime archaeology. I hold recreational, technical, and commercial diving qualifications, along with professional certifications in coastal and marine law, international heritage protection, archaeological heritage conservation, media presentation, and project management. I have also invested heavily in developing my cultural intelligence and in building up my ecosystem-based altrocentric leadership skill set, so that I can provide psychologically safe working environments for my project teams.

My career began at the Nautical Archaeology Society in the United Kingdom in outreach, education, and stakeholder engagement. I knew then that if I wanted to be the best maritime archaeologist that I could be, I needed to gain experience in all aspects of the discipline, so I moved to a state government regulator's role managing maritime heritage in Australia. From there, I went into development-led archaeology, where I climbed the consulting ladder to project director level before moving into academia. My most helpful career tool has been my network. Why? In my entire twenty-year career, I have only had to compete for one role. Even then, I was invited to apply for it. Archaeological skills are essential, but it is your network that will give you the chance to use them. Nurture it.

There is no such thing as an 'average' week in my world. That is one of the things that I love about my job. It is as practical as it is intellectual, and it is that unique mix of activities that keeps me motivated. I spend about three months a year on-site, undertaking prospection, site identification, survey, excavation, and monitoring. I spend a similar amount of time with my team post-processing, analyzing, and interpreting data. The balance is spent in a mix of project planning, management, and dissemination. I love the fluidity and mobility that archaeology provides, and I feel incredibly fortunate that it has allowed me to live in five countries and work in thirty-five.

My top tip for pursuing a career in archaeology is to get grit and a growth mindset. That is not to say that practical and intellectual skills are not important. They are. Being competent and qualified for the task at hand is critical. But beyond that, passion, perseverance, and persistent long-term effort are paramount in becoming an archaeologist. Know that failure is part of the process. Do not be afraid of it. At some point in your journey, you will fail. We all have. Fail fast, and then move forward. Celebrate effort, not achievement (although that is nice too) and have the courage to keep going. I see so many people give up when they do not get the grades they want, their first archaeology job, or when their tenure is turned down. Do not let that be you.

There are so many incredible organizations to assist you in becoming an archaeologist that it is difficult to choose just one, so I will share two with you. First, the Nautical Archaeology Digital Library is an open-access online nautical archaeology archive freely available for anyone to use (see https://nadl.tamu .edu/). Second, my home university, DMU, is working with me to develop a series of special scholarships for women in maritime, in support of the United Nations Ocean Decade (see www.dlmu.edu.cn/). Why? Because you cannot be what you cannot see, and the world needs more women scientists.

## Choosing Your Degree Specialty

As outlined in Chapter 1, there are several different thematic routes into archaeology, practical as well as theoretical schools of thought. In part, these routes are a consequence of geography, drawn along national lines, and also partly a question of regional environmental specialty, such as African, American, Asian, Australian, Chinese, European, or Indian archaeology. These different approaches have a direct impact on the types of degrees available at both the undergraduate and postgraduate levels.

As previously noted, the anthropological archaeological school of thought is most dominant in the United States. Therefore, most archaeological degree courses in the United States are in anthropology departments, and most undergraduate degrees will involve a major or minor in anthropological archaeology or even just in anthropology. Historical archaeology, however, is now almost as important a specialty, so there are also many departments and undergraduate degrees involving a major or minor in historical archaeology, or even just archaeology. As a result, choosing a course of study in the United States is a relatively straightforward choice between an anthropological or a historical archaeology department or school, a decision likely to significantly influence future training and specialization.

In contrast, in the United Kingdom and Australia, anthropology departments rarely offer degrees in archaeology unless directly associated with an archaeology department – here, anthropology is a distinct and separate subject from archaeology. In these locations, 'pure' archaeology departments are the norm, although their teaching will usually include a similar series of themes to those in US anthropology departments. In these locations, the choice of degree type is ostensibly even easier than in the United States – archaeology, be it anthropological, prehistorical, or historical, is likely to be offered by, simply, an archaeology department. Further confusing the situation, the structure of UK university courses means that students there can usually apply directly for specific types of archaeological/anthropological degrees, selecting *before* their arrival a dedicated degree program on a period, topic, or theme (e.g., prehistoric or historical archaeology, Roman or medieval archaeology, British or European archaeology). This is the opposite of the situation in the United States, where the minor/major structure and broader general requirement courses of the credit-based university system mean that students make such specialization choices much later on, once at university and well into their studies.

When looking around to pick a university and a degree program, students should be aware that each university might offer archaeology courses in anthropology, archaeology, classics, and even history departments and schools. There may also be specialized departments, such as departments of Egyptology. Some universities even have more than one department that teaches aspects of one or more specialty in archaeology, such as an anthropology department and a history department. Prospective students need to look widely at what is offered across any university in which they are interested, and not be afraid to ask for advice. Similarly, when trying to decide what degree program or course for which to apply, students should be aware that some universities (especially in the United Kingdom and Australia) offer very tailored programs with limited options once study has commenced, often on defined or prescribed topics (e.g., a BA in prehistoric archaeology). In contrast, other programs (especially in the United States) will have more general requirements and an ability to pick a major/minor in different subjects, building up credits and allowing flexibility throughout the course of study, with the decision on the type of degree and field of study not being finalized until relatively close to the end of a program. Again, prospective students need to look widely at what is offered and not be afraid to ask for advice on what is taught, when it is taught, and how flexible a course or program is. In addition to the preceding information, for students in the United Kingdom, the Council for British Archaeology's 'Guide to Studying Archaeology at Undergraduate Level' is very useful.[4] A similar resource in the United States is the American Anthropological Association's AnthroGuide webpage,[5] and in Australia, the Australian Archaeological Association's Study Options webpage.[6] Similar guides exist in many other countries around the world, usually provided by different national voluntary or professional archaeological organizations. The World Archaeological Congress (WAC) also has an active student committee that links student archaeologists across the globe.[7]

The following pointers should help the choice of degree specialty at both the undergraduate and postgraduate levels:

- *BA or BSc study (broadly focused on humanities or sciences)*: In many cases, this decision will be made in relation to your A levels, Scottish Highers, or high school test subjects and results. Most BSc programs will not accept students without a background in the sciences, whereas BA programs will accept a broader range of entry backgrounds. BSc courses will have a heavier focus on archaeological science – some may even be dedicated programs in archaeological science or a specialty of that. All BA archaeology programs will include at least some of these more scientific aspects too, and normally will allow further specialization once the program is under way, so getting a BA degree does not necessarily stop a student from going on to further study at the graduate level in the sciences. Moving on from a BA to an MSc, or from a BSc to an MA, is merely a question of whether you wish to specialize slightly earlier on in your career or not.
- *Single or double/combined degrees*: This is a decision that must be made only in the United Kingdom and Australia: as noted previously, the US major/minor

[4] See https://new.archaeologyuk.org/Content/downloads/3320_Factsheet3b_Study_Undergraduate.pdf.
[5] See www.americananthro.org/LearnAndTeach/Landing.aspx?ItemNumber=24168&navItemNumber=736.
[6] See https://australianarchaeologicalassociation.com.au/careers-resources/information-for-students/study-options/.
[7] See https://worldarch.org/students/.

credit-bearing system does not focus so early on specialization. Many UK and Australian universities offer both "single honours" programs in archaeology (or specialties such as classical or historical archaeology), and "double/combined honours" programs in archaeology and many other subjects, most commonly archaeology and history (or art or ancient history), archaeology and Egyptology (or classical archaeology), archaeology and anthropology, archaeology and a language (both ancient and modern), and archaeology and geology or geography. The benefits of single honours study are a deeper focus on "pure" archaeology and a smaller peer group; the benefits of double/combined honours study are a broader appreciation of the place of archaeology and a larger peer group. But this is not a decision that should cause undue worry, as it is usually easy to swap between single and combined honours programs during your study if your preferences change.

- *"Pass" or honours courses*: This is a decision that must be made only in the United States, Scotland, and Australia, where honours courses are the result of taking a degree program with a longer duration and/or more credit. Making this decision (which is usually undertaken during the program of study, not at the start) is thus a commitment to longer, harder, and thus more expensive study overall, but the reward is a more 'merit worthy' degree that will better impress future employers. The result is that most students in the United States, Scotland, and Australia choose to pursue an honours degree if possible. In contrast, in England, Wales, and Northern Ireland, honours are awarded not for the duration of the course of study but for the program chosen at the start of study, given sufficiently good overall grades. Therefore, most English, Welsh, and Northern Irish students graduate with an honours degree unless their performance is exceptionally poor, unlike students in the United States, Scotland, and Australia, where honours are more closely tied to higher academic endeavours.

## Getting into the University of Your Choice

The decline of entry-level pre-university training in archaeology should not be taken as indicative of the lack of need for such qualifications later on; the reality is that without at least a bachelor's degree in archaeology or anthropology, even the most naturally brilliant of archaeologists will find it hard to get work. Prospective professional archaeologists have a clear career path to follow: they need to do what is required to get in the university archaeology program of their choice. In the United Kingdom, this means getting good A levels or Scottish Highers (ideally, all A and B grades) in appropriate subjects; in the United States and Australia, good high school SAT scores, along with a log of those all-important extracurricular activities that make an application stand out to college admissions staff.

A diverse array of A level or high school subjects is appropriate for an application to an archaeology or anthropology department for undergraduate study. This is unlike an application to study most STEM subjects at university, for which extremely high grades in specific subjects are a must to stand any chance of gaining entry. But subjects relevant to the archaeological curriculum include obvious choices such as history and geography; core subjects such as English, mathematics, and any of the hard sciences; as well as more unusual options such as economics. Languages, both ancient and modern, are also a definite bonus – from the ancient world, Latin being the obvious choice, and for the modern, German (Germany has a long tradition of archaeology and remains a publishing powerhouse in the subject). Italian and Spanish are also other excellent second-language choices; the latter is especially valuable in the United States. Indeed, a thorough command of at least one other language is arguably the most important skill that any aspiring or indeed active archaeologist should have.

Beyond the undergraduate level, application criteria get much tougher. Applicants for graduate study at the MA, MPhil, or PhD level need to have an excellent undergraduate degree (in the United Kingdom at 2.1 level or above, in the United States with a GPA of 3.4 or above). A proven ability in two languages is also a common requirement for PhD study in many universities, along with excellent GRE scores, if one expects to go on to any type of graduate study. International students studying outside their home countries in the United States, United Kingdom, and Australia are also likely to face stringent English language proficiency tests as part of their applications – together with increasingly stringent, government-enforced immigration procedures.

Beyond formal qualifications, there can be no doubt that various other things can be done to help gain entry onto the course of your choice. These will come up for discussion in the personal statement or interview that some universities require for prospective students. The aforementioned experience of archaeology with a voluntary society is obviously an excellent start, if possible – if nothing else, archaeologists like to hear about other people's fieldwork, so your experience on that summer dig is a good topic to bring up in discussion. But archaeologists are, by and large, kind and generous folk, and rare is the admissions tutor who will hold a lack of formal experience against a potential student; these tutors know how hard it is to get such experience. Enthusiasm for archaeology, shown through evidence of reading around the subject, even your thoughts on the approaches of the latest popular archaeology TV show, can go a long way. If nothing else, a bit of background research on the specialties of the department, its staff, and their research and publications can help a lot. Being able to briefly discuss the latest book by Professor Y from the department, for example, is a good application or interview icebreaker; even if the admissions tutor thinks that Professor Y is an idiot and their new book an abomination, at least you have shown an interest and are conversant with the subject. The worst possible thing is to be either so tongue-tied or, worse still, simply so uninformed that you have nothing to write or say about archaeology in response to the series of kindly – but probing – questions that the interviewer will ask.

Even if you cannot find anything to talk about regarding archaeology, then above all, in a personal statement or an interview situation, you must show enthusiasm for *something*. Archaeologists are people too – they have opinions on sports, current affairs, and TV as well, and your application is the admission officer's moment to judge not what you currently know, but rather your capacity to learn and to develop yourself in the future. An agile and inquiring mind and a willingness to think a question through and provide a logical response are the characteristics that will help win that coveted place in a course. An uncommunicative or unenthusiastic candidate is the one who will *not* be getting that place. If you cannot summon up serious enthusiasm now, then the admissions officer will have gained a strong impression of what your attitude is likely to be if you are accepted and they then have to deal with similar disinterest on a rainy morning on site.

## Choosing a University: Courses and Locations

Until the 1960s, choices of location for archaeological training were few and far between; perhaps two dozen universities spread across the globe offered some aspect of the subject, frequently at the postgraduate level only. The archaeologist Mortimer Wheeler believed that archaeology should be offered only at the postgraduate level, available after students had gained a thorough grounding in ancient/classical history and languages at the undergraduate level. Fast-forward half a century, and there are hundreds of undergraduate archaeology programs available all over the world. Some of these universities and their archaeology departments are extensive and world famous. Deciding between such an array of options can be tricky, and there is no perfect way to decide – the department of archaeology/anthropology and the program of study that suits one person will not suit another.

As a prospective student, you should carefully consider the following archaeological and non-archaeological issues, including asking questions about these when you visit the various campuses. Above all, you ought to try to visit a campus in person; there is no substitute for your gut instinct of a place in which you could end up spending years. You should also ask to meet current students during your visit; any good university will have prearranged such opportunities, and some may also arrange for recent graduates of their program to be around as well, to provide a longer-term view of the benefits of study at their institution.

### *Non-Archaeological Factors*

- *Location*: Does the location suit you and your family? For example, if you grew up in a big city, are you sure that a small, rural college will work for you? Similarly, if you are from the countryside, are you ready for inner city life? Try to visit a campus twice – once during the working week, and once at the weekend – that bustling weekday square lined with shops may be a deserted and depressing dustbowl on a Sunday.
- *Student body*: Do at least some of the current students come from a similar social/cultural background to yours? If, for example, you grew up in a multicultural inner-city environment and attended a coeducational state school, how do you feel about going to a college at which most of the student body was educated at private, expensive single-sex schools with much less demographic diversity?
- *Size/facilities*: How big is the university and how large is the school/department? How large will class sizes be, particularly in comparison to the library and lab

facilities? Try to visit the library when teaching is fully underway, for example, to see how much competition there is for space and books between students. What about other non-subject facilities, such as leisure and sports facilities, or public transport infrastructure? What are the living accommodations like, and where are they located in relation to the campus? Some dorms are virtually luxury hotels located right next to the campus (and with the prices to match); others are of much lower quality and may be a considerable distance from the campus.

- *Costs/finances*: What are the tuition fees of the university, and what can you normally expect to pay on top of that in terms of living costs? Does the university and/or the department offer financial aid, general hardship grants, merit-based scholarships, and/or specific allowances for fieldwork? If so, how do you apply for these funds and what, realistically, are your chances of getting such assistance – for instance, one in five, one in fifty, or one in five hundred?

## Archaeological Factors

- *Specialty*: Does the department offer archaeological specialties that you either know you want to study or think you might be interested in? You do not need to have any strong feelings either way, as plenty of students do not specialize until well into their studies; if you do, however, then this will likely be a deal maker or deal breaker. If the specialty of interest is offered, find out about the facilities supporting it, such as the provision of dedicated lab space, specialist equipment, and the like – offering a specialty is one thing, but following through on that offer in a meaningful way is quite another.
- *Fieldwork opportunities*: How much field experience do students gain as a part of their studies? Where and when does this experience take place, and is such work credit-bearing or not? Does the department arrange such work, or it is up to students to do this? Does the department offer financial assistance for travel and/ or living costs? Is related training (e.g., scuba training for underwater work) available, and does this carry an additional cost? (See Figure 11.)
- *Professional experience/training*: Does the university offer work placements with archaeological or related organizations such as CRM archaeology firms or museums? As for fieldwork, does the department arrange such work, or is it up to students to do this? Does the department offer financial assistance for travel and/or living costs?
- *Post-degree pathways*: What do graduates of the school/department go on to do after they graduate? How many graduates remain in the department for postgraduate study, and what are the funding opportunities available to support such studies?

## Selecting Courses at University

Congratulations – you have arrived at university! Your career in archaeology has begun. In addition to a busy social life, a bewildering array of courses awaits, some compulsory and others optional; and then there are other opportunities – possibilities

Figure 11. Archaeology in the university curriculum, part 1: Practical training plays a major part in the university archaeology curriculum. Here, a final-year student experiments with spindle whorl creation at UCL Institute of Archaeology's Experimental Archaeology Course, an annual practical training course for undergraduate students (copyright Charlotte Frearson/UCL Institute of Archaeology 2009).

of taking courses without credit, public lectures and seminars, discussion and reading groups, field trips, and so on. All this comes before you have even considered all the other non-specialist training courses in languages, presentation skills, CV writing, and the like that the university offers. It can all seem like way too much to take in. Therefore, no matter what you see yourself doing in the future – hardened field archaeologist or pampered industry CEO – some basic planning now will reap untold rewards in the future.

The key thing to remember is this: *you do not need to have your future all planned out at this stage.* Some people may feel on arrival that they are destined to become famous archaeologists; such people tend to talk loudly in the cafeteria and can be wildly intimidating. Perhaps they are right, but it is too early to tell. Getting the right balance of academic and field skills amid this hustle is by no means impossible but does require some solid thinking. Everyone should begin with the following simple step: At the *start* of your first academic year of study, and then at the *end* of each subsequent academic year of study, plan out roughly (this can be notepad-while-sitting-on-a-park-bench territory) your coming year and file this plan away somewhere. When drawing up your next year's plan, review the previous year's one and think ahead. Near the start of your final academic year of study, think about your post-degree options – what do you need to achieve these aims?

Figure 12. Archaeology in the university curriculum, part 2: Practical training in the university archaeology curriculum takes many different forms. Here, undergraduate students at UCL's Institute of Archaeology undertake an aerial photography interpretation practical as part of their studies (copyright UCL Institute of Archaeology 2010, courtesy of Ian Carroll).

This planning should, as noted, be simple; it is designed to make sure you get the required number of course credits to gain your degree. Confusingly, virtually every university in the world seems to operate a different credit scheme, so I will not even try to generalize here. It does not help that UK universities tend to work on a more chronological-year model of a set number of courses per term or semester, whereas US and Australian universities are more focused on credits, which can be taken at any time and build up towards a total and which offer more flexibility. However, by mapping out the skills you already have and the skills you would like to get, you will have a clearer picture of your goals (see Figure 12).

By the start of their last year of study, most people who go on to become professional archaeologists have probably been bitten by the bug and want to at least try to get a job in the profession at some time in the not-too-distant future. The result is then, in many cases, what becomes the most crucial decision of one's career: whether to remain in education and gain a higher, postgraduate degree or to go out and get field experience of one kind or another.

## Compulsory Courses/General Requirements

These are the courses that you *must* take. You must take them for a reason – they provide the basic tools of understanding and practicing archaeology. In the United

States and many other countries, there will also be other nonspecific general requirements in a broader range of subjects. *Do not avoid these courses.* Some will be general introductory courses on the history of archaeology, basic field methods, and core archaeological concepts (e.g., material culture) and principles (e.g., the laws of stratigraphy). Others will focus on honing your analytical skills: almost every university requires students to take a core option in archaeological theory, for example. You are also likely to have core courses on basic research skills.

## Option/Elective Courses

These are the courses from which you get to choose. The risk here is that you pick only what sounds like fun, or what your friends choose, or what that cute classmate is taking. If you pick courses this way, you risk ending up with an odd range of experience and no clear way forward at the end of your studies.

This is where the planning is important. You should choose some courses that just sound fun – ones where you are interested in a topic, period, or location. You always need to have at least one course that you are excited to be taking, one that gets you up in the morning. But make sure you get a balance of these with some strategic courses – these are ones that might sound less fun but provide useful transferable skills. Examples are particular lab-based courses that introduce you to specific archaeological techniques such as petrology, osteology, or environmental sampling, or particular skills-based courses such as finds drawing, remote sensing, the application of geographic information systems (GIS) or statistics in archaeology, and the like. All the latter courses are currently in demand in the field and are likely to be so in the future – a solid working knowledge of and experience in using them could be a clincher in a future job interview.

Some of those harder lab- or field-based classes might also carry a higher credit than the ostensibly easier lecture-based courses; such harder courses might also have longer dedicated class time but require much less personal study time. There is something to be said for knowing that you are done after four hard hours in a lab, rather than having one hour of a lecture but six more in the library. You also do not have to take a course for credit to get the benefit from it; the lecturers of most courses, except for those that have a lot of lab-based or practical work where you might take time away from students who *are* taking credits, will be happy to have students sit in on lectures and seminars but not be graded. It is important not to take too many of these non-credit options – at most, one or two per year – but this can be a great way to get experience of a specialty that intrigues you but in which you do not ever see yourself actively being involved. This might include courses from outside your own department/faculty – for instance, in anthropology, history, classics, or departments that specialize in particular cultures.

## Selecting Fieldwork: Choosing Your Ideal Field School

Almost all university archaeology courses require some participation in fieldwork that is at least monitored, and in many cases formally assessed, to gain a degree qualification (see Figure 11). The length of time required, forms of monitoring and assessment, and variety of work offered varies considerably among universities. Some require only a few weeks of work, others the equivalent of several months; some specify only fieldwork organized by the university itself, and others accept any active work (such as an archaeological survey or excavation but also lab or museum work) organized by a reputable organization. Increasingly, such training is focused into dedicated field schools run by universities or allied training organizations. There are numerous searchable online portals that can guide you to different opportunities: to give three such examples, there is the Archaeological Institute of America's fieldwork list,[8] the Council for British Archaeology's fieldwork guide,[9] and *Current Archaeology* magazine's digs guide.[10]

The reality is that most archaeology students want to get as much field experience as possible – summer digging in glorious weather is generally what people had in mind when they signed up for a degree in archaeology. For many, the fieldwork undertaken in the spring or summer of their first year of study will be their first real exposure to the formal practice of archaeology. Some already knew this was what they had long wanted to do and love it from the first moment; others may be less sure, but rapidly fall in love with the process. And a minority of participants realize, often painfully, that this is not what they thought it would be – such students frequently switch to another degree program entirely in their second year.

Picking fieldwork is as important as picking courses; find out as much as possible beforehand about what the field project in which you want to participate will be doing, what your role will be, what skills and experiences you will gain, and what the working and living conditions will be like – refer back to the points raised in the section earlier in this chapter about going on your first archaeological project. Many universities give a lecture on the available fieldwork opportunities some time in their spring term, at which time the various project directors tell people about their proposed work, to help students choose; other universities simply have one excavation that all students must attend. If you do have an option, think also about how the fieldwork you are considering fits into your overall program of study. Do not be afraid to speak to students who have previously attended any field school to hear of their experiences, both positive and negative.

## Dissertation/Thesis

Another component of university study that many students face is a dissertation or thesis – a longer piece of independent research work. This is usually begun towards the end of the undergraduate degree program. Again, situations vary among universities: many have a compulsory dissertation, but in a few it is only an option; some require only 5,000–10,000 words (approximately 20–40 pages of text), others as much as 15,000–20,000 words (60–80 pages of text); some require original or

---

[8] See www.archaeological.org/programs/professionals/fieldwork/fieldwork-list/.
[9] See https://new.archaeologyuk.org/fieldwork.    [10] See www.archaeology.co.uk/digs/fieldwork.

field research, and others require only secondary-source, library-based work. This is useful work for a variety of reasons:

- The dissertation/thesis helps to focus your thinking on a topic or specialty that you might want to study as a postgraduate, so it may crystallize your career aspirations.
- It is a useful document to bring along to a job interview – for non-archaeological as well as archaeological employment – as it demonstrates your capacity for clear thinking and writing, discipline, and independent working.
- It often carries considerable credit – so by taking a dissertation/thesis option, you may considerably reduce your class workload.
- It can be fun – you get to follow through an issue from beginning to end, which is (in theory) what real-world archaeology is like, or at least should be like. If, as an undergraduate, you find that you really like doing this research, this is one indication that you might enjoy postgraduate study.

## Non-specialist Courses

Universities also offer a host of other (usually non-credit-bearing) courses and training. You are well advised to make good use of these, as a portion of your tuition fees is contributing towards the cost of running these whether you take them or not. Such opportunities are usually offered through campus-wide rather than school/departmental facilities, and include the following:

- Computing skills, on different types of software or applications.
- Language skills: Languages are incredibly useful for archaeologists, and this may be your last opportunity to pick up such skills at no additional charge. The benefits of being multi-lingual are numerous, and too few people take this issue as seriously as they ought to. If you do not already have a second (or third, or fourth) language, avail yourself of the opportunity now!
- Professional development skills, such as how to create a CV and present yourself well in a job interview.
- Academic skills, such as how to write clearly and effectively. Training in the creation and giving of presentations can be particularly useful, as almost every-one – archaeologist or not – needs to be able to give a good public presentation these days. It is better to learn how to do this now, in the safety of a university in front of your peers, than later in front of your new boss.

## Extracurricular Activities

Extracurricular activities at university fall into three broad camps. Most people sample a bit from all three, but no one should ever feel under pressure to do any of these. They are as follows:

- *Archaeological*: These are the extra opportunities that most archaeology depart-ments offer not only to their students but also to their staff – public lectures and seminars, reading groups, field trips, and the like. When chosen carefully, such opportunities are a great way to keep up to date on a subject; find out about new sites, concepts, or methods; and meet other archaeologists from elsewhere. A top tip for those interested in archaeology but not studying at a university is that most of these events are also open to the public and are free to attend; you just have to find out when and where they are held, as they tend not to be widely publicized. Why not check out the webpage of your local archaeology depart-ment and see what is being offered?
- *Career-oriented*: These are those aspects of life at university that, undoubtedly fun, also have at least some tentative career benefits. Volunteering in the community in different ways is a classic example. In the current economic climate, every little thing you can do to make your CV stand out from the hundreds of others on offer to an employer is worthwhile.
- *Social-oriented*: These are all those remaining aspects of life at university in which many students participate, with varying degrees of benefit and/or success. Social, cultural, sporting, political, and religious organizations of every possible variation exist on every campus in the world. For example, many skills or sports have at least a passing applicability to archaeology – in the author's own career, the knowledge of rock climbing, sailing, and scuba diving picked up in college has come in handy several times.

## Postgraduate Qualifications: Graduate School and the MA/MSc

Most professional archaeologists now have a postgraduate qualification. Whereas at one time a good BA/BSc (graded overall at 2.1 or above in the United Kingdom, GPA of 3.4 or above in the United States) was sufficient to get a job as an archaeologist and/or to do well in the non-archaeological job market, an MA/MSc is increasingly common. This is particularly so for certain archaeological careers. Those intending to go on to get a PhD, for example, can usually proceed only if they first gain an initial postgraduate qualification. Even for those who never intend to work as archaeologists, such a higher degree is increasingly common, a means of distinguishing oneself from the mass of other applicants for a job.

A range of issues surround the decision to undertake postgraduate study, and such a course of action is not to be entered into lightly (see Table 3). In the United Kingdom, an MA/MSc program will normally last twelve months; elsewhere, especially in the United States, they can last much longer, twenty-four months or more. Such courses require extensive coursework commitments and prolonged periods of self-study; in all cases, the costs involved are considerable, and the demand for merit-based financial support outstrips supply. Government-secured loans for study are usually available, but this still means committing yourself to

TABLE 3. The pros and cons of studying towards a higher degree in archaeology

| Pros | Cons |
| --- | --- |
| Often the only way to get certain types of specialist training such as in ceramic analysis or environmental or conservation work. | Some employers prefer to hire based on practical experience, and they may be dubious of university-based training (but there are programs that offer work placements). |
| A good way to learn about a specialty before you commit to pursuing a career in it. | Pursuing a degree can be costly and time-consuming, with no guaranteed return on your investment such as a job or higher pay. |
| A good way to meet people and network for future jobs – decent courses introduce you to possible employers, and you may well end up working with former classmates. | Fewer and fewer programs offer much practical training experience (except for certain dedicated programs – usually the hardest ones to get into). This lack of practical experience can be a barrier to future employment. |
| A good way to build up generic transferable skills such as research, report writing, and presentation skills. | |
| Many employers like to see a higher degree these days – it is a way to distinguish the mass of potential employees from one another and is often seen to be evidence of greater maturity and common sense. | Some employers – and some family members – are worried that going to graduate school means you simply did not know what to do with yourself upon graduation and so decided to spend yet more years in college to avoid settling down. |
| If you are hoping to move into some specific sectors of archaeology (particularly academia, but to a lesser extent government and museums) a higher degree is virtually essential – you are unlikely to get hired without one. | Although an MA or MPhil may be looked on in a kindly light, some employers, both archaeological and non-archaeological, are scared off by a PhD, as they feel that you may be too much in an "ivory tower" to work well in the real world. |
| If you are already employed, it is always worth asking about taking leave to allow part-time study (any decent employer will be keen to encourage your personal development and may be able to help – some organizations even give training stipends or interest-free loans). | Sadly, some employers are stuck in the dark ages of their employees' professional development and simply will not help out in any way. Others might like to but are too small or too poor to be able to help. You may have to quit and move jobs to get this kind of support. |
| If you are working and paying your own way you may be able to claim some of the expenses as a tax deduction and/or apply for government loans at preferential rates. A small number of people also get grants, awards, and other bursaries to pay for study. | |

significant financial outlay and, for most people, personal debt, alongside years of hard work. And not everyone is suited to the pressures of this type of study, even those who did well in their undergraduate studies.

For some students, the choice of what course to study is self-evident; the author's main interest at this point in his life was maritime archaeology, so an MA in that archaeological specialty was the obvious way forward. Others may feel the same way about a variety of period, subject, or regional specialties. This is the reason why there are so many hundreds of specialist MAs on offer. Some students may also know that they want to gain skills in a dedicated field or technical skill, such as remote sensing or osteoarchaeology. Other prospective postgraduate students, though, may simply know that they would like to study for an MA/MSc to enhance their career prospects, without a driving special interest. For such individuals, the choice of which course to pick can be much harder. All MA/MSc degrees require specialization to a greater or lesser extent, which makes them markedly different from BA/BSc studies. Once one has embarked on a postgraduate qualification there is also usually much less room for manoeuvring in terms of course options. A badly chosen course may lead to the painful decision either to study specialties in which you are not particularly interested or to drop out altogether, neither of which is a particularly appealing option. Therefore, it is important to carefully study the content of an MA/MSc program for which you are considering applying to make sure it is the right program for you.

Assuming you have made the decision to undertake postgraduate study, the process of picking a university – choosing courses and locations – discussed earlier must be revisited. Entry requirements vary widely among universities, but most require a high first-degree score – at the very least a BA or BSc graded overall at 2.1 or above in the United Kingdom, or with a GPA of 3.4 or above in the United States. More popular courses will require substantially higher overall grades than this. A proven ability in two languages is also a common requirement for PhD study in many universities, along with excellent GRE scores for any type of graduate study. Entry will also usually depend on a successful and often intensive interview, as well as two or more supportive letters of reference from your previous/current university. Even if all these hurdles have been successfully negotiated, some courses remain oversubscribed, and entry may come down to timing and luck.

The process of applying for postgraduate study begins for many students during their final year of undergraduate study, another burden during an already busy period of one's life. Getting an attractive package of application forms, references, CV, and supporting documentation together is a task in and of itself. Visits and interviews can drain funds and spirit alike. Some students, in fact, wait a year, applying for graduate school after they have graduated from their first degree; such a gap year, if used thoughtfully, is a good period in which to build up finances for the coming study and to gain direct archaeological experience as a volunteer.

Choosing a graduate course comes down to a series of factors; all the issues discussed previously in relation to picking an undergraduate program apply again here. Many students, in fact, choose to return to the same university for postgraduate qualifications; there are obvious benefits to this, such as knowing the university, local area, facilities, and the like. The specialty you wish to study may well not be offered at your old university, however. And in addition, you may wish to have a change of scene after several years in the same place. Even more so than for undergraduate courses, many postgraduates pick a university based on cost: the prices charged by different universities for postgraduate study vary markedly, sometimes by many thousands, and when added to the varying costs of living in different locations, this can add up to significant sums of money over the long term.

## Studying for a Doctorate

The ultimate form of archaeological qualification remains that of the doctorate, most frequently known as a PhD, sometimes as a DPhil. This is based around a sustained period of independent and original research and writing that concludes in the submission, and in many countries a verbal examination, of a dissertation/thesis anywhere between 80,000 and 200,000 or more words in length.

The decision to study for a PhD in archaeology should be made only after considerable thought and discussion with your tutors, friends, and family. Doctoral study can be incredibly stimulating, enjoyable, and worthwhile. The production of the dissertation alone can be one of an individual's greatest achievements. A PhD can also lead to a distinguished career at the highest professional levels of archaeology. However, such study can also be financially crippling and emotionally destructive – the knowing joke in academia is that the initials PhD stand for 'permanent head damage'. The quandary is that the path to a successful PhD is littered with the metaphorical corpses of failed doctoral students and abandoned theses, but equally, almost all the people who have completed a PhD consider the work taken to achieve this to be one of the high points of their lives.

The PhD is not a route that suits everyone, and it is not always the best career path. Unlike BA/BSc and MA/MSc qualifications, which almost all employers will welcome, a PhD can actively harm some careers as much as it helps others. For those who wish to pursue an academic or related career in, say, a museum, a PhD is just about essential; but for many others, both archaeologists and others, the PhD can prove to be a waste of time, money, and effort. Although some CRM, government, and other archaeologists have PhDs, there is an argument to be made against these in such experience-based job sectors. It may prove better to have spent the time doing the job itself and working up to a position of seniority, rather than doing a PhD. Others have completed a PhD in archaeology only to find themselves unable to find work as archaeologists, outcompeted for the few academic jobs that exist and out-skilled for the posts in other sectors of archaeology. Meanwhile, the non-archaeological world is even less understanding of a PhD in archaeology. A few employers may be impressed by the qualification, but many more will be actively put off by it, feeling that it represents at best an unnecessary luxury and at worst an otherworldliness fatal to the successful running of a business. Therefore, a PhD is the best option only for a minority.

If you are still seriously thinking about undertaking a PhD, then bear the following in mind:

- *Topic*: Can you write a coherent, referenced, 1,000-word essay on your proposed topic that your parents/partner/best non-archaeological friend can understand? After you hide this essay away for a fortnight, when you reread it, does it excite and energize you? If none or only some of this is true, then are you sure that you want to do a PhD on this topic at least, or even do a PhD at all? Such an essay is often required by universities as part of any PhD application. Fewer and fewer departments provide prearranged research projects (unlike the sciences, where such a situation is common), so it is normally up to applicants to come up with their own topic and to sell their ideas as worthwhile and feasible to their university of choice.
- *Method*: How are you going to actually do the PhD? What data do you need access to produce your thesis? What facilities do you need, and at what cost? How and where will you analyse your data? If you plan on doing any fieldwork, what are the logistics of such work, such as getting to and from the site? What happens if you go into the field to collect your information and it either proves impossible to collect or, worse still, just isn't there – do you have a 'plan B'?
- *Supervisors*: Your supervisors will be your main contact with your university, and so a good working relationship with them is essential. You need to be able to talk to them about your work, trusting them to advise you well and in a timely manner. *Choose your supervisors wisely*. PhDs regularly come to grief through a breakdown of the supervisory relationship. As any relationship, it requires both parties to work at it. If you know that Professor X is a brilliant researcher, but you have never hit it off with them on a personal level, then you need to find another supervisor – you must be able to work well together from day one. Similarly, think very hard about being supervised by Dr Y, whom you know socially as the funniest member of the faculty, but who has a reputation for not bothering to read students' work quickly.
- *Timing*: How much time, realistically, can you devote to your studies, and thus, roughly, how long will the PhD take? Remember, a full-time PhD student takes, at the very least, three or four years to submit the dissertation or thesis; many take double that time, and part-timers will take even longer. A decade-long period of study is not uncommon, and at peak periods may involve long hours of work into the evenings and weekends. This kind of lifestyle gets tiresome very quickly, and it can put a strain on the calmest of individuals and strongest of personal relationships.

- *Family*: How do your family and close friends feel about this? If you are in a long-term relationship, what does your partner think of this in relation to their own life goals – a work promotion, having children, or simply the desire for you to not work (too many) weekends and during otherwise free time?
- *Finances*: How are you going to pay for it? Given that the speediest of doctorates takes at least three or four years, how do your long-term finances stack up? What are your other financial goals in this period, such as buying a house? Bear in mind that the competition for any sort of financial aid for a PhD is intense, with dozens of high-calibre applicants for every grant given out.
- *Outcome*: What do you see being the result of the process, beyond those colourful doctoral robes and the fancy letters after your name – a job? If so, what sort of job – based where, doing what, being paid how much? Speak to people with PhDs who have jobs and ask them how they got their current post and how they feel about it.

## Focus on: Jessica Thompson (US)

My name is Jessica Thompson, and I am an Assistant Professor at Yale University in the United States. My research focus is on the archaeology of human origins, so I spend some time each year at field locations in Ethiopia and Malawi (see Figure 13). My job is split into the three main aspects of academic archaeology: research, teaching, and service. In theory, my time is divided about 40/40/20, but in reality it varies depending on my commitments at any given time. I live my life by the rhythm of two semesters and a summer, with most summer spent on research – typically fieldwork – overseas.

Archaeology combines my childhood desire to be an author and tell stories with a keen interest in science that I developed in high school. I went to university with interests in biology and anthropology, but at a field school in the Illinois River basin I fell in love with the experience of archaeological fieldwork. Although field conditions can be uncomfortable, there is just nothing like the feeling of uncovering something that was last held by someone thousands (or even millions) of years ago. Through my BS, MPhil, PhD, and six years of post-doctoral experience I have maintained this fieldwork-focused thread. Today, my primary expertise is in human origins research, and my practical specialization is in the study of fossil animal bones recovered from ancient archaeological sites.

I have taken an entirely academic-focused pathway, which is very much a long game. It requires a lot of up-front education, plenty of time volunteering and gaining experience at one's own expense, and an enormous amount of persistence. Academic positions are scarce, and job descriptions can be quite specific, so there may be only a few posted each year that apply to you. Application-writing and interview skills are the intangibles that make a difference in the process but do not appear on your CV. After four years in a tenure-track position at a different university, I moved to my present job. The most helpful aspects of my CV were my experience as a project leader and a demonstrated capacity to do research (publications, grants) across a range of 'big question' human origins topics.

My job is an incredible source of both passion and stress. I love that every day I will go to work and learn or maybe even discover something new. Introducing students to the field for the first time, or mentoring experienced students to the next level, is also incredibly rewarding. However, I feel I am never really 'off the clock', and there is always a long to-do list. An average work week during the semester would see me engaged in daily correspondence and meetings, preparing and delivering classes, supervising activities in my lab, and trying to partition out time for manuscript and grant writing. A lot of these activities follow me home for nights and weekends. Fieldwork during the summer typically goes for about two months, after a year of preparation. It is logistically challenging and can be frustrating, but I have never lost the excitement and freedom of being in the field.

My top tip for pursuing a career in archaeology is that thinking big but staying practical is the best way to stand out in a crowd of motivated, accomplished people. It is important to have a primary, broadly applicable skill (say, a particular type of analysis), complemented by a suite of underlying skills (e.g., in computers or fieldwork) where you can involve students and other stake-holders. However, you also need to be able to link these skills to a bigger picture that holds broader intrigue. In my case, I can analyse bones from archaeological sites, run a field project, and work with GIS. But in getting an academic job, I needed to be able to embed these skills in a meaty research question. Mine is the origins of our species, *Homo sapiens*.

My fieldwork takes place primarily on the African continent, and there are heritage resources available only there (e.g., fossils relevant to early human evolution) that are of global significance. However, the results of their analysis are not always broadly available even to people in the countries from which these resources derive. In addition to limited specialist capacity, the lack of community knowledge about these resources can inadvertently hasten their destruction. The future of palaeoanthropology, and the archaeologists who operate within this research framework, must rely on actively growing capacity within the countries where we find ourselves working. There is no perfect solution, but we have a duty to explicitly address this problem as an integral and ethical part of our research, rather than as an add-on.

## Additional Training and Skill Sets

One of the greatest joys of working as an archaeologist is the continual process of learning that is inherent to doing archaeology. A good archaeologist is always

Figure 13. The realities of fieldwork, part 4: Work ongoing at the Hora 1 site in the Mzimba District of Malawi (copyright Jessica Thompson/CC-BY 2021).

learning and, perhaps more important, is driven by the desire to learn – sometimes formally, through training, lectures, symposia, and the like; sometimes informally, through observation and participation. As new sites are discovered, new theories expounded, new techniques developed, and new laws and management structures proposed, so an archaeologist continually refreshes their knowledge and expertise.

Although a career in archaeology has many practice-specific training requirements, many other skills can usefully be developed by both practicing archaeologists and those wishing to enter the career. It is worth it to everyone to take the time to think about the array of skills that archaeology brings. This is especially important for students considering pursuing a career, who may have the opportunity to pick up additional skills at no additional cost while still in college. Examples include the following:

- *Bush craft*: Many of the bush craft or wilderness skills that have become increasingly popular of late have an applicability to archaeology. Some of these come down to good common sense. It is valuable to know to how to safely handle sharp tools (and how to keep them sharp), use a compass, read a map, and move efficiently through the landscape with minimal disturbance. Other skills may be more esoteric or equally mundane: a detailed knowledge of plant species, for example, might be helpful on one site, an ability to tie a secure knot on another. In many other countries, a basic ability to handle firearms safely can be useful (e.g., when working in an area with a large bear population). This is in marked contrast to the United Kingdom, where the lack of dangerous species, on the one hand, and tight gun controls, on the other, mean that such a skill would be looked upon oddly.

- *Business/financial*: Do you know how to read/create a budget spreadsheet and associated report? How to do basic financial planning? How to develop and run basic statistical analyses? If the answer is yes to any of these questions, then you are one up on many archaeologists. If you have a formal qualification such as an MBA, you will be even more rare in the industry.

- *Computing*: Business-related information technology (IT) skills, such as a high level of competency in a particular type or product of financial management software, can be extremely useful; expertise in building/maintaining websites, databases, and geographic information systems (GIS) is of particular value. The latter are hugely important to archaeologists, and they are becoming ever more so as we collect both more, and higher-quality, digital data. An archaeologist with well-honed experience in GIS will always be welcome on a project and is unlikely to ever struggle to find work.

- *Drafting and surveying*: Although aspects of these skills are taught to most archaeologists, shockingly few archaeologists are really adept at these skills. People properly trained in landscape and/or building surveying and drafting are incredibly useful in archaeology. So, too, are those who can draw up and/or interpret formal building or architectural plans.

- *Editing*: Here, editing means an ability to write clearly on the one hand (decent schooling in the basics of grammar and sentence construction is a good start; formal/professional training in how to write effectively even better), and specific word skills, on the other – such as knowing how to edit work effectively, how to work as a professional editor (including journalism-specific skills such as copyediting), how to proofread, how to create book indexes, and so on.

- *Environmental*: Archaeologists of many guises increasingly use environmental sampling of various types. The broader principles of sampling are also highly relevant to archaeology at heart; the 'polluter pays' principle behind CRM archaeology is taken directly from similar principles and funding of environmental work, especially environmental impact analyses. Consequently, specific skills such as knowing how to take soil, water, air, or species (flora/fauna) samples can be useful to archaeology, as can broader analytical modelling skills relating to the calculation of statistics, such as species density, threat, and the like.

- *Lab*: Core laboratory skills – how to work in a lab without breaking things or hurting yourself or people – are useful; more specialized skills, in particular, biological or chemical sampling, processing, and analysis, are even more valuable.
- *Languages*: To repeat what was said before: language skills are incredibly useful to archaeologists – the more numerous and extensive the better.
- *Mechanics*: A host of skills can prove useful under this banner – mechanical skills such as engine maintenance of various forms, on the one hand, craft skills such as carpentry and metalworking, on the other. If you can get a generator working, make up a serviceable wooden storage box, or undertake similar tasks, you are likely to be welcome on most archaeological sites.
- *Media*: This does not mean the ability to present a TV show; it means the ability to design, produce, write for, and edit different types of media – websites, videos, books, and so on. This encompasses a wide array of practical skills, including computer skills such as website design and maintenance as well as film/video recording, direction, editing, and post-production.
- *Teaching*: This can comprise basic teaching competencies – can you create a decent presentation in PowerPoint or similar software, and then give a clear, enjoyable presentation to an audience of between five and five hundred people aged anywhere between eight and eighty? This is something that most archae-ologists, especially academics, should be able to do but, surprisingly, many cannot. More specialized competencies – up to and including formal teaching qualifications – can be even more useful.
- *Transport*: A valid driver's license, plus experience with different types of vehicles (manual and automatic transmissions, two- and four-wheel drive, the latter especially off-road), is always useful; a driver's license for larger vehicles such as trucks, buses, and the like is even more valuable, and everyone ought at least to know how to do basic maintenance tasks such as changing a car tire and checking oil levels. Many maritime archaeologists also have various boat-handling qualifications, from basic leisure boat-handling skills right up to formal merchant navy ship-handling ratings; even more have commercial/industrial rather than sports diving qualifications. In a different light, a few archaeologists even have private pilot's licenses.

## *'Soft Power' Skills*

For the second edition of this book, I have added this new section of 'non-archaeological' people skills that are of importance to all the heritage professionals whom I know and work with. Put simply, this is about a range of people-focused skills that enable individuals, and teams, to work more effectively, both on their own and as part of a group. There are many terms for these skills, and many books, online sources, and formal training programmes are available to learn more about them. For the purposes of this book, I split these into three as follows:

- Influencing and networking skills
- Conflict management, resolution, and negotiating skills
- Policy skills.

These transferable 'soft power' skills are useful in terms of getting as well as succeeding in a job. The UK civil service, for one, and many comparable governments and businesses around the world, use assessments based on such skills-sets as part of their recruitment processes. In the UK government this is called the 'Success Profile Framework'. This moves recruitment away from using a purely competency-based system of assessment by introducing a more flexible framework that assesses candidates against a range of elements using a variety of selection methods. This gives the best possible chance of finding the right person for any job, driving up performance and improving diversity and inclusivity[11].

On the first of these groupings, 'influencing and networking skills', there are a range of different terms in use, but commonly these can be called 'authentic' and/ or 'inclusive' behaviours. They are often used in the context of leadership development for people formally leading and managing people, but their value goes far wider than that. You do not have to be a 'leader' of a team to benefit from inclusive ways of working that help you positively influence an outcome and work effectively in a network. Authentic/inclusive behaviours are also ones that, through both instinct and environmental conditioning, many archaeologists excel at. These are the skills that make the best archaeological fieldwork both appealing and successful. The six signature traits of authentic/inclusive behaviour are shown in Table 4.

On the second issue of 'conflict management and resolution skills', these are a distinct range of 'soft power' skills related to how to negotiate with people in difficult circumstances, through both actions and behaviours. As before, there are many terms for these skills, and many books, online sources, and formal training programmes are available to learn more about them. But knowing how to remain calm and potentially to defuse tense situations is a skills-set useful in many different circumstances, not least in archaeology, where you may interact with many different people of many different backgrounds, often in challenging circumstances, either physical or emotional. Keeping cool and calm under pressure, maintaining a dignified and respectful approach to others, thinking long-term and so de-escalating 'flash point' conflict situations are all skills that can be useful in archaeology.

---

[11] See www.gov.uk/government/publications/success-profiles.

TABLE 4. The six characteristics of authentic/inclusive behaviours

| | |
|---|---|
| **Curiosity**<br>(about people, places, and ideas) | Asking about and respecting others' experience and ideas; recognizing that everyone is an expert in something and that there is value in diversity of experience and opinion |
| | Deploying active and inclusive learning styles and approaches: practical learning, oral and other forms of non-textual transmission of information and skills |
| **Cultural intelligence**<br>(collecting and analyzing data and acting upon it) | Seeing links and building bridges between theory/policy and delivery/practice |
| | Deploying different mental 'band-withs' – always collecting, analyzing, and sharing data, thoughts, and ideas |
| **Collaboration**<br>(building and sustaining partnerships) | Thinking like and working effectively in a team, internally and externally |
| | Bringing a range of contacts and collaborators together, people who bring different perspectives on and approaches to an issue |
| **Commitment**<br>(being present, showing commitment through deeds and not just words) | Treating every opportunity as a learning opportunity; central to this is thinking about our own personal development – how do we learn, and how do we apply that learning? |
| | Being hands-on, showing commitment through action, and challenging hierarchies – e.g., putting aside one's ego for the greater good by volunteering to do 'drudge' work |
| **Courage**<br>(being bold and being brave) | Being honest in a situation, sharing and giving people the space to process any news – good and bad |
| | Using formats like '360 feedback' to give constructive advice on personal and professional development |
| **Cognizance**<br>(recognizing and challenging unconscious bias in oneself) | Being on one's own journey of self-discovery; this will include some potentially painful periods of reflection |
| | Undertaking activities like unconscious bias training, reflecting upon our own backgrounds and experiences |

On the third issue of 'policy skills', this is then perhaps the most practical of the three groupings, and which may seem the easiest to comprehend – but beware. What I mean by 'policy skills' is understanding the complex networks, both formal and informal, of any community that you work within. Some of this can be gained through ensuring familiarity with the various vision and strategy documents of any organization that you might interact with, across the public and private sectors, government, and industry. But much else here is left unsaid and can be far harder to comprehend – the network of links between different government departments in a particular nation, for example, or in those areas of life where the public and private sectors intersect. Getting to know such 'soft power' connections takes time – there are no guidebooks written about these linkages. This requires you to build up knowledge of the different organizations involved; of their relevant aims and objectives; of government policies and practices – and thus of associated laws and regulations; and then of 'big picture', usually national and often inter-national, geopolitical interconnections. And it also requires you to deploy the 'soft power' skills identified above to network successfully with individuals in such organizations, sometimes with people in identifiable positions of power, and sometimes with the less obvious powerbrokers, the people in the shadows and behind the scenes.

As an example, in the author's former role as a local government archaeologist in the English county of Surrey, I needed to network within the following communities and organizations:

- County council (my employer): the unelected civil servants in the culture/heritage, planning/development (of which I was one), and infrastructure/environment departments; and beyond these, the elected county councillors who chaired the different committees that set policy and made decisions on such issues.
- Borough and district councils: the unelected civil servants of the eleven different local planning authorities, each with their own range of policy concerns linked to the county council, and the elected councillors who again chaired the different committees that set policy and made decisions on such issues.
- Local/national political intersections: especially with the local Members of Parliament, and influential/politically connected locals, e.g., members of the House of Lords in the area who served in various official and unofficial capacities.
- Local/regional/national business/industry links: for example, mineral/aggregate producers and housing and infrastructure developers, including organizations (both public and private) linked to the road and rail networks.
- Local, regional, and national community, including religious, groups and organizations, especially with the clergy and lay staff of the Church of England, a major owner of land and historic buildings in England.
- Local and regional culture/heritage/environment organizations, including local museums and cultural organizations; the various local archaeology and history societies; local environmental and ecology groups and trusts, including the

county wildlife trust; universities both in the county and those based outside it that undertook fieldwork within it; and local and regional elements of national organizations, especially the National Trust, which runs operationally on a devolved structure, so local managers have immense on-the-ground power.

- National culture/heritage/environment organizations, notably Historic England and English Heritage (linked to the Department for Digital, Culture, Media and Sport (DCMS)) for the historic environment; the Environment Agency and Natural England (linked to the Department for Environment, Food and Rural Affairs (DEFRA)) for the natural environment; national archaeology organizations including the Council for British Archaeology (CBA), Chartered Institute for Archaeologists (CIfA), Portable Antiquities Scheme (linked to the British Museum), and the Associations of Local Government Archaeological Officers (ALGAO) and the Federation of Archaeological Managers and Employers (FAME); Arts Council England (ACE), the national development agency for creativity and culture; and the National Lottery Heritage Fund (NLHF), the single largest and most influential funder of cultural and natural heritage activities.

## *Apprenticeships and Traineeships*

Another change between the first and second editions of this book is the formalization of apprenticeships and traineeships within the sector. These are professional development opportunities designed to up-skill individuals, embed skills (especially in-demand or highly specialized skills that it may require additional time or training regimes to develop), and improve the overall career 'flow' of the sector, so that there are appropriately skilled individuals operating at all different life-stages, ensuring that the next generation of such skills exists in early, mid, and late career groups. Apprenticeships and traineeships are also used in some circumstances to improve demographic diversity, targeted specifically at individuals whose social or cultural background is under-represented within the sector in comparison to the demographic make-up of the wider population.

When the first edition of this book was written, although such opportunities existed, they were usually so informal in nature, and so hard to consistently identify and share, that the author did not include mention of them. I am pleased to report that at the time of writing the second edition, there is now both a much clearer structure for such opportunities, and many more available. Such a change in behaviour relates back to the earlier section of this chapter on accessibility and equality in archaeology, for it is essential that such opportunities are open to all, based on an individual's skill and determination, not because of whom they know. And such opportunities ought to be real opportunities, with the same rights of pay and working conditions as any other job. The latter point is important to emphasize here. There remain many highly dubious, 'voluntary' opportunities – often referred to as internships, a term that I specifically avoid using in this book – within the heritage sector, even among some of the best-known and well-financed of cultural organizations. Such roles are both exploitative and exclusionary, taking advantage of individuals' enthusiasm to develop a career to pay them little or sometimes even nothing at all (in some cases not even providing reasonable expenses) to undertake tasks and even fulfil entire roles that are properly paid in other circumstances. The organization Fair Museum Jobs (https://fairmuseumjobs.org/, @fair_jobs on Twitter) does excellent work calling out such abuse and abusers online, and the main points of their manifesto that pertain to career development opportunities are included below.[12] This neatly summarizes what true apprenticeship and traineeship opportunities will offer to applicants, and how such opportunities are as fairly and equitably made available as possible. If any reader comes across a development opportunity that runs contrary to these terms, then they are advised to proceed with caution.

### Internships

[Fair Museum Jobs Manifesto Points 3.2–3.7] Internships must be paid at Real Living Wage, or London Living Wage as set by the Living Wage Foundation. Internships must be of fixed length; must have clearly defined learning and development outcomes, which are clearly set out on the role advert; must be provided with adequate training and support, and a named manager or supervisor; [and] must not replace roles which were previously paid jobs. For the avoidance of doubt, internships should be advertised with the word 'paid' in the role title.

### Voluntary Roles, Placements, and Unpaid Labour

[Fair Museum Jobs Manifesto Points 4.1–4.5] When advertised, a voluntary role must clearly and unambiguously be stated as such and must not be allowed to pose as a paid job. For clarity, the word 'volunteer' should be included in the role title. Entitlement to reimbursement of expenses (or absence thereof) must be clearly set out in the job advert. Voluntary roles should not be advertised with a requirement to commit more than 1 day or 8 hours per week (except for shorter-term periods) and ideally the volunteer should be able to commit as much or as little time as they like, within reasonable bounds. Volunteers can be free to choose to commit more of their time beyond this minimum. Voluntary positions should not ask for minimum qualifications or prior experience of specialist technical knowledge (e.g., collections management systems or documentation standards). Voluntary positions must not be used to replace roles which were previously paid, or which carry duties and responsibilities one would normally expect from a paid role.

[Manifesto points 4.6–4.10] Adequate training and Personal Protective Equipment must be provided, depending on the nature of the role. Each volunteer should have a designated supervisor, manager, or mentor; and appropriate volunteer agreements should be in place between volunteers and hosting organizations, so that the expectations of both parties are understood. Organizations should not seek to claim title to Intellectual Property produced by their volunteers; and commercial, profit-making organizations should not advertise for voluntary roles, with the sole exception of placements. Placements are understood to be fixed-term periods of unpaid work, within the context of an educational programme, with clearly defined learning and development outcomes and adequate training and support.

---

[12] The most recent edition of the manifesto dates to 2021 and is available at https://fairmuseumjobs.org/manifesto/.

As an example of the types of apprenticeships and traineeships available, I flag below some recent examples of best practice. The UK-based umbrella heritage organization the Heritage Alliance regularly flags such opportunities (globally, although primarily focused on the United Kingdom) in its free 'Heritage Update' bulletin that it is well worth subscribing to (www.theheritagealliance.org.uk/news-and-events/news/). Similarly, the UK-based 'British Archaeological Jobs and Resources' (BAJR) regularly advertises such opportunities on its website (www.bajr.org/):

- **Association of Heritage Engineers** (AoHE) (heritage skills network based in the United Kingdom) (www.associationofheritageengineers.co.uk/). This association facilitates the cascade of specific industry skills and experience to young people as part of its Sustainable Skills Network. These skills are not just about motor vehicles – they span the whole world of heritage engineering, including different types of historic engine (e.g., steam engines) and marine, aviation, and specialist engineering skills.
- **Heritage Skills Academy** (HCA) (heritage skills network based in the United Kingdom) (www.heritageskillsacademy.co.uk/). The Academy works with employers, apprentices, and industry leaders to train the next generation of heritage engineers and promote exciting opportunities within the heritage industry.
- **Historic England** (HE) (English national heritage agency based in the United Kingdom) apprenticeships (https://historicengland.org.uk/about/jobs/apprenticeships/). These opportunities vary in type, location, and duration across the English heritage sector and emphasize the desire to be inclusionary, the website stating that 'most importantly, our apprenticeships are open to everyone. When considering applications, we do not always look for the most qualified applicant. We consider who would gain the most from the learning opportunity provided by the apprenticeship. We also want you to make a fully informed decision about whether an apprenticeship is right for you.'
- **Museum of London Archaeology** (MOLA) (CRM firm based in the United Kingdom) (www.mola.org.uk/about-us/work-us/early-careers). MOLA offers training and development opportunities accredited with the UK Chartered Institute for Archaeologists (CIFA), with 'Trainee Archaeologist' and 'Graduate Archaeologist' programmes tailored to provide the experience, skills, and knowledge needed to work on site as a professional field archaeologist.
- **The National Trust** (NT) (conservation charity based in the United Kingdom) (www.nationaltrustjobs.org.uk/find-your-place/apprenticeships). The NT regularly offers a range of apprenticeships of varying length, challenge, and structure, working on many different aspects of the cultural and natural historic environments, including in archaeology. They deliberately offer varied opportunities at different levels that include opportunities for people to develop new skills as well as furthering existing ones.

- **Society for the Protection of Ancient Buildings** (SPAB) (heritage charity based in the United Kingdom) (www.spab.org.uk/learning). SPAB's 'Fellowships' and 'Scholarships' are designed to broaden the skills and experience of craftspeople who work with old buildings, as well as offering training opportunities for architects, surveyors, and structural engineers in the early stages of their careers.

# Chapter 3

# Cultural Resource Management

## Introduction

Cultural resource management (CRM, sometimes known as cultural heritage management) refers to those archaeological jobs that are paid for directly because of 'polluter pays' laws and policies in different countries. Although the details, terms, legal status, and format of implementation vary widely (particularly because of issues of applicability on different types of land and the overlap of national/federal and local/state/county laws and regulations), the core principles of such policies tend to be the same. Ultimately, such principles are derived not from archaeology or even the wider historic environment lobby, but rather are modelled on the policies and principles in much longer use within the natural environment sector.

The principle has become enshrined in both common practice and legal statute in some, but by no means all, countries around the world that when developments such as the construction of houses, commercial buildings, transport, energy, or other infrastructure or extraction of primary resources such as minerals take place, then the *historic* environment, alongside the natural environment (i.e., flora and fauna), should be taken into consideration from the outset. This occurs whether the development is done for profit or by a government, charity, or other organization for the communal good – in some cases on all lands and properties irrespective of ownership, in other cases only on government-owned or government-controlled lands or on specific types of land such as Tribal or Indigenous-controlled land.

Consequently, a small percentage of money – usually less than 1 percent of the total costs of a development – is spent on the following:

- Assessing the likelihood of the discovery of an archaeological site.
- Partially or fully surveying or excavating the site (if the likelihood of archaeological discovery is thought to be low, the latter may simply involve monitoring the development in case of unexpected discoveries).
- Analyzing and publicizing the archaeological materials discovered.

Archaeologists, alongside other specialists such as historic buildings experts, ecologists, and biologists, are employed to undertake this work in advance of development. Mostly, they are employed by commercial archaeological organizations. These organizations are businesses just like any other, and generally they bid for an advertised piece of work put out for tender by a developer, competing against other firms to win the job on the basis of their proposed costs, services, timescale, practices, standards, and a host of other factors, in a manner akin to construction firms competing to provide equipment, materials, or specialist construction skills on site. In some cases, a developer may also employ consultant archaeologists who will not undertake the primary archaeological work themselves, who will act as advisors to and liaisons between the developer and CRM archaeology firms and also to the local/central government officials who advise on the legal responsibilities of developers and who monitor work undertaken on such sites.

The impact of the competitive bidding process on the practice of archaeology has been much discussed within the community. It is one of the most loathed aspects of the modern practice, felt to drive down standards of pay, and conditions alike, as developers frequently choose the lowest-priced bid, not necessarily the bid that will provide the best quality or treat the archaeologists undertaking such work well, particularly regarding pay, contracts, and working conditions (see Figures 14 and 15).

Figure 14. The structure and interrelationships of the CRM archaeology sector.

Figure 15. The realities of fieldwork, part 5: In many parts of the world, CRM archaeology means long working hours in tough conditions. Here, an extremely wet and muddy site in southeast England does not stop the work from continuing (copyright Archaeology South East UCL 2010, courtesy of Dominic Perring).

As a result of the circumstances described above, some academic archaeologists do not take this type of CRM archaeology seriously, because the low funding and quick turnaround times of such work tends to place an emphasis on site identification and preservation rather than intensive study and analysis. In return, some CRM archaeologists counter that few academic archaeologists have the expertise in site survey and excavation that comes from working on so many different types of sites – in other words, what is the point in spending so much time on a site if you're going to dig it badly? The reality is that, as discussed later, CRM archaeology accounts for the majority of archaeological fieldwork in the modern world, and this situation is unlikely to change any time soon, so academics who criticize such work are, to some extent, missing the point. CRM archaeologists would love to spend more time on sites, but market forces usually mean this is impossible; furthermore, in most cases, if CRM fieldwork were not done on the site, then no archaeological work would be done at all, leading to a loss of potentially unique data.

CRM and academic archaeology sit alongside one another and are simply different expressions of a greater archaeology – much like, say, different branches of medicine or the law. What both branches need to do more of, however, is cross-working. Shockingly few academic archaeologists have ever visited, let alone worked on, a CRM site, and hardly any more use the reams of data produced from such work in their research. Similarly, it is rare for CRM archaeologists to teach university classes on aspects of their fieldwork (although many do undertake research, usually in their spare time). The situation of mutual misunderstanding – in some cases, outright distrust and even dislike – is only exacerbated by modern insurance and health and safety laws that make it difficult for noncontractual staff, especially university staff and, more importantly, students, to work on CRM archaeology sites.

## Types of Work Undertaken by CRM Archaeologists

The options open to archaeological officers for archaeological consultations include requiring CRM archaeologists to undertake some or all of a broad remit of possible types of archaeological investigation – from simple, non-invasive desk-based assessments (reports on the archaeological significance of a site using existing data) right up to total area excavation of an entire site, and going on into post-excavation work, analysis, and publication. These give a sense of the breadth of employment as well as the array of skills used in CRM archaeology (see Figures 14–16). Most of these different types of work are subject to varying degrees of local and/or national guidance on best practice regarding the precise detail and quality of the work involved. An example from the United Kingdom (similar peer-reviewed guidelines exist around the world) are the Chartered Institute for Archaeologists (CIfA) Standards and Guidance, which include detailed specifications for the following:

- Archaeological advice provided by historic environment services.
- Creation, compilation, transfer, and deposition of archaeological archives.
- Investigation and recording of standing buildings and structures.
- Collection, documentation, conservation, and research of archaeological materials.
- Commissioning work or providing advice on archaeology and the historic environment.
- Desk-based assessments (DBAs).[1]

---

[1] A desk-based assessment (DBA) is defined by the CIfA as 'a programme of study of the historic environment within a specified area or site on land, in the inter-tidal zone or underwater that addresses agreed research and/or conservation objectives. It consists of an analysis of existing written, graphic, photographic and electronic information in order to identify the likely heritage assets, their interests and significance; the character of the study area, including appropriate consideration of the settings of heritage assets; and, in England, the nature, extent and quality of the known or potential archaeological, historic, architectural and artistic interest. Significance is to be judged in a local, regional, national or international context as appropriate.'

Figure 16. The realities of fieldwork, part 6: CRM archaeology involves many different skills and working environments. Here, an archaeologist surveys a historic sluice system (dating to the 1930s) in southeast England prior to its refurbishment (copyright Archaeology South East UCL 2010, courtesy of Dominic Perring).

- Archaeological excavation.
- Field evaluation.
- Forensic archaeology.
- Geophysical survey.
- Nautical archaeological recording and reconstruction.
- Stewardship of the historic environment.
- Watching briefs.

## *General*

- Environmental impact assessments (EIAs), including a cultural heritage component.
- Desk-based Assessments (DBAs).
- Field walking and/or field surveys, as part of predetermination/EIA or as a stand-alone nonintrusive survey, including in some cases a related or stand-alone geophysical survey.
- Watching brief: monitoring the excavation of foundation and service trenches, landscaping, and any other intrusive work to identify and record any

archaeological finds or features (which, if so discovered, might lead to amendments to the project design requiring additional evaluation or full excavation).

- Evaluation: appraisal of the archaeological potential and significance of a site by way of sample area excavated as trial trenches, usually 5–10 per cent of the total area of the site or as negotiated, especially on long survey lines for pipelines, roads; this might take the form of test pitting – small survey excavations at regular intervals along a route.
- Full excavation.

## Specific

- Historic building surveys to varying levels of detail.
- Historic area assessments and appraisals.
- Human burials and remains assessments and excavations (which might include the requirement to leave these totally undisturbed and entirely in situ).
- Environmental sampling.
- Historic environment assessments, such as assessment of historic woodlands and trees, hedgerows, and the like.
- Coastal and marine environment: especially intertidal surveys.

## Allied

- Post-excavation work (a broad rule of thumb being that every day on site = three days of post-excavation work).
- Mitigation and preservation of remains in situ.
- Community archaeology and outreach.
- Publication.
- Archiving.

### Focus on: Tom Irvin (Canada)

I am Tom Irvin, and I am the Principal Archaeologist for my own archaeological consultancy, Irvin Heritage Inc. I am based in Newmarket, Ontario, in Canada, and I conduct archaeological assessments throughout my home province of Ontario. My role is to assist clients in meeting their obligations under various forms of provincial legislation that pertain to archaeological concerns. In practice, this means conducting archaeological and historic research, land (and at times marine) surveys, and site excavation and mitigation, in order for development to proceed. I have previously been employed by both large and small archaeological firms, as well as within an oversight capacity as a Review Officer within the Archaeological Program Unit at the Ontario Ministry of Heritage, Sport, Tourism and Culture Industries.

I was first introduced to archaeology when I was five years old, having spent many summers visiting family in North Yorkshire in the United Kingdom. I was fortunate to be exposed to ruined castles, archaeological sites, and beached shipwrecks, which sparked a lifelong fascination with history. When I was seventeen years old, I attended the Boyd Archaeological Field School, run by the Toronto Region Conservation Authority. I spent a few weeks assisting with the excavation of a Woodland period village site. I then attended the University of Toronto where I obtained my Archaeological Specialist BA, followed by an MA in Marine Archaeology from University College London in the United Kingdom. Having worked for various private sector firms and the provincial government, I have learned various skills from GIS and site-mitigation procedures to project management and archaeological budgeting.

I began my career as a field technician for a small private archaeological firm just before completing my undergraduate degree. I worked there for a few years before relocating to the United Kingdom to complete my MA. Upon moving back home, I began a series of careers at various international engineering firms, forming part of their archaeological team. I took advantage of many career opportunities, as during that time there was a boom in archaeological employment in Canada. I was fortunate enough to have also worked for the provincial government's Archaeological Program Unit. This was the most valuable career move for me, as it allowed for deeper understating of both the provincial archaeological standards and their intent. Owing to my experience in both the consultant and regulatory sides of archaeological work, I started my own consulting firm in 2014. I can now foster staff with a passion for archaeology and leverage our team skill set to tackle any archaeological project.

In an 'average' week, I spend about half my week in the field lending my experience to complex projects, such as burial and Indigenous site excavations. The other time is spent in the office, with much of my time spent addressing clients' needs and writing technical archaeological reports. I often work on three to five projects at a time, so there is a large amount of paperwork, reporting, and business management such as payroll, proposals, invoicing, and taxes (things that often have a steep learning curve). What I love about my role is that I can share my archaeological experience with a hand-picked staff who all have a passion for history and archaeology. We are always self-evaluating, and always trying to learn more. Working for myself allows me to navigate the complex balance of a 'for profit' archaeological firm with my own ethics and archaeological code of conduct.

My top tip for pursuing a career in archaeology, which I used myself, is networking! You can have all the right academic qualifications, but you need to know the 'players in the game'. I have been an extremely fortunate person as I have never had to apply for an archaeological position. I have always been approached by others who either knew me or knew of me. Having a cheerful disposition, being able to work well with others, but also being a professional and competent archaeologist are key assets. Another key asset is being able to admit when you are in error or when you don't know something.

For any young archaeologists in Ontario, I highly recommend attending a field school, and I highly recommend the Boyd Archaeological Field School. This field school (when I took it back in 1997!) was a completely life-changing event that cemented my desire to pursue a career as an archaeologist. Some twenty-three years later I still speak with staff and students from the course (https://trca.ca/conservation/archaeology/boydfieldschool/)!

## Significance of CRM in the Profession

In many parts of the world, CRM archaeology is the single most important component of professional archaeology, which is why, of all the thematic chapters on archaeological careers discussed in this book, it has been placed first. Globally, CRM archaeology employs more archaeologists than any other archaeological sector; it is responsible for more money spent than any other archaeological sector; and its work leads to the discovery, analysis, and understanding of the largest number of archaeological sites. Some estimates suggest that as much as 90 per cent of total global archaeological spending comes via CRM archaeology. Even the more conservative estimates put this sum at somewhere between 70 and 80 per cent. Three reports from the United Kingdom published in 2019 and 2020 highlight this:

- Historic England's (2019) *Heritage and the Economy* reported that £7.1 billion in gross value added (GVA) was generated by heritage-related construction activities in England in 2018. Some 6,000 people were employed as archaeologists on such sites; 24,000 architects, building and civil engineers and chartered surveyors were involved in heritage-related activities; and 100,000 construction workers were involved in heritage-related activities.
- Rocks-Macqueen and Lewis' (2019) *Archaeology in Development Management* reported that the total estimated revenue generated by commercial archaeology in 2017–18 was £239 million, of which £218 million was related to development management, and that 74 per cent of all archaeologists are employed because of the developmental management system (i.e., either in CRM jobs or related jobs in local and/or central government).
- Aitchison and Rocks-Macqueen's (2020) *State of the Archaeological Market 2019* reported that 73 per cent of all funding for archaeology in the United Kingdom comes from private sector.

For an older example of similar data on the scale of the CRM industry from the United States, Altschul and Patterson (2008) reported that 'annual expenditures for services by public and private sector clients have been estimated between $683 million and $1 billion ... based on actual public expenditures and optional surveys of CRM senior management on the scale of private sector funding'. In the previous ten years this scale of development-led investment in archaeology in nations such as the United States, as well as in many other nations around the world, is only likely to have increased along similar lines as reported in the United Kingdom, although hard evidence for this is hard to come by (see Rocks-Macqueen (2014a) for some discussion and Aitchison (2012) for wider context). Quite simply, without CRM archaeology, archaeology could hardly be called a profession at all – there would barely be any jobs to be had for archaeologists. Comparable data for spending on other sectors of archaeology – that is, figures for university and public sector spending on archaeologists – do not exist, but by sheer comparison of the number of archaeologists employed in each sector, the spending is undeniably much smaller.

The 'polluter pays' principle that funds the majority of this archaeological activity is a well-established system that works, if not perfectly, then of a fashion, which has at heart a positive objective if not necessarily a positive outcome, and which is accepted both as an economic imperative as well as a social necessity. By any standards, archaeology contributes to society more than it costs, even in terms of pure financial profit/loss. Some of the products of archaeology are tangible: publications and reports, websites, and TV and radio media that people pay for; lectures, seminars, and presentations given to public and private audiences alike, usually in return for a fee of one sort or another; excavated materials that end up on display or in storage at museums and archives that people choose to visit; and even whole historic sites that are open to the public, as well as the archaeological projects that people volunteer, some even pay, to go on. Other products are intangible: the benefits to society of an enhanced understanding of our common past, the trans- ferable skills that students gain from their studies, and the pure economics of the 'polluter pays' system, in which legislation requires industries to pay for work on sites in advance of development. As noted earlier, such forms of regulated capital- ism pay for an estimated 90 per cent of all archaeology; only some 10 per cent of money spent comes from the public purse or private philanthropy. That 90 per cent of industrial funding represents, at most, a very few percentage points of the total costs, let alone the end profits, of any development, so such environmental regulations are not the burden to or block on development that might be supposed. The broader intangible and purely economic benefits of archaeology and, more broadly, heritage to society are then incalculable – these include the money made through public interest and participatory payment when visiting historic sites, people choosing to pay a premium to live in old houses or historic districts, and people buying themed books, toys, and computer games and/or watching related TV shows.

## A Day in the Life

CRM archaeologists get to do, see, and handle the largest amount of 'real' archaeology of all archaeologists. If the thought of spending the greater proportion of every year out of doors doing field archaeology – surveying, digging, drawing, and the like – appeals to you, then realistically CRM archaeology is the way forward. Government archaeologists get to spend only perhaps 5–10 per cent of their time doing field archaeology; academic archaeologists, perhaps 20–30 per cent of their time; but CRM archaeologists, especially in junior and mid-level posts, will regularly spend 80–90 per cent of their time in the field.

Trying to sum up an average day in the life of a CRM archaeologist is extremely hard. By the very nature of this type of work, which is reactive, responding to the needs of development, there is a limited 'average' to be drawn. Thankfully, a few CRM archaeologists have written down their stories. In particular, the American CRM archaeologist Trent de Boer produced the marvellous book *Shovelbum* (the nickname some US CRM archaeologists give themselves – the British equivalent term is 'digger') that offers an insight into their experiences (de Boer 2004). See also Jourdane's (2017) *Fieldwork Fail* for a broader view of the lifestyles of similar scientific fieldworkers around the world, and King (2002) for a more formalized but equally impassioned view of the situation. The British archaeologist Paul Everill has also published a formalized study of the similar situation in that country entitled *The Invisible Diggers: A Study of British Commercial Archaeology* (Everill 2009, revised 2012), and readers ought also to see Smith and Burke's (2007) *Digging It Up Down Under* for experience of working as a CRM archaeologist in Australia. Everill's and de Boer's books, both the products of archaeologists with wide experience of CRM fieldwork, share many similarities in the highs and lows of this section of the profession (Table 5).

The United Kingdom and the United States also have websites dedicated to these communities: in the United Kingdom, British Archaeological Jobs and Resources (BAJR),[2] and in the United States, Shovelbums.[3] These are no mere dusty web archives of life on the dig, though – both are actively used by practicing CRM archaeologists to share best practices, search for jobs (both include regularly updated archaeological job sections), and gripe about the realities of their daily grind. The BAJR also has a fascinating archive of the now defunct UK CRM archaeologists' newsletter *The Digger*, which ran between 1998 and 2006. This provides a fascinating, if at times brutal, insight into the world of CRM archaeology in that period (see Figures 17 and 18).

Some CRM archaeologists spend the majority of their working lives moving from one site to another within a relatively small area – for example, archaeologists working within major cities such as London, New York, San Francisco, Sydney, or Melbourne, which have a rich history as well as a fast-paced process of near-constant redevelopment. Such an archaeologist is doing CRM archaeology just as much as a colleague who travels thousands of miles yearly, moving among extensive rural sites in advance of new housing developments, mines, roads, or pipelines. Indeed, these two archaeologists might even be employed by the same archaeological firm, as well as by the same developer. However, the realities of the fieldwork that these different archaeologists do would be radically different. Urban CRM archaeologists will often work within the tight footprint of an existing building that has been torn down and is shortly to be replaced; they may

---

[2] See www.bajr.org/.     [3] See https://shovelbums.org/.

TABLE 5. The pros and cons of working in CRM archaeology

| Pros | Cons |
| --- | --- |
| Greatest amount of time spent actually doing archaeology, i.e., fieldwork such as excavation and surveying | Poor pay and conditions, with few benefits, long hours, and limited job security |
| Constantly on the move – changeable locations/sites, so you see a lot of places, meet new people, and so on | Employers may be unable or unwilling to offer leave for career development or training opportunities. |
| Challenging – working on new sites, new types of archaeology, in face of changing environmental conditions – almost always intellectually stimulating | Many employers require staff to organize their own accommodations and/or provide some of their own equipment. |
| Can pick up wide range of skills and get to know the distinctive characteristics of the archaeology of a region, the subtleties of its soil types and features, and so on | Projects are often relatively short-term, so you may not get to see the long-term development of a site and its analysis – or, indeed, see anything beyond the confines of your small section or trench. |
| Sense of community on project – most people doing these jobs are in their twenties and thirties, so it can be a friendly, lively working and social environment | Being constantly on the move also means you often see nasty neighbourhoods and stay in seedy accommodations. |
| | No stable base makes relationships/ family life hard, and can be lonely too – fieldworkers have a particularly hard time if they are in a committed relationship. |
| | Workers can suffer other problems common to transient employees, such as sporadic access to health care, quality accommodations, and access to credit or loans because of regular changes of address. |
| | Can get stuck in a rut doing only one thing – once you have refined your skills, there can be virtually no skills or career progression. |
| | Limited career structure – most people advance by leaving one job and trading up to another post with a different employer on the basis of their CV – which often works but can be risky. |

Figure 17. The realities of fieldwork, part 7: Many CRM archaeology projects follow the routes of new pipelines, roads, or other long-distance developments, surveying the route in advance of development. Here, CRM archaeologists work along the route of a pipeline in southeast England (copyright Archaeology South East UCL 2010, courtesy of Dominic Perring).

work many meters below street level, possibly even under cover in a basement area; they will almost certainly work right alongside ongoing construction, and may excavate and plan a feature only to move on and see the feature be destroyed immediately, covered in concrete or with a foundation pile driven through it. Urban archaeologists may deal with many meters of archaeological stratigraphy (vertical layers of archaeological remains), surveying early twentieth-century features, then nineteenth-century ones, working their way down systematically century by century to, in cities such as London, the Roman or prehistoric uses of the site. Urban archaeologists may travel to sites using public transport, and eat their lunch in a busy city square, surrounded by suited office workers who probably do not even realize that they are archaeologists: their clothes will be almost identical to those of the construction crews with whom they cohabit the site, with safety boots, high-visibility jackets, and hard hats required. At the end of their day, the urban archaeologist may return home to a small apartment or house in the suburbs shared with friends or family.

In comparison, rural CRM archaeologists may work on an extensive 'green' (undeveloped/farmed) or 'brown' (previously lightly developed) field site. Their excavation may cover, in one or a series of large trenches, dozens or even hundreds

Figure 18. The realities of fieldwork, part 8: CRM archaeology often works in response to the tight timetables of industry, and extremes of weather have to be allowed for within this. Here, archaeologists work on through the winter snows of 2009–10 on the site of a housing development in southeast England (copyright Archaeology South East UCL 2010, courtesy of Dominic Perring).

of square meters, or, equally, it may comprise thousands of single, meter-square test pits following the line of a new road or pipeline for hundreds of kilometres. The rural archaeologist is likely to be working at approximate ground level, but that level may be anywhere from a field in the midst of a bucolic farm by way of a densely wooded hillside, muddy riverbank, or even worse. For example, the archaeological work undertaken in advance of London Heathrow Airport's Terminal 5 in the late 1990s and early 2000s was mostly on the site of a former sewage treatment plant. And plenty of fieldworkers in more remote rural areas have stumbled upon illicit drug- or alcohol-producing sites in the course of their work, alongside the more expected threats of territorial wild and domesticated animals, together with farmers, ranchers, and loggers who range from the friendly to the openly hostile. The work of such archaeologists might comprise deep stratigraphy to rival that of their urban counterparts but could equally comprise the shallow and fragmentary remains of a prehistoric hunter-gatherer encampment distinguished only by subtle changes in soil colour and a few pieces of worked flint. Rural archaeologists may travel to sites by car, van, or pickup truck, perhaps driving many miles down narrow roads to reach their site; they may eat their home-packed lunches sitting on top of a hill with a view one day, and then crammed into a truck to get away from rain or mosquitoes the next. Their site may be right alongside an ongoing development, similar to that of the urban archaeologist, but it might equally be so far away from, or well in advance of, a development that they never see anyone other than their colleagues. At the end of the day they are most likely to drive back to cheap, short-term rental apartments or motels rather than their own homes.

For all this generalization, there are certain commonalities of all CRM archaeology, no matter where it takes place. These commonalities are the result of the interplay of circumstances of CRM archaeology, in particular, two factors reacting to one another.

## Archaeological Factors

CRM archaeology is almost always reactive, responding to construction and other socioeconomic developments. As a result, although the principle of in situ preservation (leaving the site intact, proposed by many organizations as the preferable option for cultural resources) remains an objective, the reality is often that in situ preservation is simply not possible – an archaeological site will be partially or wholly destroyed by development, and the archaeologists must mitigate for this by following the complementary principle of preservation by record – creating as comprehensive a documentary record of the site as possible, through detailed survey, excavation, and recording. The impact of this principle on CRM archaeology sites can mean that detailed and comprehensive recording takes place; however, the impact of industry-focused factors can also mean that this recording is less than ideally detailed and/or partial – for instance, fully excavating and recording only certain selected features, not all features.

The priority to record effectively has also seen the rise of a system known as *single-context recording* – that is, ascribing to every significant feature (be it a stratigraphic or non-stratified layer, pit, posthole, or other) a unique reference number, and then recording the details of each feature on pre-printed/pro forma record sheets to ensure accuracy and consistency of the type and extent of recording. Alongside feature records a host of other specialized records will also be maintained, each with its own dedicated record sheet – for instance, for different types of archaeological finds and environmental samples, as well as broader logs of all survey information and photos taken on site, drawings and diagrams, site plans, and so on. Together, these documents comprise the site archive that can be worked on after the end of the fieldwork component of any project, used first to assist post-excavation analysis, then to assist publication, and finally stored in perpetuity alongside physical samples of material from the site to allow future scholars to analyse the primary data from the project.

## Industrial Factors

Clichéd it may be, but following the principle of 'the one who pays the piper picks the tune', CRM archaeologists must make all sorts of compromises on archaeological practices when on such sites. Such compromises are worth making, though, because the alternative would be to not have the funds and the time to be on site at all – it is far better to get some archaeology done than none.

Some of these compromises are shared by all archaeologists, however and wherever they work. These are environmental impacts – problems with site access, adverse weather, or staff illness during the dig, and accidents of chance such as trenches only partially running across a major feature. Other compromises are not unique to CRM archaeology but are more common on such fieldwork than on other types of projects funded by other means. These usually have to do with the amount of time and money available – operating in advance of multimillion or multibillion pound/dollar/euro developments, many CRM archaeology projects run on tight timelines and even tighter budgets. Failure to deliver on both these promises can spell disaster for a CRM archaeology firm, and except under exceptional circumstances, an unexpected significant archaeological discovery during a project will not be given extra time or change the mind of a developer about leaving the remains in situ.

Finally, the distinctive nature of competitive bidding in CRM archaeology also undoubtedly means that corners are often cut on such projects. To win a bid, CRM archaeology firms are known to cut costs in all sorts of ways. Some of these cuts will have an impact on the quality and quantity of archaeological work undertaken – choosing, for example, to survey, excavate, sample, or record only a certain percentage of a site, feature, or context; choosing to use only certain remote sensing, sampling, or dating techniques; or choosing to take only digital rather than digital and film photographs. Other cuts will affect the life of the archaeologists – the general bad pay, short-term contracts, and few benefits that make CRM archaeology notorious are a wider reflection of this, but on a site-by-site basis this may be seen in other ways, for example, a lack of specialist staff on site, failure of a firm to provide clothing or tools (requiring the archaeologists to bring these along themselves), failure to provide facilities such as a break room or proper toilet/washing facilities on site, and failure to arrange any (appropriate or not) temporary accommodations.

## Focus on: Gai Jorayev (UK)

I am Gai Jorayev, and I am a research fellow at UCL's Institute of Archaeology in London. Our Institute is one of the largest centres of archaeological research and teaching globally. I participate in several research projects, and I coordinate the MA degree programmes in Managing Archaeological Sites and an MA module on Digital Heritage. My current research interests are in the modern uses and management of heritage, cultural tourism, community engagement, and digital approaches to documentation and dissemination of archaeological information. Geographically, my research focuses mostly on Central Asia, but I have also worked in wider Asia, Africa, and Europe.

My first degree was in tourism, and I worked in Turkmenistan – my country of birth – on development projects with various international agencies. Thanks to my mentors Tim Williams and Mike Corbishley, I got involved in the Ancient Merv Project, which is a long-term, multifaceted UCL project in Turkmenistan, to help with local education and tourism work. Over several archaeological seasons, I developed a strong interest in the issues of heritage management and studied for an MA at UCL. My PhD in the role of heritage in nation-building followed that. My work in European projects, with different UN bodies including UNESCO, and involvement in heritage consultancy work gave me certain skills that I rely on daily. I learned research skills and GIS as part of my MA studies and developed strong digital competences over time.

Most of my archaeology-related work is associated with UCL. I gradually transitioned from my PhD studies into my current position, but between my start as a part-time research assistant (2011) and present (2020), I worked in many different capacities at the same institution. My skills in managing projects and ability to operate in international, multicultural and multilingual settings helped enormously. Flexibility and readiness to take on a diverse range of research and practical projects brought me to where I am now. Over the years, I have been able to work on capacity building, documentation, management planning, and public engagement in some of the world-famous archaeological sites (such as Merv, Olduvai, Otrar, and many others) and I wouldn't have been able to do that without agreeing to take on many different, sometimes fragmented initiatives.

The variety of initiatives that I am involved in also brings challenges. My weeks involve a patchwork of different engagements. At present, teaching and working with students takes priority during study terms. Most of my research and practical project work involves a range of international partners and stake-holders, and the majority of my time goes to working with them, providing advice and support. I enjoy hands-on digital tasks, from modelling large land-scapes to coming up with new approaches to digital presentation of data, but I often end up doing those in non-working hours. I love the diversity of the work that I do, but it also requires commitment and hard work.

My top tip for pursuing a career in archaeology is that archaeology is a broad discipline, and unless one is interested in a specific specialist area, it is essential to have a diverse range of skills and competencies. I believe it is not only about gaining academic knowledge, but also about continually learning, formally or informally, new skills and gaining new knowledge. That is a challenging but also exciting side of the discipline. Adaptability is often the key. My career path was not linear, and serendipity certainly played a role. However, adapting to new positions and adhering to principles of lifelong learning was crucial for me and I absolutely enjoyed the journey (so far, at least). More importantly, I was, and am, able to help others – from students to colleagues in all corners of the globe – and that is an extremely rewarding experience.

Currently, I am part of a large research team of the Central Asian Archaeological Landscapes project (www.ucl.ac.uk/archaeology/research/CAAL/). With a goal of creating an open geospatial database, we are attempting something on a scale and complexity that had never been attempted before this. I hope this will enable greater awareness of the region's heritage and support education and research. Additionally, I collaborate with international development agencies on heritage-based sustainable tourism initiatives that will support the livelihoods of very local people on the ground. As someone who grew up in a small, distant village, I feel very passionate about working with communities.

## Career Structure and Qualifications

Stuck in an apparently endless cycle of short-term, low-pay contracts but driven by a great love of the practice of archaeology, many CRM archaeologists would laugh at the suggestion that there is *any* career structure in their industry. University graduates who choose to go into CRM archaeology are at a distinct and permanent career disadvantage compared with their peers who go into virtually all other sectors. Across their careers, CRM archaeologists will consistently find it harder to get, remain in, and advance at work; will consistently be paid less; and will enjoy fewer benefits. Archaeology regularly comes out at or near the bottom of surveys that balance qualifications against pay levels – archaeology is regularly the lowest paid of all graduate careers.

Most CRM archaeologists hold archaeology or anthropology undergraduate degrees. As discussed in Chapters 1 and 2, an increasingly large proportion have postgraduate qualifications as well, usually an MA or MSc. Their careers thus commence similarly to the careers of millions of their peers: during the end of their last year of university study they polish up their CVs and apply for jobs. Before the financial crash and consequent global recession that began in 2007, entry-level CRM archaeology jobs were relatively easy to get – an enthusiastic graduate with an archaeology/anthropology degree who could write a good letter of application and CV, persuade a tutor to provide a good reference, and show some savvy in an interview stood a good chance of being taken on, albeit at the lowest pay grade. Since 2007 the situation has become more difficult, however, and employers are increasingly vociferous about a problem they have long been experiencing: a BA/BSc in archaeology rarely prepares an individual for a career in CRM archaeology adequately, with university training failing to deliver on the following:

- *Pre-excavation work*: Employers note that few students know how to undertake tasks such as collecting and analyzing secondary (published and unpublished) data in relation to the creation of a desk-based assessment, or even what such assessments should look like and contain. In relation to this, many students have not been introduced to the basic laws, principles, and other concepts that underlie not only CRM archaeology but also related aspects of archaeology, such as the existence and role of local and central government archaeologists.
- *General fieldwork skills*: Employers complain that students have limited field experience in general, having rarely been introduced adequately, if at all, to

basic skills such as surveying, excavation, or recording. Employers also note a lack of related core skills such as an inability to read maps/grid coordinates or ignorance of how to lay out trenches with right angles (i.e., basic competence in mathematics).

- *Specific fieldwork skills*: Employers note that students lack familiarity with specialized fieldwork skills, such as the correct handling and use of survey or geophysical equipment such as total stations and resistivity meters. As noted in Chapter 2, it is well worth developing skills in such specializations, as they are always in demand.

- *Post-excavation work*: Employers note that students lack familiarity with post-excavation skills, both generic skills such as the construction, writing, and editing of reports and the application of specific scientific techniques.

This is the classic 'catch-22': although the vast majority of students have worked on some sort of excavation, many have been on only a few types of sites, and may not have had the time to build up these fundamentally time-based competencies. The universities involved are not to blame, and many academics take such accusations from CRM archaeology firms very badly: they argue in return that the point of an archaeology degree is to enable students to think broadly about the concepts and processes of archaeology, not to turn out generically skilled CRM 'worker bees'. The argument sometimes made is that it is up to the firms to provide such skill-specific training, just as, for example, law firms expect to teach new employees about the practical realities of working in a commercial law environment. Equally, the CRM archaeology firms have a point: archaeology students come away with less and less field experience, a result of universities cutting costs, on one hand, and being fearful of fieldwork for legal and health and safety implications, on the other; in addition, students themselves have less free time to go on fieldwork, as so many now need to spend some or all of their vacations earning money. This situation is exacerbated by similar legal/environmental implications making voluntary work on CRM archaeology sites difficult. Consequently, even though it is no one's 'fault', it is an undeniable fact that most recent graduates of archaeology programs have less field experience than comparable graduates would have had ten years ago, and those graduates of ten years ago have less experience than those of twenty years ago.

The question that obviously arises is: is an archaeology degree necessary to pursue a career in archaeology? Despite what the preceding discussion might seem to indicate, the irony is that it *is* necessary. CRM archaeology firms expect their employees to have university degrees in the subject not so much because they feel that these degrees adequately prepare students for life as CRM archaeologists, but more because there is no other real indicator of experience or expertise.

## Lifestyle

Given these facts, one can see why CRM archaeology is harder to break into than ever before: it requires applicants to get a degree that will not adequately prepare them for life in the sector, and it is almost impossible to get voluntary experience of the sector because of legal and health and safety restrictions. Once one starts working within CRM archaeology, there is no clear career structure – advancement is possible, but usually requires a mixture of tenacity and luck.

The lack of formal career structure, however, does not suggest that CRM archaeology itself is unstructured. There are clear hierarchies at work – based on experience, on one hand, and expertise, on the other – and these hierarchies affect pay, job security, and working conditions. Very few archaeologists proceed all the way through the model laid out here; in part, this is because reality is much less clear-cut – there is much more grey area between the levels discussed here than this model suggests, much more blurring of responsibility and, consequently, of working conditions. It does not help that the levels of experience and expertise needed to progress from one level to another are less than clear. In an industry such as commercial legal practice, for example, seniority tends to be clearly linked to different levels of experience and expertise, which in turn are linked to distinct pay and contractual grades. This is not so in archaeology, in which this relationship is murky, and in which there is also no formally required professional association (and limited union representation) to demand clearly defined promotional levels, salary grades, and associated contractual benefits. Finally, plenty of people do not progress all the way through this hierarchical model because they cannot do so – because there are more good people than jobs, because what at first seems a fun lifestyle moving from job to job can become boring, because people get tired of the low pay and tough conditions. CRM archaeology has a high entry rate but also a high turnover/dropout rate: once people hit their late twenties and early thirties, those who remain in the industry will have seen many friends and colleagues leave.

## Junior Field Tech Posts

These are the entry-level positions open to recent university graduates. Like such positions all over the world and in every industry, they have their good points. Junior CRM archaeologists get to do the most active archaeology – although this can be tough and tiring, and sometimes very boring, it can also be incredibly interesting and fun, moving from site to site, seeing new places and new types of archaeology, surveying and digging new features, working out contexts and relationships, and physically finding new archaeological evidence.

Such positions also have their benefits in the lack of responsibility that comes along with them. Many such position holders will have responsibility only for their immediate area and will not have to manage others or think about the big issues of the project. In such circumstances someone can turn up, do a day's hard work, finish up with a cold drink in the evening, and repeat this cycle for weeks, months, and in some cases years at a time. One can get to become an incredibly capable field archaeologist, visit many sites, and meet many archaeologists. The physical rigors and professional/personal insecurities of this life mean that it tends to attract a young and lively crowd, mostly single people in their twenties or thirties; the consequence can be an active social life, and given the low pay and generally

116

constrained living circumstances, the result can seem like college without the classes, essays, and exams.

Although this may seem seductive for a while, however, most people get fed up with this after a time; responsibility, both professional and personal, can begin to appeal, as can better job security and a larger pay packet. Furthermore, such positions offer little follow-through – archaeologists move from dig to dig, rarely getting an opportunity to stick with a site from discovery through investigation, analysis, and publication. This can be very frustrating.

## Mid-Level Posts: Managing a Section of a Site

If the junior field techs are the entry-level ranks in the military of an archaeological site, then mid-level managers are the NCOs of archaeological life. Found mostly in charge of a section of a site, or possibly all of a smaller site, such individuals will most often have been promoted from junior field positions and will be of a similar age and background – the only difference will be their levels of experience as CRM archaeologists. Their responsibility remains relatively limited – to manage the crew on their section of the site and the work there only, not to make any broader decisions or take charge of issues such as timescale or logistics. But such individuals nonetheless wield considerable indirect power, for they are effectively the ultimate arbiters of the quality of the physical archaeological work in their section; sloppy digging, surveying, or recording techniques can be theirs to fix or let slide. Such positions bring with them many of the pros and cons of junior positions – the difference is that the pay will be slightly better (although not by much, and job security is unlikely to be any better at all), and in such a position one can begin to gain at least some vague overall appreciation of the site and its archaeological significance.

## Senior Field Tech/Junior Management Posts: Managing a Site or Project

Continuing with the military analogy, these are the junior officers of the archaeo-logical army. Just as in the military, they must trust their NCOs to keep the detail of things running on the ground, and again just as in the military, whereas some will be good and experienced souls promoted from the trenches, so others will either have been overpromoted beyond their ability or parachuted in from above by management. The result can be very mixed in terms of both the quality of the person and the person's age and experience – brilliant young managers no older than many of their crew may work alongside tired, older managers in their forties who have spent a long time getting to where they are.

The responsibility for managing an entire site or project, even a small project, is a big one for any archaeologist, but this responsibility is particularly acute for CRM archaeology site managers, with a fine balance to be maintained between archaeo-logical sensibility, on the one hand, and industrial sensibility, on the other (how to do good archaeology within the time and financial constraints that apply), over which, at this level, they have no control; a site manager will be given a timescale and a budget and told pretty much to get on with the job within those constraints.

Going back to the military analogy, such individuals also face a potentially difficult professional and personal series of challenges akin to those of junior military officers. Promotion and responsibility are appealing, especially advances in pay and conditions, but this is the stage at which an individual is literally drawn further and further away from the trenches – doing less and less of the physical fieldwork that so often attracted them to this career in the first place.

A manager may be physically based on site but is unlikely to do much, if any, real digging; rather, the manager will be focused on overseeing the program and timetable, monitoring the quality and speed of work, managing the site paperwork archive, and, at heart, thinking about, rather than doing, archaeology – piecing together the three-dimensional jigsaw puzzle that is the site, both in the manager's head and on paper. Individuals at this level may also be asked to make tough decisions regarding the aforementioned balance between archaeological and industrial sensibilities, such as the amount of time to be spent working on a particular component of a site, the techniques, and even field crews to be employed. Many archaeologists promoted to this level have balked at what they see to be impossible compromises to their integrity as archaeologists in the face of demands to dig faster, cheaper, or differently. Similarly, on a personal level, such responsibility may prove very hard if an individual has been promoted up the ranks – friends who have not enjoyed similar promotion may choke at taking orders from them.

On the other hand, being responsible for a site or project can be incredibly rewarding. To make the key decisions, to lead the project from beginning to end, to link method and theory on the investigation, analysis, and reporting of a site is very fulfilling. It sounds hackneyed, but responsibility at this level ensures a bit of immortality – a project director will have been primarily responsible for a project of both individual and communal significance to the understanding of the past. This significance might be immediately apparent – a unique find or an unexpected date – or might become clear only months or years later when compared with other data.

## Middle-Management Positions: Managing Multiple Sites/Projects

Archaeologists working at this level in CRM archaeology are unlikely to fit the stereotype of the 'make-work' middle manager who costs a lot but does very little. Yes, pay and job security are better at this level than in more junior positions; so too are the fringe benefits – if nothing else, these managers do not have the time or the need to be standing in a freezing muddy trench on a wet November afternoon, which is a big deal for most people once they are in their mid-thirties. The responsibility for managing a number of projects simultaneously, however – thinking again about both the archaeological and industrial sensibilities only on a larger, multiple scale – is not a responsibility to make light of; the financial commitments alone may run to hundreds of thousands or even millions of pounds/dollars/euros from multiple clients, and the personal commitments to the well-being of dozens of field crew are significant as well.

Archaeologists who reach this level are never going to be dumb or lazy: the competition for posts, the demands of the job, the need to multitask and be ruthless with their time and priorities all mean that managers at this level will be the cream of the crop. Consequently, such middle managers are likely to be relatively young – in their thirties or perhaps early forties – and to be experienced field archaeologists with years of work on dozens or even hundreds of different sites under their belts. They will often have postgraduate degrees in archaeology, some will have PhDs, and they may well publish and lecture on archaeology alongside their main responsibilities. Such a lifestyle clearly is not for everyone – the professional demands placed on such individuals, on one hand, and the lack of doing archae-ology in the field, on the other, put off many people from ever wishing to reach this level.

Many managers at this level also end up with the unenviable role of having to write up different projects – taking the site archive of notes, plans, maps, and photographs produced by a field crew perhaps weeks or even months earlier and piecing it together in a report for the employer and local government archaeologists alike. This post-fieldwork editorial work can be a very tough thing to do when working to a tight deadline, as such work will usually have to be fitted in by a manager working at this level simultaneous to the management of one of more 'active' sites.

## Senior Management Positions: Managing Sections of or an Entire Organization

The top of the CRM archaeology tree is, honestly, the place where it is hardest to provide any defining characteristics. Until the mid-1990s, CRM archaeology firms were traditionally small businesses employing perhaps a few dozen staff at most. This meant that the hierarchical structure tended to be relatively flat – many people did many different jobs, and everyone was on direct speaking terms with the senior managers. Under such circumstances, many managers were originally diggers themselves, who had started off as enthusiastic field archaeologists in their twenties and slowly been given more and more responsibility until becoming managers in their forties or fifties; in some cases, the firms had been created by old friends joining to form a small private company, of which they were the directors. This structure still exists in a few places, for even the larger firms that now exist may well have been created from the merger of smaller firms, with their senior management at least partly intact. Under such circumstances, managers at this level will have the skills, as well as the desire, to physically go out on site at least some of the time to keep a direct eye on a project, to talk directly to clients about their needs, or even simply to feel dirt under their boots and do some real archaeology to keep their old field skills up to date.

As the profession expanded and 'professionalized' in the 1990s, there was the emergence of a new breed of managers, with either limited or no direct field experience. These were purely and simply managers, people with the business/industry skills to manage what, in some cases, have become firms employing hundreds of staff based at multiple locations and with annual budgets that run into tens of millions. Working in archaeology at this level is, clearly, not something to which many people might aspire. It is also obviously not something that is easy to achieve – there are not all that many archaeological firms in existence around the world, so the number of managers is correspondingly small. The benefits, although not commensurate in any way with those of other industries, can nonetheless be considerable in comparison with the pay and contractual conditions of most other CRM archaeologists – a point of some contention.

## Specialists

Every organization has specialists who do not fall into a clear hierarchical structure. Archaeology, with its demands for so much specialist knowledge and with so much new information, theories, and methodologies being developed, is particularly prone to such circumstances. Some specialists may be dedicated field crew: examples are landscape/topographical and/or building surveyors and geophysical survey experts, people who use very specific tools, requiring very specific expertise, at a key point in most projects, sufficient to keep them solely employed in this one task. Others may have expertise in a particular analytical technique, and so spend time both on site and in the lab when required: examples are environmental sampling, dating, and other specialists, on the one hand, or those with particular material experience, on the other, say, in osteoarchaeology, ceramics, or water-logged wood. Finally, there are specialists who play a role at certain times in a project – for example, conservators who will take care of any finds recovered from the site or who will stabilize any standing archaeological remains to be left on site. With the size and quantity of digital data, imagery, remote sensing, and similar evidence being produced, stored, analysed, and manipulated, there is also a distinct community of archaeological data managers employed by many organizations these days, people with both computing and data-management qualifications alongside their archaeological expertise.

Bigger archaeological units may also have dedicated photographers (although many archaeologists will take this responsibility on themselves as part of their broader duties on site). More and more CRM archaeology firms also have dedi-cated education/outreach teams to engage with the local community – such people may have a background in school teaching along with their archaeological knowledge.

The pros and cons of such specialization are obvious: what happens if you get bored with the specialization you used to love? Once pigeon-holed as the specialist, it can be incredibly hard to move into another specialty or into a general field role. On the other hand, if you really, really like what you do – and many specialists do – this can be an incredibly stimulating life. Such specialists are often world-renowned experts, many with a PhD or equivalent experience and publications in their area of specialty.

## Focus on: Lynley Wallis (Australia)

I am Lynley Wallis, and I am Associate Professor in the Centre for Social and Cultural Research at Griffith University in Australia. I am an archaeologist and cultural heritage professional based in Brisbane, Queensland, but I do a lot of fieldwork in places beyond Queensland, including the Pilbara (Western Australia) and Arnhem Land (Northern Territory) (see Figures 19 and 20). My main role is research-based, carrying out archaeological surveys, recording sites, and undertaking excavations, as well as helping train Indigenous ranger groups, providing assistance to help them build capacity to manage their own heritage places. Although I mostly work with Indigenous heritage, I also work on historic sites, and more broadly in ethnobotany and environmental management.

As a child, my family tell me that I was apparently always intrigued by the 'old people' and the 'olden times'. I started my BSc degree without a firm idea about what I wanted to specialize in, thinking that archaeology would be interesting. Towards the end of my first year, one of the archaeology graduate students attended our lecture and asked if anyone would like to volunteer over the summer on his PhD fieldwork at a beach in southwest Western Australia. When he flashed a photo of his field area up on the screen, I realized that it was where my family had a beach shack and that I would be down there anyway, so I volunteered, and my journey in archaeology began. I completed my BSc focusing on archaeology, human biology and anatomy, and geology, and I then did an honours year undertaking residue and use wear analysis of Aboriginal stone artefacts. Throughout my undergraduate degree, I volunteered for every field and lab project that I could find, and because of that experience I was invited on several research projects that my university lecturers were leading. I then went on to do a PhD, focusing on microscopic plant remains in archaeological rock shelter sites dating back to 45,000 years as a means of exploring long-term vegetation and, by proxy, climate change.

Unlike many of my archaeological colleagues, I have pursued a non-traditional career path, moving continually between academia, government, and private industry, blending scholarly pursuits with commercial activities. I have held lecturing positions at universities (and have actually twice given up tenure to take up other opportunities, to which my colleagues have often asked, 'Are you crazy?'; the response might be 'a little' but I like to constantly challenge myself and not become 'institutionalized'), worked as a government heritage officer, run my own heritage consultancy business undertaking cultural heritage assessments and providing expert advice, and worked with Indigenous ranger groups. I do not like to be weighed down by constant administrative and bureaucratic tasks, and I love being out in the field visiting fascinating places and meeting interesting people. When I secured a very large research grant leading a

Figure 19. The realities of fieldwork, part 9: Environmental and geographical extremes faced by archaeologists change around the world. Here, Flinders University graduate student Danny Markey undertakes a total station survey of an extensive open Indigenous campsite along the Woolgar River in north Queensland during July 2009 (copyright Lynley Wallis 2010).

team of outstanding scientists, I was fortunate to be offered a research position at Griffith University. My wide-ranging experience and strong professional networks were considered attractive by the university, who were looking to continue to build strong community partnerships and expand their growing archaeological research and teaching program.

My weeks vary, depending on whether I am in the field or the office. When I am in the field, a typical week involves getting up early, heading out for a day in the bush finding and recording amazing rock art sites. We do a lot of four-wheel driving, followed by hiking and climbing. At the end of the day, we download and label the hundreds of photographs that we took during the day. When I am in the office, a typical week involves sorting excavated archaeological materials, analyzing artefacts (often involving a lot of measuring, weighing, and peering at them down a microscope), writing reports and papers, reading papers, editing papers, meeting with colleagues, and supervising graduate students (see Figure 20). This mix means that there is always a lot of variety. And because I do most of my fieldwork in northern Australia, I have been able to avoid winter for about five years now!

My top tip for pursuing a career in archaeology is that having a wide range of experience working in different places, on different types of sites, and with

Figure 20.  The realities of fieldwork, part 10: Fieldwork in remote and arid environments like many parts of Australia requires extensive planning. Here, Flinders
University technical officer Louise Holt uses a drawing frame to construct detailed
feature plans of Indigenous heat retainer fireplaces along the Woolgar River in
north Queensland during July 2009 (copyright Lynley Wallis 2010).

different people will ensure that you have a great set of general skills that are
transferable to a lot of different scenarios. If you can continue to build on those
skills throughout your career, it will stand you in good stead. In gaining all that
experience, you will also get to meet and work with many people. You should
always treat everyone kindly and fairly and be a good team player who pulls
their weight. You just never know where you will be in the future, and a
random person who you worked alongside for a couple of weeks ten years ago
could end up being on your next interview panel and hold your fate in their
hands. Especially in a country like Australia, where there is only 'one degree of
separation' between all archaeologists and cultural heritage professionals, your
reputation will precede you. It does not matter if you are a genius who can think
outside the box, churn out research papers and reports with alarming regularity,
or who topped your class at university – if you do not get along well with others
in a work environment, then people will not want to employ you.

As an archaeologist, I am privileged to work alongside some amazing
Aboriginal communities and to visit some spectacular places across Australia.
I am committed to social justice, and I see education as a means of non-
Indigenous Australians moving towards reconciliation with Aboriginal and

Torres Strait Islander communities. Only if we understand and acknowledge the complex and intertwined history of our country do we have a chance of addressing the social inequity that unfortunately persists in it today. Working in partnership with numerous Aboriginal communities and people across Queensland, together with colleagues I have developed an extensive online database that brings together a wide range of historical and archaeological sources that deal with the topic of frontier conflict and the Native Mounted Police, a notorious paramilitary government agency whose job was to subdue any Indigenous resistance on the colonial frontier. All of the material we have compiled is available for the general public, including teachers and students, to develop their own understandings of what the 'settlement' of Australia truly involved, at https://frontierconflict.org; blog posts about the project are also available at https://archaeologyonthefrontier.com.

## Consultants and Specialists within Larger Non-archaeological Organizations

As archaeology has become increasingly professionalized over the past twenty years, not only have CRM archaeology firms increased in number and size, but other organizations have also begun to appear in relation to this process. Some specialized consultancy firms have sprung up, many with their origins in CRM archaeology or local government, providing industry clients with advice on development-led archaeological responsibilities, laws, and strategies. Such firms will often not undertake archaeological mitigation work in advance of development themselves; rather, they will act on a developer's behalf in arranging all the necessary paperwork, liaising with the local and central government officials who oversee the process, finding their clients a CRM archaeology firm to actually do the work, monitoring their output, and so on – 'hand-holding' their clients through what may often be an unfamiliar process in return for payment.

Archaeologists who work for such firms come from local government or CRM archaeology. They tend to be attracted into this sector by the traditionally higher pay, better conditions, and improved job security it offers. As with any form of consultancy, this is a relatively risky and high-energy enterprise, particularly when dealing with something as unpredictable as archaeology. Deals need to be struck with clients and archaeologists alike, often in advance of the actual work to be done – unexpected archaeological finds that raise costs and cause delays to a construction program can be most unwelcome, and in such circumstances a client is likely to blame a consultant. Clients, CRM archaeology firms, and government alike frequently distrust such consultants, all secretly (or not so secretly) fearing that they are being taken advantage of in some way. So the rewards can be considerable, but the risks can be considerable as well.

The step beyond dedicated CRM archaeology–related consultancy is the inclusion of archaeologists into much larger firms, either environmental assessment firms or major industries. On one hand, a number of firms that were already doing natural environment consultancy noted the rise in cultural environment work and so began to hire single archaeologists at first, and then entire teams, to work alongside their existing staffers and so offer industry clients a package of advice covering all the necessary predevelopment advice and work that might be needed – from lawyers to archaeologists through architects, botanists, engineers, ground-water specialists, and so on. On the other hand, some larger industry clients have taken such impact assessment teams into their own organizations – cutting out the consultant intermediaries altogether to have dedicated teams and sections just as they have dedicated teams of structural engineers, architects, and the like. Archaeologists working in such organizations can, on one hand, expect many more benefits than their friends working in CRM archaeology – far more generous pay and benefits such as leave entitlement, pensions, and work-based professional as well as leisure facilities. On the other hand, archaeologists working in such firms sometimes report that they feel isolated – the archaeological team will often be the smallest and least important in the building, struggling to have its voice heard and respected in meetings alongside the big guns of other, larger teams with more of the project's overall costs/profits riding on them.

## Freelance Archaeology

A large – but, by definition, hard to define – group of archaeologists are free-lancers: self-employed and/or working for different archaeological organizations on a case-by-case basis. The motivation behind being a freelancer is varied: in some cases it is simply the best way for an archaeologist to earn the maximum income; in other cases, it may be a decision based on personal or family circum-stances, even simply a preference for working quietly on one's own, often in one's own home, rather than in an office environment with all the politics that can entail. Others may have been driven into this position by necessity – in some cases, through being laid off by a previous employer but realizing that they had the skills to branch out and provide the same service as before, but on their own terms. As can be imagined, there tends to be considerable competition both between them and between non-freelance specialists based in archaeological organizations such as CRM firms.

Freelancers in archaeology tend to fall into one of four inherently specialized groups:

- *Technical specialists*: in pottery, dating, environmental sampling, and the like.
- *Thematic or site-specific specialists*: in landscapes, parks and gardens, and so on.
- *Education and outreach specialists*: those leading education and training workshops, public archaeology events, and contributing to media online and in print, TV, and radio.
- *Consultants*: individuals specializing on advising industry on major infrastructure projects such as new airports, port installations, and road networks.

Even more than in other aspects of archaeology, there are distinct pros and cons about being a freelancer. A major long-term pro/con is financial: by being your own boss no one can fire you, but equally it is up to you to run the business, make the decisions, and, above all, make a profit from which you can live – and there is no one else to blame if things go wrong. Many people also dislike the idea of becoming a freelancer because of the management responsibility that this inevitably entails – running a business, dealing with tax and other administrative issues, and so forth.

A more day-to-day concern is the reality of the daily schedule. Some people like working on their own, absorbed by a particular task; for other people, this would be their worst possible working environment. A surprising number of people who become freelancers return to a larger organization after a short period realizing that, after all, they did not like working on their own as much as they thought they would.

People choosing to become freelance archaeologists, therefore, must make a series of very hard-headed decisions in advance of going freelance, about what they can offer clients – in a highly competitive marketplace for archaeological services – that will ensure a steady stream of work and so a solid income, perhaps a higher-quality or more specialized service than those offered by other existing providers. Such individuals also must take a long, hard look at their own characteristics, preferred working environments, and broader skill sets. As can be imagined, this is not a route that suits all people and is certainly not something that people leap into or come to by accident or as junior archaeologists. Most freelancers are highly skilled archaeologists, usually with many years of prior experience, who reach the decision to go freelance after much thought.

## Focus on: Kevin Wooldridge (UK)

I am Kevin Wooldridge, and I describe myself as a freelance archaeologist. By that, I mean that I have no single employer or employment type. I work for commercial archaeological units and for Historic England in the UK on a contract basis. I also work overseas in Europe, mainly in Norway but also in Sweden and Germany, largely in a research environment for universities and not-for-profit organizations. At present, due to the Covid-19 pandemic, my fieldwork has been suspended, and instead I am engaged on post-excavation work for Historic England on a backlog project and editing a journal article for a Norwegian colleague. My specialism is archaeological GIS and illustration, and I consider myself first and foremost to be a field archaeologist.

I got into archaeology when I was working in a London borough social services department. A colleague (and thankfully a *Guardian* reader) showed me a small advert in the newspaper seeking volunteers to work on an arch-aeological project in Scotland. In those days (pre-internet) you had to write a letter of application. I did so, and surprisingly I was accepted on to the project. At that point, aged twenty-one years old, I knew nothing of archaeology, had never studied it, and I had everything to learn. But from a small start on that project in Scotland I learnt of a project in Orkney (by which time I had ditched my job in social services) and then was taken on by the government's Central Archaeology Unit in England. Since then (1981), I have always been employed in archaeology. My early training was all 'on the job', but in 1986 I attended a survey training course at City University in London, and later I took an MA in Landscape Archaeology and GIS at University of Birmingham. The earlier course was paid for by my employer, but my MA was self-funded, although I did receive facility help from my then employer, particularly in allowing free access to university resources and time off to prepare and present essays. At the time, I was working for a different university to that at which I was studying. I should add that I was the first person in my family ever to attend university. I do not think that would have happened if I had not become an archaeologist.

I have worked in every capacity in field archaeology: as a volunteer, field assistant, supervisor, site director, and project officer. I have also worked, more often in recent years, as a survey specialist. The fieldwork has inevitably led to post-excavation and publication projects, and I have several publications to my name. I have also been involved in several field schools, for both universities and non-academic bodies. The field schools have taken place in the United Kingdom and overseas. My current position working for Historic England is due to a lucky chance. I was fully employed by a Norwegian university during the spring and summer, but I am no great fan of the Norwegian climate during the winter. I happened to see an advert for a Historic England project in London in a location where I had previously worked for the Museum of London. It also happened that Historic England had just begun using the Swedish Intrasis data-management programme on its archaeological projects, and I had lots of experience of using the same programme in Scandinavia. A combination of fortuitous circumstances thus led to my being employed on a contract basis ever since on this project. I alternate my work for Historic England with my seasonal work in Scandinavia and commercial work else-where in the United Kingdom. So my most recent job and current work I guess is all down to my being a known and trusted resource, although I am still required to formally apply for most projects.

My average week varies depending on whether I am engaged in field work or post-ex work. Fieldwork invariably takes me away from home, so I will be staying in rental accommodation, normally good, but sometimes less so. Obviously, that makes some difference to the lifestyle one normally enjoys – it is probably more sociable than would be the case at home! My post-ex work I try as far as possible to do at home. That requires perhaps a little more discipline, just to make sure that budgets and quality of output are maintained. It is of course much easier these days to stay in touch with colleagues based elsewhere, and to some extent the Covid crisis has not required much change to my normal working practice. The best thing about my different roles is that every day is different, even working with familiar data. Every new project is a challenge, probably in a new location, offering a great deal of variety. I am an archaeological 'generalist' happy to apply myself to sites from all periods and of all types of complexity.

My top tip for pursuing a career in archaeology is that flexibility is very important, and I realize that often results in a clash with other lifestyle choices. It is crucial to find that balance early in one's career. I would also suggest that it is important to acquire a specialism, particularly one that allows the freedom to be able to moderate the impact of the job on your lifestyle and provide employment when fieldwork opportunities are limited. My experience in Scandinavia has taught me that, where the climate has a much more limiting effect on fieldwork than it probably does in the United Kingdom. I was also taught a very important maxim early in my archaeological career: 'Be respectful and caring towards colleagues on your way up the slippery pole, because it can be damn painful if you meet them again on your way down.'

I believe the most significant organization to arise in UK archaeology in recent years is the British Archaeology Jobs and Resources (BAJR) project. Not only has it become the single most important outlet for archaeological job advertising, but I believe it has, through its online forum, led to much greater harmonization of workplace standards and self-regulation, as well as a brilliant source of archaeological news, opinion, and gossip. As for my wider interests, I am particularly grateful to the University of Bergen, Norway, for allowing me access to some marvellous sites and finds alike.

# Chapter 4

# Academic Archaeology

## Introduction

In the public eye, the academic is the archetypal archaeologist who springs to mind when the career is mentioned. This is the career path that most people assume archaeologists take, either because there are thought to be the most jobs in this sector (wrong), or the best pay (partly right and partly wrong), or the best working conditions and status (again, both right and wrong). Ever since Professor Henry 'Indiana' Jones Jr.'s academic credentials were highlighted in the movies of that franchise, the general perception is that at the end of the day, however dirty and tired the archaeologist may be, they will be stopping off at campus to drop off their kit and pick up their mail on the way back from the field (see Figure 21).

As discussed in Chapter 1, for a very long time all the above assumptions would have been correct. The first professional archaeologists were, arguably, academics – people with a formal educational background in classical, ancient, or medieval history who were employed by major academic-oriented organizations to work as archaeologists. This career is thus the origin of 'professional' archaeology, and so of the popular misconception of the 'definitive' archaeologist. However, Chapter 3 made clear that the CRM archaeology world accounts for most archaeological jobs these days, and it handles most of the money too. Those in these academic posts are thus a lucky – I would emphasize that this does not necessarily equate with 'elite' – few. There can be no doubt that when this sector works out for an individual, such a career can be one of the best in archaeology, both personally and professionally rewarding in terms of lifestyle, pay, conditions, and status. However, academia can

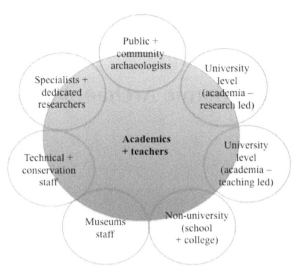

Figure 21. The structure and interrelationships of the academic archaeology sector.

also be an exceptionally demanding place to work, placing particularly heavy pressures on its denizens in terms of their employer's expectations of performance and delivery. Sadly, over the past decade between the first and second editions of this book, academia has also witnessed similar market forces to those that already negatively impact pay and conditions in CRM archaeology. The result has been an increasing move towards fixed-term and/or part-time contracts in place of permanent (sometimes referred to as 'tenured') and full-time positions, and a subsequent drop in pay and conditions. This shift is not unique to archaeology alone; nor is it a problem exclusive to any single country – it is a wider socioeconomic change witnessed across the university sector around the globe.

## Focus on – Stefano Campana (Italy)

I am Stefano Campana, and I am an Associate Professor of Archaeology at the University of Siena, Italy. My work is focused on the understanding of past landscapes from protohistory to the present day. The principal context for my work has been Tuscany, but I have also participated in and led research work in the United Kingdom, Spain, Turkey, Palestine, Iraq, and Asia. Since 2006 I have been a faculty member of the University of Siena, in the Department of History and Cultural Heritage, where I have engaged in teaching and research as Associate Professor in Landscape Archaeology. Between September 2014 and June 2016, I was a Senior Research Fellow at the University of Cambridge in the United Kingdom, in their Faculty of Classics. There, I initiated a totally new project aimed at stimulating change in the way archaeologists in the Mediterranean world study the archaeology of landscapes, moving from an essentially site-based approach to a truly landscape-scale perspective. From 2017 I have also been invited from the Department of Social, Political and Cognitive Sciences of the University of Siena to teach 'Cultural Diplomacy and Archaeology' within the international master course in Cultural Diplomacy.

I do not think that I am a valid example of how to choose the subject of study and the university! I always wanted to become a mechanical engineer, and I always thought that I would study at the polytechnic of Milan or ETH Zurich. However, at the end of high school I changed my mind completely, and I decided to study history and archaeology. I decided to come to in Siena mainly because it is a beautiful city, rich in art, history, and culture. I did not know at that time that it was also one of the best universities for the study of archaeology in Italy and perhaps in Europe. In Siena I met my mentor, Prof. Riccardo Francovich, and I did my degree and doctorate on the study of the archaeological landscapes of southern Tuscany. My training was based on the study of archaeology, a lot of fieldwork (field walking survey, aerial survey, and archaeological excavation), and computer science.

My career path has been very linear and apparently simple. After my degree and my doctorate, I became an Assistant Professor at the University of Siena. A fundamental role in my training has undoubtedly been played by the opportunities offered by the European Union's research framework, which allowed me to connect with a large international community of researchers. At present, among the most important turning points, I would consider the opportunity of spending two years at Cambridge University as a research fellow. Moreover, my activities have also had an impact in the fields of archaeological conservation and commercial practice, through creation in 2009 of the spin-off company ATS and through its use under my direction of the innovative approaches to its assessment work on the Brescia-to-Milan motorway, as well as in subsequent projects throughout Italy and beyond. Today, the company is fully independent from the University of Siena, involving up to ten archaeologists.

It is difficult to describe a 'typical' week in my life, as one of the most interesting aspects of my business is that every day is different from the other. I have a great deal of freedom of movement. I am required to teach three courses per year at the university that I can organize as I prefer, and for the rest of the time I have no set obligations. This is undoubtedly a great privilege. In addition to lectures and ongoing research, and the continual drafting of new proposals, I travel a lot for conferences, as a visiting professor and for fieldwork. As they say: it is hard work, but someone has to do it!

My top tip for pursuing a career in archaeology is that in the first place it takes passion, a lot of passion. That said, it is good to do the opposite of what I did! I believe it is important to plan your choices well: carefully identify a good university, have targeted experiences abroad consistent with your interests, and gain a lot of experience in the field with highly experienced archaeologists. If during the first university years it is important to acquire a broad and general vision of the problems in the various eras afterwards, one must choose and specialize in something without losing the general vision of the problems.

Among the most important projects that I am working that I would like to point out are Emptyscapes and SottoSiena. The first one is aimed to challenge past landscape and theoretical paradigms, moving towards a more complex and comprehensive understanding of ancient urban and rural layouts including transformations across time and the blurring of boundaries between urban and rural environments. SottoSienna is a new project aimed to build upon the experience developed in previous survey work in urban and formerly urban areas and within historical towns, with particular regard to a case study in Siena.

## A Day in the Life

The average day in the life of an academic archaeologist is likely to be driven by two things: the time of year and the individual's seniority (see Table 6). Taking time of year first (for it is undoubtedly the more important factor), the year splits roughly into two portions, commencing anew at the start of each academic year. The first (two-thirds) share of the academic year is more or less focused on teaching and its administration, management, and examination (I say 'more or less' as this depends on an individual's workload, which is in turn associated with the second issue above, seniority). The latter, one-third share of the academic year is, at least by intent if not outcome, broadly focused on research, which often includes physical fieldwork on archaeological sites but may also mean work in a library, lab, or archive undertaking both pre- and post-fieldwork study, or writing up work for publication. Some time is also likely to be spent attending conferences and symposia, presenting new data, and learning about the work of others, even visiting new sites and museums; other time might be spent being involved in various different types of public and community archaeology, sharing results with the wider community. In the gaps in this busy schedule then fits, hopefully, at least a little time off, although plenty of archaeologists both within and outside academia never take a real holiday, and some even maintain a perverse pride in this fact (Table 6). Alas, while this basic model still holds in principle, the marketization of academia makes it less and less of a reality for many. With the reduction in permanent and/or full-time roles mentioned above has come the emergence of a new academic 'underclass' paid only during the teaching term and left in a precarious position out of term. Such individuals will often take on other work (archaeological and otherwise) during and between terms to account for the financial shortfalls that such gaps generate, and in these gap periods will be juggling work with job applications alongside course preparation and their own research – all of this work unpaid, unlike their luckier, permanently employed peers. The emergence of this precarious lifestyle is one of the most shocking aspects of early twenty-first-century

TABLE 6. **The pros and cons of working in academic archaeology**

| Pros | Cons |
| --- | --- |
| Prestigious: university academics are still seen as being in one of the historic professions (such as being a medical doctor) and working as part of a generic organization that employs many thousands of people; such roles usually provide associated benefits such as cultural/sports/social facilities on campus. | Poor pay and often surprisingly poor conditions: fewer and fewer posts are permanent/tenured, many are fixed-term or part-time with heavy workloads. |
| Academic books are generally held in high regard by the community and general public alike. | You can end up working very long hours; it is hard to turn off when in many ways you are your own boss. |
| Best opportunities to 'write your own ticket' in terms of balance of field/office/lab work, types of sites, or materials studied. | Hierarchical structure of university systems can be frustrating and stuffy. |
| Opportunities often exist to do additional consultancy alongside your main job, which can generate additional income. | Many women report a glass ceiling based on gender for senior appointments – which, in the twenty-first century, is shocking – and illegal. |
| Good research, funding, and other opportunities; stimulating intellectual environment | Competition for posts is cutthroat – which the employers know, hence the poor – and worsening – labour conditions. |
| Teaching can be rewarding and exciting. | Once in a post you can get trapped there for lack of other opportunities – which can make it hard if you are in a relationship and your partner wants to move for their career. |
| | Not all university towns are great to live in – for every university in a big and lively city there are half a dozen based either in an older industrial dump or in a tiny town with nothing to do on the weekend. |
| | Career structure and progression is slight – you often must move to get promoted in any way. |
| | Once definitely in or out of the academic track, it can be hard to make a move to/from another aspect of archaeology. |
| | Demands of teaching, administration, research, and grant-winning place constant pressure on academics to produce to meet ever-higher targets. There is consequently a high rate of stress-related problems. |

academia. It is often a source of bewilderment to many friends and family that an individual they love and respect, who is likely to hold a PhD and may well be a highly respected specialist in their field, can nonetheless be living literally pay check to pay check and may have to resort to handouts of food to keep themselves and their family going. And akin to CRM archaeologists, such individuals increasingly find themselves having to travel widely to take up such temporary employment, which impacts negatively upon their personal lives.

When employed in the early 2000s as a relatively junior and part-time academic, the author had a fairly heavy teaching load, including the administration of several courses (i.e., preparing handbooks and assessments, teaching classes and giving lectures, advising students and undertaking marking, and so on) and also being responsible for the management of and admission into an MA program (including recruitment to the MA, marketing it, interviewing students, and the like). Other junior and mid-ranking academics are likely to have similar roles, balancing out what are effectively middle-management administrative tasks – such as being admissions or examination tutors on degree programs, chairing various committees (exam, staff-student consultative committee, research, and grants and publications are just some of the internal committees of the author's former employer), or acting as the senior tutors for a year or subject group, and so responsible for their overall leadership. Many staff also have 'pastoral' responsibilities, acting as personal tutors to students (advising their studies and professional development); some may also sit on the management panels of internal or external organizations such as archaeological charities and trusts.

More senior staff are likely to undertake broadly similar roles to those described here; what differs may be that they chair the various committees on which others sit and may well have additional management responsibilities, especially if they are the coordinators of large research grants employing specific junior staff. Others may be the chairs, heads, or other types of leaders of the structure in which the archaeology section/department/school sits. Senior staff may also have to sit on university-wide committees, or even be a part of the higher administrative team of the university.

From this description, the benefits of the academic archaeologist's lifestyle may not seem clear – it sounds like a lot of rushing and administration in return for only a little archaeology. Although this is true in some ways, it depends on what is meant by 'archaeology': for those interested in a career based around fieldwork on archaeological sites, there can be no doubt that academia offers fewer opportunities than, for example, CRM archaeology. Furthermore, the fieldwork that does occur within an academic's remit will usually be very different from that of a CRM archaeologist – and may not be fieldwork in this sense at all, but rather archival research, non-invasive surveys, or lab work. Academic or research work in general, particularly excavations, tends to be proactive, driven by different objectives than CRM archaeology work, usually the single-minded pursuit of a research question or questions. Because the research on academic-led projects takes place on sites selected by the project director and is financed privately (by government or private grants), this mean that timescales, both short- and long-term, are also different.

Research fieldwork is undoubtedly more physically leisurely than CRM archaeology work; rarely will the research archaeologist working on a site discovered as a result of development or industry have to work to a predetermined deadline in advance of a site's loss, or even work alongside such destruction, plotting features literally days, or perhaps even minutes, prior to their loss. Research archaeologists also generally do – or at least should – get to be involved in the entire archaeological process, starting with the formulation of research questions and objectives, moving on to site identification and discovery, then analysis (perhaps involving excavation, but just as easily taking the form of non-invasive survey), continuing with data interpretation and secondary analysis, through to post-fieldwork conservation, curation, and publication. This level of control over the choice of sites, manner of investigation, and the pace and format of the process is undoubtedly one of the major appeals of research archaeology.

Another big plus, especially for younger researchers, is the ability to personally lead smaller, self-contained projects. An academic archaeologist in their thirties who can write a successful grant application can be placed in charge of an entire project in the format described earlier. Although such a situation is possible for a CRM archaeologist of the same age, it is far less likely, as the CRM archaeologist usually is part of a much larger project team and perhaps has responsibility for only certain aspects of an archaeological investigation or site, ultimately reporting to others. Indeed, this managerial freedom is one thing that most academics in general, including archaeologists, normally cite as a major perk of their jobs.

Although influenced by the shifting cycle of the academic calendar and affected by the weekly requirements of tutorials, classes, and lectures at set times, academics are overall some of the least managed people in modern society: as long as they turn up to teach at the right times and attend essential meetings, the plan for the rest of their day, week, month, or year is usually left up to them, with minimal external interference. There are plenty of deadlines, usually self-set: complete these lecture notes, finish that book chapter, send off that grant application, and so on; but only very rarely does an academic have a line manager setting the priorities, noting when they are in the office, or setting a deadline or new urgent priority. As a result of this freedom, most academics spread their time across a number of locations and times when they work best – early-bird archaeologists might well be writing a site report over the first cup of coffee in their kitchen at 5 a.m.; night owls might equally be sitting in their studies at 2 a.m.; in between will be a series of different people spread across their homes, offices, labs, libraries, archives, and sites.

This managerial freedom is also, unfortunately, the source of a good deal of misunderstanding about the academic lifestyle in general. A commonly cited complaint is that non-academics may see an academic leaving the office building in the mid-afternoon, apparently on their way home, and equate this with a laid-back lifestyle. But in a career in which one never really turns off, supported by a modern world full of broadband Internet connections, mobile phones, and laptops, the 'office' is anywhere one can sit down for more than five minutes, and most academics are some of the least laid-back people out there. It is impossible to succeed in modern academia without a work ethic bordering on the obsessive-compulsive. In a discipline such as archaeology, a social science focused on understanding humans and their behaviour, inspiration can strike anywhere – most archaeologists have had a moment when they sat bolt upright in bed, woken by an idea their brain had been mulling over for days or weeks, and rushed off to tap it into their laptop before they forget it. Similarly, a discipline with a tradition of living in rough-and-ready fieldwork camps has no doubt about doing academic work in such conditions. When working in academia, the author once wrote a major grant proposal while sitting cross-legged on the floor of an old house that was functioning as the site HQ, kitchen, and bunkhouse rolled into one, a floor that was so damp that I could feel the moisture rising up through the carpet into my jeans. I balanced the laptop on my knees both to keep me warm and as the only definitely dry location in that old dump (thankfully, the grant application was successful).

The career benefits – the sheer pleasure – of teaching archaeology are also not to be overlooked, both preparing to teach and the teaching itself. This, in itself, is a part of the broader research commitments of academics, and when well done, teaching and research intermesh to a considerable degree – what an academic is reading, writing, and researching, whether in the library, lab, or field, influences their teaching, and vice versa. Some 'general' classes require lecturers to have a very broad knowledge of site types and locations – for example, the author's old graduate classes on the topic 'global issues in maritime archaeology' comprised twenty, two-hour, linked lectures and seminars encompassing sites above, across, and below water from across the entire world, ranging in date from around 10,000 BCE to 2000 CE. The classes included details of project planning and methodology, site discovery and exploration, post-excavation and analysis, as well as legal and management frameworks in global marine archaeology. Keeping on top of the best and latest work for such a broad-reaching class is a job in and of itself, and an extremely stimulating one at that. Teaching preparation is one thing, however – teaching itself quite another. Any schoolteacher, as well as most academics, will tell you that the buzz one gets from teaching well, to a responsive class, is one of the finest natural highs obtainable (equally, all have horror stories of classes or lectures that just didn't seem to work and classes on the verge of, or even under, revolt).

## Focus on: Ethan Cochrane (New Zealand)

I am Ethan Cochrane, and I am an Associate Professor in anthropology at the University of Auckland in New Zealand. I teach undergraduate and postgraduate courses, supervise postgraduate and PhD students, and conduct field-based archaeological research in the Pacific islands, in Samoa for the last decade, but also in Fiji, Hawai'i, and other archipelagos. Like academic staff around the world, my job comprises teaching, research, and administration or service, including working on committees, and leading departments. At Auckland, the official division of these responsibilities is 40/40/20.

I have always had an interest in academics: maths, chemistry, as well as humanities, social sciences, literature, and so forth. At university in the United States, I was inspired by an archaeology teacher in my first year and realized that in archaeology I could combine the sciences and social sciences. I also learned to love research, and researcher became a dream job for me – to get paid to answer compelling questions and think about topics that interest you. I took a year off between my undergraduate and postgraduate work and I then completed an MA and PhD in anthropology with a specialization in archaeology. Throughout my postgraduate training I tutored university classes, worked for a cultural resource management firm, and ran archaeological field schools for my university. Through these opportunities I have learned how to encourage and lead multiple people with different skills and backgrounds to work together on a common problem – an important skill in archaeology.

I have been on the academic staff of two universities in different countries, and I have also held cultural resource management positions in a third, from entry-level shovelbum to project manager. I was offered my current position through the standard academic interview process. I think I was successful in this process (and for my previous academic post) because I fit the job description (i.e., I was not pretending to be something that I am not), I was future-focused on my interview and application, and I play nicely with others. Academic employers and colleagues want to know about your future plans and how you will grow the university; they already know what you have done from your CV. And academics want to hire someone whom they will not mind having in the office next door for many years to come, someone who positively contributes to the intellectual life of the discipline and academy beyond their own specialty, someone they want to spend time with at the department BBQ.

My weeks vary throughout the year. In my office most days I am preparing lectures, working on administrative tasks, meeting with students and reviewing their work, and writing research. I teach during the semester, both lecture-style undergraduate courses and postgraduate seminars. I try to get research writing or analysis done every day, even just a little bit, as there is always some adminis-trative chore or immediate teaching-supervision task that can draw time away from research. I have a lot of overseas field research too, so multiple times each year, between semesters, and in the summer I am in the Pacific Islands leading fieldwork, working with local communities, and negotiating the challenges (and joys!) of this. By far, the intellectual freedom afforded academic staff is the highlight of my role. My job is thinking, something I enjoy above all else, whether I am paid for it or not.

My top tip for pursuing a career in archaeology is, perhaps counterintuitively, to acquire both diverse training and have a specialized skill that makes you a desirable colleague. Archaeology is an 'all-trades' field, so having a variety of talents makes you more employable, but also a specialized skill means that you can fill a role that perhaps few others can. Also, archaeology is a small profession, so try to nurture positive relationships with your colleagues as you will undoubtedly, years in the future, meet someone who worked with your first field supervisor.

Almost all archaeological knowledge is produced with public financial support. This knowledge should be publicly available, within the bounds of descendant communities' culturally appropriate dissemination. Therefore, I encourage you to support high-quality open-access publishing.

## Career Structure and Qualifications

It goes without saying that most research archaeologists are academic high-flyers. Ask almost any academic about their childhood, and a familiar story normally appears of a kid who liked reading and got good grades. Put bluntly: academics are often the nerds. This is admittedly an exaggeration, but not a gross one. Academic success requires a peculiar form of single-minded dedication, a dogged pursuit of often-intangible goals that are constantly replaced by another set of goals even further away. This is not a lifestyle that suits everyone. People who like to work as part of a noisy, friendly team may make great CRM archaeologists but would rapidly lose their sanity when they have to sit for days or weeks in an archive, and people who are very shy may simply not be able to cope with the thought of teaching large groups of lively students. The author left academia partly because of this issue – to put it bluntly, I prefer working as part of a team, and I dislike spending extended periods working on my own.

Going against the stereotype, however, academic archaeologists are increasingly extroverts – enthusiasts for the subject of archaeology in general and for their own specialty in particular. Perhaps the fastest-changing aspect of academia is the balance it increasingly requires of its practitioners to be at once both introverted loners, good at solo research, and extroverted performers capable of giving a lecture to a hundred or more students. This is not an easy mix to find. Although it used to be joked that many academics were hopeless public speakers, scruffy, forgetful, and vague, this is an image less and less based in reality. As universities pursue ever more external funding as well as come under increasing public scrutiny, an academic who cannot perform is much less welcome. This is not to say, of course, that all academics give lectures so good that they could be filmed as light entertainment, but it is to say that most can give a well-structured, as well as decently presented, talk to a mixed audience without falling over the podium or boring everyone to sleep.

Almost uniformly now, a lecturer at a university will have a BA in archaeology, anthropology, or a related subject (e.g., classics or, at a stretch, history); an MA, usually in a subject or period-specific specialty; and a PhD. Up until quite recently the PhD was not nearly as essential, but that time is now just about over: although it is conceivably possible to get a post without a PhD, such positions are infrequent. The real questions are not 'Should I get a degree?' but rather, 'What programs, where, and what else?' That is, how should prospective academics focus their studies, should they travel to different universities for their different degrees, and what additional archaeological skills make people more attractive to prospective academic archaeological employers? The first two questions are discussed in detail in Chapter 2. The last question is simple and can be answered in one straightforward way: *everything*. An archaeologist who has the requisite academic qualifications – and, thus, research credentials – is one thing, and may get jobs; but an individual who brings such qualifications along with other skills is going to stand a better chance. Crudely speaking, however, there is undoubtedly a skills hierarchy of what universities as employers want, and it goes something like this:

- *Publications*: Peer-reviewed journal articles at least; ideally, chapters in or entire books of original research from major academic presses (university presses and the major well-known independent academic publishers). These are the highest-valued parts of the various research exercises undertaken by government monitors of the university sector. Edited works show signs of commitment to the process of academic endeavour, but do not rate so highly in such research assessments, as most unfairly edited works do not count as 'original' work by editors in such assessments, despite the great effort and originality put into them.
- *Grants and awards*: Most important are those from major research institutions, others are less so. The larger the sum, the better! In the United Kingdom, this means funding in the tens and hundreds of thousands or millions of pounds from the Arts and Humanities Research Council (AHRC), the Natural Environment Research Council (NERC), the Leverhulme Trust, and similar organizations – and/or major government funding streams. That being said, it is understood that young academics cannot be expected to immediately raise very large sums, and that early in one's career, small grants of thousands of pounds from many different sources are perfectly acceptable, showing ability and potential to consistently engage in original research.
- *Field experience*: Academic archaeologists tend to have an extremely wide range of field experience these days; some are highly competent and experienced fieldworkers, others far less so. But field experience does not necessarily have to include being out in the field: it may mean, rather, experience or research in a laboratory, museum, or archive. Such projects tend to be linked to the aforementioned grants and awards, and are a major selling point for universities when making hiring decisions: academics who can bring existing grants tied to a specific project with them, and/or are involved in an ongoing project in which students can get experience, are highly attractive to universities.
- *Teaching and supervisory experience*: Academics increasingly must teach both within and outside their research specialty: the benefits of being a multifaceted lecturer capable of teaching several different subjects and/or general courses and surveys to undergraduates and postgraduates alike cannot be underestimated, especially for younger academics who generally carry a heavy teaching load than more

senior colleagues who are likely to have to do more management and administration. Academics also must recruit and supervise research students – candidates for PhDs – an exciting, if at sometimes extremely challenging, process.

- *Administrative and management experience*: Universities require a growing administrative role from academics, from the everyday tasks of logging student attendance in class, recording tutorials, marking in a timely and fair manner, and attending departmental and examiners meetings to the highly specific, with certain roles in particular taking up a lot of time, especially those of examinations officer and recruitment/admissions tutor, where the decisions they make influence the future lives of hundreds or thousands of students. The latter role can be extremely time-consuming, dealing with hundreds of applications per year that need to be assessed.

## Lifestyle, Career Progression, and Employability

The availability of jobs and the pay, benefits, and working conditions in academia vary greatly and are, as noted above, generally in the decline – there is currently a corporate rush to the bottom globally in terms of academic pay and conditions. Partly, this is a question of professional structures drawn up on national lines. In the United States, academics of all types – not just archaeologists – work within the tenure system. A declining number of junior US academics are on the tenure track – their performance over a set number of years in terms of teaching, publication, fundraising, administration, outreach, and other factors is monitored and assessed. At the end of a specific period, their tenure position is reviewed; if successful, they are awarded tenure – effectively, the right not to have their contract of employment terminated without just cause. Once tenured at one institution, an individual usually will be granted tenure automatically at another institution if they move there. Tenured – even tenure-track – positions are highly sought after but are also highly stressful – the pursuit of tenure takes many years, and if an individual fails to be awarded tenure at the end of this process, it can seriously harm their professional and personal social standing. Tenured positions also cost universities relatively more, as these tend to be more highly paid; as a consequence, more and more positions in US universities are not tenured or tenure-track or even full-time – archaeologists in such positions can, in theory, be hired or fired at will, although in many cases they may see their contracts last for years or even decades without threat of termination. And as noted above, a growing number of academic jobs have the same expectations of applicants – a PhD, research experience, publications and successful funding applications, teaching and management experience – but none of the benefits of tenure in terms of pay, conditions, or job security.

Below this level are also an army of those who are usually referred to as 'TAs' – teaching assistants. Many of these are graduate students – usually PhD students – who undertake a large measure of teaching, and especially grading, of undergraduates on behalf of more senior tenured or tenure-track staff. Being a TA is good professional experience, and it also provides at least some salary. But the downside is a lowly academic status and comparably poorer pay and conditions. Many TAs are paid only by the hour or class they teach, with little or no paid preparation time; TA contracts usually are renewed only each term or semester, dependent on student demand, so are extremely insecure; and most TA contracts do not accrue additional benefits, such as health insurance. The model is that a bright graduate student works as a TA while undertaking work toward a PhD; completes this PhD and moves on to a tenure-track position; and, after many years, is awarded tenure, teaching the next generation of graduate students in a self-sustaining cycle. The increasing reality is a partial breakdown of this system, with fewer tenure-track or tenured positions being chased by more and more TAs. The result is that more and more professional academics, archaeologists, and others alike are trapped working as TAs even after they have their PhDs, caught in a cycle of poor pay and conditions that make it hard for them to find the money and time to research, write, and produce materials that may help them escape this trap.

In the United Kingdom and Australia, as well as in many other nations, the situation of academic employment is less clear-cut than in the United States. Tenure is not an issue in the United Kingdom and Australia in particular; rather, contracts of employment are either permanent (broadly the equivalent of tenure, and with the greatest benefits and job security, including substantial compulsory payments if terminated) or fixed term for a set number of weeks, months, or years. In the United Kingdom, in particular, if someone has been on a continuous fixed-term contract for more than four years without break, then at the end of those four years they are legally entitled to apply to have the position made permanent, although institutions have been making this transition harder and harder to achieve through the use of break periods for such employers. Just as in the United States, therefore, there are fewer and fewer permanent positions and more and more fixed-term positions being offered to academics in the United Kingdom and Australia – in some cases for only a few months, or a term of one semester at a time. Academic archaeologists around the world thus fall broadly into two distinct groups. On one hand are a small group of fully tenured or permanent positions. These posts are stable, well-paid for archaeology (tied to standardized university pay grades for all academics, irrespective of their research specialty), and come with benefits such as health care and child care provisions, private pension and life insurance funds, access to campus facilities, training and so on, and the many other benefits that can come from working for a large institution. On the other hand are a growing army of untenured staff, TAs and the like, paid either by the hour, day, or period (six-, eight-, or ten-month contracts are growing increasingly common). These individuals may well have the same academic qualifications, teaching, and field experience as their tenured colleagues. Often such post holders are relatively young, making their first steps on the academic career ladder; worryingly, though, more and more are older and have simply been unlucky in their hunt for a permanent or tenured position. The result is that the nice university archaeologist you meet, whom you imagine teaching bright young students from the comfort and security of a job for life and a wood-panelled study, is increasingly likely to be a nervous soul running toward the end of a short-term contract and worrying about how they will pay the rent or feed their family in a couple of months.

Modern academics, whatever their tenure position, also must juggle an increasingly complex workload. Traditionally, academics divided their time roughly 50/50 between teaching and research, the two aspects cross-fertilizing each other. Nowadays, an increasing administrative burden has crept in, and with staff cutbacks the teaching workload has generally risen in association; thus, on average, the balance is now more something along the lines of 50/30/20 spent on teaching, research, and administration, respectively. Some academics may have wildly different balances, with a lucky few having far fewer teaching commitments and thus more time for research, but a worrying majority are teaching more and more and researching less and less. To this can also be added the new demands to publish, on one hand, and to generate external grant income, on the other.

Although the negatives are numerous, there are also positives in this archaeological career path. As already mentioned, there is a tremendous amount of freedom within academia, a factor that arguably outweighs all other comparable benefits. This freedom is certainly one of time management and prioritization, but it is also the even more intangible issue of intellectual freedom and the social environment that comes with such freedom. Under the right circumstances, the sheer joy of working alongside so many different, dedicated people thinking along similar, but not prescribed, lines in the pursuit of the wider understanding of the human past can be incredibly pleasurable and stimulating.

Assuming that the longed-for nirvana of a tenured position has been achieved by the academic archaeologist, it is also possible to have a good long-term quality of life with, for archaeology at least, a better-than-normal semblance of a career and career progression, working through the hierarchies of academic responsibility described previously. Perhaps more important, however, it is also possible for individuals to identify a professional level that they want to achieve and then stay at without penalizing their status, job security, or salary. Plenty of academics, including plenty of tenured academic archaeologists, have no aspiration to rise beyond their current position within the university hierarchy, to become a senior professor or head of department or a dean or head of school, let alone a vice-chancellor; with the higher pay and perks that such positions undoubtedly bring also comes a loss of involvement in what first drew individuals into this world – archaeology itself.

The downside of what is undoubtedly an appealing lifestyle is also the relative lack of jobs; just as in the rest of archaeology, demand for jobs exceeds supply, and for every academic position that opens up there are likely to be dozens, if not hundreds, of highly qualified and motivated applicants. Getting a post, especially a tenured post, can be hard enough; shifting jobs because of personal or other professional commitments can be even more difficult. Ask most academic archaeologists why they have a job in institution X rather than Y, and their answer will usually be, 'Because X was hiring.' Even if X is not the ideal university in the ideal town or even the ideal country, most academics are glad to get whatever job they can and will adapt their lifestyle to suit. But this can mean some painful lifestyle choices – plenty of attached academics, archaeologists or not, live in a different town or even region from their family, commuting daily or weekly; precious few archaeologists live in the location of their, or their family's, choice.

## Focus on: Kate Domett (Australia)

I am Kate Domett, and I am an Associate Professor in the College of Medicine and Dentistry at James Cook University (JCU), Townsville, Queensland, in Australia. I have lived in Townsville for nearly twenty years, and because it is in North Queensland it is very warm and sunny (sometimes too sunny). It is also on the coast, with the Great Barrier Reef just a couple of hours away by boat. I have a 'traditional' academic job in that my role is dispersed across teaching (40 per cent), research (40 per cent), and administration (20 per cent) – those percentages vary quite a bit across the year. JCU has a very popular medical programme promoting health in rural, regional, and remote tropical areas of Australia. I teach these, and many other students, anatomy. When I am not teaching (or doing paperwork/attending meetings), I undertake my research on bio-archaeology. That can involve a range of things from travelling (mostly to countries in Southeast Asia like Thailand, Laos PDR, Vietnam, and Cambodia) to working on archaeological excavations, collecting data on skeletal remains from previous excavations, or back in my office analyzing data and writing publications. I also supervise several Honours, master's, and PhD students in collaboration with my research colleagues in archaeology at JCU – we have a nice interdisciplinary association.

My interest back in high school was in health sciences, so when I went to university I undertook a Bachelor of Science, majoring in anatomy (but also completing subjects like physiology, biochemistry, microbiology, and a little taste of anthropology to balance things out) at the University of Otago in New Zealand. It was in my last year of my bachelor's degree that I was introduced to the field of osteology – the study of bones. This really caught my interest – I love the skeleton as it is like a puzzle – everything fits together – and, as I gained more experience, if you know your normal anatomy really well, it is so clear when something is 'wrong' with a bone. I did a range of small bio-archaeology research projects in my fourth year – some involving hands-on work with skeletal remains, others more around literature review. I was lucky to be invited to excavate in Thailand at the end of my fourth year by my supervisor, Nancy Tayles. To have the opportunity to have hands-on experi-ence in the field (alongside very interesting travel), excavating a site with over 100 skeletal remains on my first dig, easily sold me and I started a master's degree, which I soon upgraded to a PhD. During my PhD I continued to be trained in fieldwork (mostly to do with excavating human remains, but I picked up a few broader archaeology skills along the way) and the detail of analyzing human remains in the 'lab'. Our labs were, and continue to be, usually quite makeshift in whatever village we were working in, so you learn to be adaptable.

I also learnt the more usual skills like statistical analysis, writing, time management. I was given the opportunity to teach in the later years of my PhD, which set me up better for getting an academic job after finishing my PhD. My learning continues both informally from colleagues and more formally at university-run workshops on grant writing, curriculum development, and such like. I also completed a Diploma of Education majoring in Tertiary Teaching.

During my PhD, I held casual positions as a tutor in anatomy and lecturer in biological anthropology – great for the CV. I also completed short research positions (mostly for fieldwork) after my PhD, but I did not go into a post-doc research position. I was successful in obtaining my current job at James Cook University because I had the teaching skills they were after – I had experience teaching large classes on anatomy in health science programs. I had to work hard to maintain my research output in the first few years of my new job, but it was worthwhile as I now have a good balance of teaching and research activity. I have been promoted twice since my appointment – to Senior Lecturer and then to Associate Professor. These promotions were based on all areas of my work, from getting good teaching feedback to my publication record to community service.

During my busy teaching times, I prepare lectures (this takes longer than you would think) and other teaching materials, deliver lectures, and teach in the anatomy lab. I have learnt that I can create effective teaching materials for my students that are not 100 per cent perfect – the effort it requires to make fancy presentations, for example, will not equate to an increase in student outcomes. I use my time effectively: put the effort in to where you will get the most results (the 80/20 rule). I will be writing assessments for quizzes and exams and marking assessments and theses. I meet with my postgraduate students, reading and editing their work. I participate in university meetings (such as teaching and learning committees) and I communicate with colleagues about current research projects – progress with journal articles, grant applications, and writing reviews. I also plan my upcoming research trips. When I am not teaching, I undertake research-related travel, which in my case is usually to Southeast Asia. This may be for an excavation or to undertake observations in the lab of skeletons we excavated previously and/or to supervise students doing lab work overseas. As a mother, I need to make sure my research trips are completed in timely manner – over the years my family and I think three weeks maximum away works best for us, so I have to use my time effectively, working seven days a week while away, but that is okay because it is one of best parts of my job, travelling to small villages and towns around Southeast Asia and experiencing the culture and food. *The* best part of my job, though, is its varied nature – I enjoy the teaching, the travel, the excavations, the data analysis, the writing, but I would not enjoy doing just one of those all the time; I like the variety. Being a university academic also comes with a degree of freedom to carry out my work over varied hours. I am not tied to a nine-to-five office job (so long as I turn up for my classes). I have the freedom to pursue a range of research topics as I choose what interests me or what comes up with each new excavation – that keeps me motivated.

My top tip for pursuing a career in archaeology is to choose a discipline within archaeology that you are most passionate about to start with. Then it really comes down to making the most of opportunities that come your way, and being proactive about finding those opportunities, without being too pushy. Be prepared to pick up a range of skills along the way, some that you might not think are directly related to your career but help you become a more flexible, well-rounded colleague. It helps to develop good working relationships with your colleagues, whether you like them or not. It also helps to learn to say 'no' – to pick and choose which opportunities you take on (this gets easier the further you progress up the career ladder). In saying that, though, sometimes you must be prepared to do things you do not want to, especially on archaeological excavations when time and money are constrained, and especially when you are in a foreign environment. Fieldwork brings a number of pressures, including being stuck with people you might not like or in a place where the food is not to your liking, where you have to share a room, and so many things like this. I have learnt that I can put up with almost anything (scorpions and snakes in the excavation pit, cold bucket showers, sleeping on the floor, etc.) as long as it is for a limited time, and it is usually worth it, as there is nothing quite like being part of an excavation where you get to uncover the past – you never know what you are going to find.

## Working Conditions

Another undoubted benefit of academic-based archaeology is undoubtedly the generally pleasant working conditions, both in the office and in the field (see Figure 22). This is generally the case with academia as a whole, irrespective of the subject. Albeit with significant onsite variations, most academics, including academic archaeologists, have access to a similar range of different campus facilities; at best, these are among some of the finest working environments to be found in any job, but even at worst they will still usually be comparable to and frequently better than many other jobs. The most immediate of these benefits is access to an on-campus office that can range, much like inner-city apartments, from the sole-occupant and palatial to the multi-occupant and cramped. Similarly, most archaeology departments have at least some additional dedicated facilities by way of conservation or computing laboratories, laying-out space, photographic dark-rooms, and the like. Every university, by necessity, also always has a decent library to which staff have access; the common urban setting of many universities and closeness of campuses can also provide access to other external collections of books or materials. Other campus facilities can then come into greater or lesser play in the lifestyle of the academic – the food and shopping outlets, on one hand, the sports

Figure 22. The life of an academic archaeologist, part 1: Practical teaching plays an important part in university training and so in the life of an academic. Here, David Jeffreys of UCL's Institute of Archaeology teaches students object identification and recording techniques at the Petrie Museum of Egyptian Archaeology in London (copyright Petrie Museum/UCL Institute of Archaeology 2010, courtesy of Ian Carroll).

and leisure facilities, on the other; more academics than most might be willing to admit they forged their careers around allegiance to a particular sport or even a specific team.

It is in the field that the biggest difference between academic and other forms of archaeology becomes most apparent, however. It does not take any formal training to differentiate between a CRM and a research archaeological site no matter what the site's location, period, layout, or extent – nearly anywhere in the world, the CRM site will look little different from, and indeed may be a part of, a construction site, with major machinery, portable office facilities, and health and safety and other equipment present all about. A research excavation is unlikely to have much, if any, of these – site offices in particular, which on a CRM archaeology project will frequently be in portable buildings that may include light, heat, and washing facilities, can, on a research dig, be everything and anything from a tarp or tent,

146

caravan or trailer, outhouse or convenient farm building; the associated washing facilities might include access to running water and/or portable toilets, but may be very much less – down to and including a hole in the ground behind a large enough tree or rock. Similarly, CRM archaeologists, as discussed in Chapter 3, usually look almost identical to construction crews in the near-universal wearing of high-visibility jackets, hard hats, and safety boots. Research archaeologists are unlikely to wear any of these except, on occasion, safety boots if they are undertaking toe-threatening digging; the only clothing rule of plenty of research digs is 'whatever the weather demands'. Thus, a CRM archaeological project is likely to see serried ranks of near-identically dressed crews working at high speed, usually to someone else's paid-for deadline. On occasion, this can mean a crew mapping archaeology at one end of a site that is being ripped up or covered over at the other, a practice that tends to kill off a lot of site chit-chat and banter. In comparison, a research dig is likely to see a more varied array of clothing on a potentially more varied range of people working at, if not a slower speed than CRM archaeologists, then certainly a different pace – particularly so if the excavation includes an element of teaching, which most do these days; as a result, there will be rather more talking and joking than on a CRM archaeology site. Most of all, the CRM archaeology project will be at work in all but the worst of weather on all but the coldest of days; the research dig is unlikely to take place outside the main summer months. Finally, the CRM archaeology project may be difficult, if not impossible, to visit owing to site access restrictions driven by health and safety/insurance liability concerns; the research dig is likely to be open to the public at least some of the time on advertised open days, and may be willing to provide informal tours for all and any who turn up with an interest.

## Specialist Archaeological Staff

Alongside academics are arrayed a variety of both more and less specialized staff. This is not to suggest a lack of professionalism among these individuals; rather, it is a question of contractual obligations – many such specialist staff may be as qualified as, if not even more highly qualified than, the academics alongside whom they work; they may even teach classes and undertake research similar to their exclusively academic colleagues. The difference is that these individuals will usually have major commitments to undertake specific dedicated tasks, such as running and managing dedicated conservation laboratories or other technical facilities such as archaeologically focused computing research clusters; undertaking specific, highly skilled, and/or time-consuming related tasks such as environmental, petrological, or osteoarchaeological analyses; or managing and promoting collections of archaeological materials or data such as university museum or library collections. The skills required to manage such facilities, and the amount of time needed to be spent on such work, usually means that if such individuals do undertake teaching or research this will be in addition to their core employment, rather than central to it. The appeal of such work is that it allows individuals to focus more on their research or professional specialty than the average core academic, while still undertaking elements of outreach and enjoying the wider benefits of life within academia. The downside is that, as with specialists in any industry, these specialists run the risk of becoming trapped by their very own abilities, unable to get work in any other area if they become bored or disenchanted with their specialty.

A different common form of specialty is research-only staff. Usually on a contract lasting a set period of months or years, such individuals are usually hired to work on a dedicated research project in relation to an externally provided grant from a major funding organization. Frequently, such individuals will be a part of a larger team of researchers on a topic, and they will bring with them specific skills in a particular time period or archaeological specialty, complementing their team members' strengths. The pros and cons of such positions are similar to those of the specialists discussed earlier – it is very easy to get trapped in an endless cycle of such short-term contracts, a particular risk for younger staff members who have usually just completed their PhDs and are keen to work; by taking the contract or a series of such contracts, the constant demands of each particular project can make it extremely hard to build up the wider teaching and administrative experience needed to break the cycle and get a more permanent position among the core academic staff.

## Focus on: Andy Gardner (UK)

I am Andy Gardner, and I am a Senior Lecturer in the Archaeology of the Roman Empire at UCL's Institute of Archaeology in London. My office in the Institute is my normal working location, a 1950s building in central London. Having completed my degrees at the Institute and worked there for over fifteen years, I am very invested in the department. As one of the biggest academic archaeology departments in the world, and with a strong commercial presence via its commercial arm Archaeology South-East, the Institute strives to encompass archaeology, heritage, and conservation across the globe. My own role is typical for mid-career academic staff, juggling teaching, research, and administration. My teaching and research are closely entwined, connecting Roman archaeology and archaeological theory, and I have performed several pastoral roles over the years (see Figure 23).

I had a fascination with history in my teens and volunteered at my local museum, which made me realize that archaeology offered a very tangible way of engaging with the past. I had the chance to go on an excavation before university, joined the Young Archaeologists' Club, and then pursued my BA, MA, and PhD in fairly close succession, albeit with a year working for a commercial unit (and in a record shop) after my BA. At first, I did not know that I would end up being a Romanist, and I did not get into theory until my MA; at each stage of my career there have been new things to learn.

I worked as a commercial archaeologist in the mid-1990s, and subsequent to my PhD I had a number of academic/teaching jobs, before getting my current position in 2005. Both the commercial sphere, and the early stages of an academic career, can involve a series of short-term positions, but – like archaeology

Figure 23. The life of an academic archaeologist, part 2: Research-led academic fieldwork is usually undertaken under very different circumstances to CRM archaeology. Here, at tea break during the Priory Field excavation at Caerleon, south Wales, in mid 2010 the entire project is visible. The excavation and its equipment are in the foreground and the project's campsite and site offices (the caravans at extreme top right) are in the background (copyright Andrew Gardner/UCL Institute of Archaeology 2010).

itself – these help you develop a broad skills set and nurture lots of different strengths. In terms of my academic career path, I had several teaching roles before, and just after, I completed my PhD, working particularly in the adult education sector. That helped me get a couple of fixed-term teaching jobs in different universities. In turn, that experience helped me get the job I have now.

One of the things that unifies archaeologists is that very few jobs are the same all year round, whether it is switching between on-site work and writing up a project in the office, or – in my job – the difference between term-time and the 'vacation' periods. During the three terms of the academic year, life is quite hectic, between teaching and teaching preparation, tutorials and student consultations, and committee meetings. The two short vacations, at Christmas and Easter, are usually busy too, with marking, and sometimes conferences. The summer is the period where things really change for three months or so, and although there is still plenty to do, particularly working on publications, the rhythm is quite different. The best thing about my role is quite simply this rotation between different things, all of which I enjoy!

My top tip for pursuing a career in archaeology is that choosing to pursue a career in archaeology opens up a wide range of doors, but like anything worthwhile it takes a degree of patience, persistence, and dedication to get to where you want to be. It is important, at the beginning, to be open-minded about where your path might take you, and to retain a degree of flexibility, as any archaeological job will involve different activities, and need you to draw on different aptitudes. Archaeology is multidisciplinary, providing good training in lots of different skills, because it combines intellectual, practical, and social strands. The main thing is to be alert for opportunities, and do not be afraid to try new things.

A few years ago, myself and my colleague Charlotte Frearson set up a new initiative to promote archaeology as a degree subject: University Archaeology Day. With the support of University Archaeology UK, the Council for British Archaeology (CBA), and a range of other organizations and friends, this annual event is now well established as a collective enterprise involving almost all of the archaeology departments in the United Kingdom. More details can be found at: https://studyarchaeology.wixsite.com/uniarchaeologyday.

# Chapter 5

# State and Local
# Government Archaeology

## Introduction

Mention "local government" to most people and the mental picture conjured up is unlikely to be very archaeological. Local government means, at best, talk of municipal facilities such as public parks and recreational facilities; at worst, waste collection and petty politics. Many people remain oblivious to the existence and important role of archaeologists and related heritage professionals in the employ of local government. Local laws protect a vast number of archaeological as well as wider historic sites. Local taxes pay directly for a large amount of archaeology to be explored, understood, publicized, and – most important – protected. Local government archaeologists also represent an incredible pool of expert knowledge that it is easy to call upon, a more immediate and often less intimidating face of the archaeological community than commercial and academic archaeologists alike. And local government archaeologists are, almost without exception, some of the friendliest and most enthusiastic individuals that you will ever meet, always happy to share their knowledge of a neighbourhood's history and make introductions to other interested individuals.

Archaeologists are employed at the local government level because various national, regional, and local laws make this service statutory (e.g., legally mandated) or semi-statutory (strongly encouraged/recommended by central government). The principle has become enshrined in both common practice and legal statute that when development (such as the construction of houses, commercial buildings, utilities, and transportation networks) or the extraction of primary resources

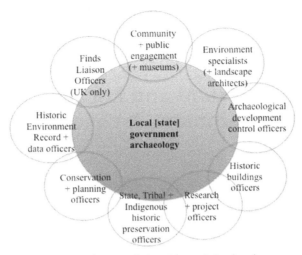

Figure 24. The structure and interrelationships of the local government archaeology sector.

(such as minerals and construction materials) take place, then the impact of such work upon the historic environment should be taken into consideration from the outset, alongside associated impact on the natural environment (i.e., flora and fauna). This process occurs no matter the wider circumstances – whether by a firm that undertakes development for profit or by a government, charity, or the like for communal good. The only variations come in relation to whether a project is on land owned or controlled by the government (or under obligation to the government by way of funding or licensing agreements) or on private property, and thus which national/federal and/or local/state/county laws and regulations apply (see Figure 24).

Archaeologists, alongside other specialists such as historic buildings experts, ecologists, and biologists, are thus employed to undertake this work in advance of development, usually bidding for such work on a job-by-job basis; this is the domain of CRM archaeologists. Undertaking what is sometimes referred to as *curatorial archaeology*, local government archaeologists also work at this level – advising on, monitoring, and, where necessary, enforcing the laws requiring this work in advance of development. Unlike the CRM archaeologists, this role must be more formalized – the archaeologists undertaking such work cannot be hired on a contractual, case-by-case basis through competitive bids; they must be part of the permanent establishment of local government. This, then, is broadly the place, and the status, of local government archaeologists: civil servants embedded within the complex web of national and regional planning systems, enforcing the law when necessary but there to advise all who might ask for their professional opinion, by dint of their salary coming from the government and thus, ultimately, the tax system (see Table 7).

TABLE 7. The pros and cons of working in local government archaeology

| Pros | Cons |
|---|---|
| Job security: often permanent, well paid in comparison to other archaeologists | Often very reactive, which can become demoralizing: many working commitments are based on compromise, in which the archaeology rarely comes out best in comparison with the other demands on a site. |
| Pensions and other benefits provided by government sector, such as sports and family facilities, are common; there is often private health care as well as discounted rates at specific shops and services. | |
| Can make a real impact on preservation and analysis of sites. | Can be dull, in both types of sites analysed and types of decisions made |
| Stability: usually based out of one office and doing day site visits in a small region. This makes it easier if you are in a relationship/family or have regular personal commitments that tie you to one location. | Limited opportunity to do any field archaeology and/or research |
| | Opportunities for travel outside your area can be few. |
| Prestige: you are part of local government and so other people (including family) see it as reputable. | You must put up with corporate, management-heavy structure common in local government. |
| You can make good contacts for future jobs, and it looks good on a CV. | The right opportunity can take a long time to appear; people often stay in the same job for many years. |
| Good career structure within the archaeological community and government sector itself (often regular pay progression based on performance is common in the first few years of such a job). | There are not many posts in this area. |
| There are usually good opportunities for internal and external training and professional development; this can include negotiating paid/unpaid leave for further study. | |

## Focus on: Pablo Garrido Gonzalez (Spain)

I am Pablo Garrido Gonzalez, and I am an archaeologist working for the Andalusian government in southern Spain. I am based in the central bureau of the Consejería de Cultura y Patrimonio Histórico in Seville, the capital of the

153

region, but my usual tasks are concerned with research rather than rescue archaeology, in any of the eight provinces of Andalusia. The regional government is the authorizing body for heritage and archaeological licenses; my work consists of managing and supervising archaeological interventions of any historic period or subject, mainly at the office, but also in the field when necessary.

I have clear memories of wanting to become an archaeologist from my earliest childhood. When I went to university, the only possible degree related to the subject was in history, and archaeology was only a postgraduate specialization, but I was able to participate in many excavations during my student years; the first one was the digging of a Roman necropolis in Huelva, my birth city. I finished my PhD on Roman archaeology in 2011, after spending several years in the United Kingdom and Italy, thanks to my long-term collaboration with the British School at Rome and Southampton University. I feel very lucky for the wonderful experience of those years and the privilege of working with archaeologists from countries such as the United Kingdom, Italy, France, the United States, Portugal, Germany, Greece, and Croatia, to name but a few.

Archaeology is the only professional work that I have ever undertaken in my life. I spent five years after my degree at Seville University teaching and researching. In 2010, I founded a consultancy firm with three colleagues, and I worked for nine years in both research and rescue archaeology. I have participated as the principal archaeologist in more than forty fieldwork interventions, and many others as a technical assistant or expert researcher in GIS. Between 2015 and 2018 I was elected a representative of professional archaeologists for Seville, so all this experience, in both public and private initiatives, allowed me to develop management and business skills. I dare say this mixture of field, business, and bureaucratic work led me to my current job.

I began my present job at the end of 2018. I must admit it has been a radical change in my life, because I was used to working six days per week, the morning in the field and the afternoon in the office, often for around twelve hours per day. My current job, on the contrary, has strictly scheduled tasks and working hours, which, on the one hand, means a great improvement in my quality of life, but, on the other hand, supposes a very different way of undertaking archaeology, which now it is 90 per cent office-based. However, my work is really exciting, because I am acquainted with every research project in Andalusia, and it is virtually impossible to get bored.

My top tip for pursuing a career in archaeology is never to lose your curiosity. Being curious is from my view the main incentive for being an archaeologist. If you never lose your curiosity, then you will do anything to reach your objectives, and you will be in a permanent state of learning, one of most important things if you are to be an excellent researcher. With this attitude you will improve and diversify your skills, and even though specialization is necessary, it is nonetheless true that professional archaeology requires a minimum ability in a broad range of domains, techniques, and historic background. So long as you never cease to sincerely ask yourself what it is beneath the soil, I believe that you will have the main requirement to be an excellent archaeologist and feel happy about that.

There is a real need to improve the working conditions of professional archaeologists in Andalusia. In Spain there are seventeen autonomous regions, each one with its own heritage laws. This means there exist very different conditions depending on the Spanish region where you intend to develop your career or carry out your excavation or survey. Consequently, professional associations are leading the fight for improving our working conditions, among which I would like to mention the Sección de Arqueología del Colegio Profesional de Sevilla y Huelva, to which I belong: www.cdlsevillayhuelva.org/arqueologia/.

## A Day in the Life

At heart, the role of the local government archaeologist is reactive and, honestly, sometimes combative. It does not suit everyone, particularly people such as archaeologists who tend temperamentally to be conciliatory and disliking of confrontation (Table 7). Boil all the different jobs in local government archaeology down to their essence, and the role comes down to making people obey heritage laws and established conventions. In this, the archaeologists involved hope (but do not expect, and will take the time to check) that a few people will be scrupulously honest and follow the letter of the law (the golden 10 per cent of the population), expect that the majority of people will be reasonably honest and not try to take too much advantage of any situation (a good 80 per cent of the population), and with a heavy sigh will deal with the antisocial minority who have to be variously cajoled and outright threatened to do the bare minimum that the law requires of them (the nasty last 10 per cent of the population equation). Along the way, the local government archaeologists will try to find the time to add in all the 'extras' that make their jobs, and the archaeology they so deeply care about, more interesting to both themselves and their ultimate masters, the local taxpayers. To ensure that they can best provide timely, meaningful, and up-to-date advice, these archaeologists will be joined by a series of related professionals who maintain historic records, undertake specialist roles, and do other related activities.

A day in the life of a local government archaeologist, then, varies in relation to a few dependent issues:

- What precise role within local government they fulfil.
- What time of year it is.
- What their local government area/region/authority is like.

The last issue in particular will have a major impact on what and when work is done, and it is worth addressing first. For example, the author used to work partly for the local government of the English county of Surrey, in southeast England. Surrey is geographically small (covering only about 600 square miles in total), but its north-eastern corner abuts the edge of London, meaning that it is a very popular place to build homes and the facilities and infrastructure that come along with a large population crammed into a small space – shops, roads, schools, hospitals, and so forth. The result is that the closer to the edge of London that you go in Surrey, the busier the archaeological workload gets, and vice versa: the farther you go away from London the slower the workload, albeit with a few exceptions – various large towns outside of this London zone that create a bubble of development. This also means that we know more about the archaeology of the part of the county closest to London than most other parts of Surrey. Consequently, it can often be harder, not easier, to understand archaeological sites that are discovered in the undeveloped areas, as there are fewer known sites with which to compare new sites. This is the opposite of what most people expect. This situation is not helped by a series of other localized environmental factors. For example, the county has complex geology, which means that types of remote sensing commonly used in archaeology often simply do not work on many sites in Surrey. The county also has heathlands in its north-western corner that have a sandy, acidic soil that tends to destroy archaeological remains and that have been used by the military for training since the nineteenth century. This combined mix of geology and historic usage has destroyed many archaeological sites, protected others, and rendered still others unexplorable, their inaccessibility owing, for example, to military use having led to their settlement by rare flora and fauna now protected by various laws that trump archaeological concerns. The county also has lots of woodland in its south-eastern corner (an ancient woodland area known as the Weald that stretches across southeast England) that has never been heavily settled (it has dense clay soils unsuitable for farming), as well as many thousands of historic houses and gardens across the county. The county also has relatively limited farming overall, as its proximity to London means there is more money to be made from development than from farming.

On the other hand, the county does not have a coastline, so the archaeological teams that used to be led by the author did not have to deal with all the marine archaeology that lies up to twelve miles offshore in the territorial sea, as is the case in all coastal counties of the United Kingdom. The county also has a very temperate climate, which means that archaeologists usually can work outdoors all year round except in the depths of winter. The county also has very little tourism, meaning negatively that there is only a very small income to be derived from historic visitor attractions and the like; on the positive side, there is much less pressure to feed this tourist industry – the local government archaeologists of Surrey can focus far more on doing a good job serving the residents of the county rather than its transitory guests.

Compare Surrey, then, with another English county, that of Devon in South West England. Devon is geographically much larger than Surrey – covering more than 2,500 square miles in total. It has not one, but two coastlines (one each in the north and south of the county, as it is part of the peninsula forming South West England), which means that in comparison with Surrey, Devon has a far larger and more complex physical landscape to manage in terms of heritage, including responsibility for maritime archaeological sites off its coastline. Furthermore, its geology is totally different from that of Surrey, with the granite landscape of Dartmoor (rich in archaeological sites and a major tourist location in terms of both the natural and historic environment) dominating the central interior of the county and contrasting with the softer sandstone and limestone of the southern coast. Devon also has a large tourist industry, based in part on the county's rich heritage as well as the coastline (sections of which are part of a larger UNESCO World Heritage site) that is essential to its economic well-being, alongside a busy farming as well as fishing community. On the other hand, Devon has much less urban development than Surrey, with only one major town (there are two major urban centres within it – Plymouth and Torbay – but these are formally separate and distinct parts, each with its own local government). In sum: both Devon and Surrey are English counties following the same national rules and principles of heritage management, but they, and thus their archaeologists' priorities, vary enormously – Surrey's local government archaeologists' priorities are driven primarily by the demands of urban and suburban development; Devon's rather by tourism and farming.

Next, compare these two English counties with some international equivalents. All employ local government archaeologists, but the scope and remit of these archaeologists is defined very differently, by dint of both their laws and their geography. An eye-opening foreign comparison to the county of Devon is the US state of North Carolina, covering more than 53,000 square miles compared with Devon's 2,500 square miles, twenty times the total area of Devon. Despite this disparity in size, comparisons can be made in terms of Devon and North Carolina's varied geography, important protected historic rural areas, long coastlines, and dependence on tourism and other service industries for a significant proportion of their total income. An even more dramatic international comparison with Surrey is then the Australian state of Victoria, covering more than 91,000 square miles in total, more than 150 times the total area of Surrey. Again, comparisons can be made between Surrey and Victoria, not least in that both see their economies – and thus their archaeological work – driven by a major urban centre: in Surrey, London (population about 9.5 million) and in Victoria, Melbourne (population around 5 million). These are all examples of local government, but the landscape, work pressures and priorities, and socioeconomic drivers and political structures affect the work of the archaeologists employed by these governments, which varies enormously. And such comparisons can be made around the world, since most countries have local and/or national archaeological regulations of this type. The author has met local government archaeologists from dozens of different nations, from those working in densely settled urban locations like Mexico City or Hong Kong to those working far out in some of the most sparsely populated rural areas of China or Brazil. Without exception, we quickly found things in common about our jobs once we began to talk.

It can be understood from these comparisons that ostensibly "local" government deals with big (in some cases internationally driven) issues influenced by multiple, constantly competing pressures. To return to the other impacts on a day in the life outlined earlier: while the exact job the archaeologist holds is discussed in detail later, the second of these, regarding the time of year, can be dealt with quickly here. Summertime is busy, in terms of development and thus archaeology. Autumn and spring are, respectively, the wind-down and build-up periods to the summer rush (complicated in the United Kingdom at least by the fact that the British tax year runs from April, meaning that there is always a rush of development and local government spending alike in late February/early March). Winter tends to be quieter – bad weather slows development and access to archaeological sites alike, and the seasonal holidays create a natural gap.

## Career Structure: Development Control Officers

As outlined earlier, what all the different jobs in local government archaeology come down to is, ultimately, making people obey heritage laws and established conventions. It is the task of what are commonly known as development control officers to lead and oversee this process of legal compliance within the planning systems of different locations. The details of what, when, where, and how such officers undertake their work are outlined later in this chapter. The primary laws that make this requirement so – the why of development control – are the following:

- *Australia*: the Environment Protection and Biodiversity Conservation Act (1999, most recently amended in 2013) and the Australian Heritage Council Act (2003) (see Smith and Burke 2007: 126–30 and 130–61).
- *United Kingdom*: the Ancient Monuments and Archaeological Areas Act (1979) and the Town and Country Planning Act (1990), the National Planning Policy Framework (2019) in England and Wales, Scottish Planning Policy (2014) in Scotland, and Planning Policy Statement 6 (PPS6): Planning, Archaeology, and the Built Heritage (1999) in Northern Ireland (see Aitchison 2020; Barber et al. 2008; Hunter and Ralston 2006).
- *United States*: the National Historic Preservation Act (NHPA) (1966, most recently amended in 2016; see Hinds 2017), the National Environmental Policy Act (1969), the Archaeological Resources and Historic Preservation Act (1974), and the Archaeological Resources Protection Act (1979, most recently amended in 1988) (see King 2009, 2012, 2016a, 2016b).

As explained later in this chapter, there are also many Australian and US state laws (too numerous and varied to list here) that protect the historic environment of those locations, and which follow the basic principles of these nations' federal laws. And as King (2012: 37) makes clear, for the United States in particular:

> The law is seldom so straightforward. There are lots of national, State and Provincial, Indian Tribal, and local laws and regulations requiring that some kind of attention be

paid to archaeological sites, but there's no universally applicable legal requirement that they be excavated before something destroys them. The federal laws in the US apply only to projects in which there's some kind of federal agency involvement – federal funds, for example, or a federal license, or the use of federal land. State and local laws vary widely in their requirements; some apply pretty specific requirements to a wide range of state and locally regulated or funded projects, while others don't. Many privately funded projects on private land are subject to no archaeological requirements at all. In other countries ... archaeological sites or at least the stuff they contain are regarded in law as government property, by virtue of being parts of the national patrimony, but that doesn't mean that the government systematically imposes requirements on property owners and developers.

Many other nations of the world also have similar federal-level laws: in Canada, for example, the Canadian Environmental Assessment (2003) has stipulations requiring that any impact on archaeological resources be assessed or evaluated, in a manner similar to these British, American, and Australian laws. However, state laws and regulations (as well as Tribal and other local laws) that protect heritage vary widely from nation to nation and within those from state to state. For example, in Canada, most heritage protection and preservation legislation is enacted by the ten different Provincial and three different Territorial governments, each of which has its own legislation and policies to protect and preserve cultural heritage, including that of Canada's Indigenous Communities (often referred to as First Nations) (see examples in Ferris 2003). A useful guide is provided online by Parks Canada.[1] To pick two more examples, in India, the overriding heritage legislation is that enacted and enforced at the national level, with the Ancient Monuments and Archaeological Sites and Remains Act of 1958 (most recently amended in 2012) protecting sites and monuments of national importance and regulating archaeological excavations. This Act also regulates the functions of the Archaeological Survey of India – the government agency responsible for archaeological research and the conservation and preservation of cultural monuments in the country. China has a broadly similar, nationally led approach to India, with its Law on the Protection of Cultural Relics first enacted in 1982 (most recently updated in 2002; see Underhill 2013; see also Yingying Jing (2019) on steps taken in China at the national level to protect its underwater cultural heritage). Other nations around the world function in a very different manner, and there is not the space available in this book to examine every example. An excellent insight into many (but not all) different nations' heritage laws, policies, and approaches can be gained from examining the documents held by the UNESCO on those nations that have ratified the 1972 World Heritage Convention;[2] see also Kalman (2014) for a partial global overview.

Australia, Canada, the United States, and many other nations also have laws protecting Native, Indigenous and First People's cultural sites, landscapes, and

---

[1] See www.pc.gc.ca/en/docs/pc/poli/grc-crm.

[2] See http://whc.unesco.org/en/statesparties/ and then search by nation: each has a tab entitled 'laws' that provides details of specific nation's heritage laws.

artefacts, including in some circumstances their intangible cultural heritage, including rights of control of land and cultural resources, and more broadly of self-governance.[3] Such laws vary widely from state to state, and if in doubt, readers should consult local state and/or Indigenous community authorities for guidance. To gain some understanding of these, see Smith and Burke (2007) for Australia, Denhez (2010) for Canada, and King (2012) for the United States. In terms of archaeology and cultural heritage, there are also particular federally mandated laws that apply across some nations irrespective of location, such as the Aboriginal and Torres Strait Islander Heritage Protection Act (1984, most recently amended in 2006) in Australia (see Stolte 2020) and the Native American Graves Protection and Repatriation Act (1990) in the United States (see Adams 2001; Chari and Lavallee 2013). There are also many different other national/federal and state/local heritage laws and ordinances regarding particular types of historic sites. For example, many countries have legislation specific to maritime archaeology – primarily submerged archaeological sites. Examples of these include the UK Protection of Wrecks Act (1973), Protection of Military Remains Act (1984), and Merchant Shipping Act (1995); the US Abandoned Shipwreck Act (1987) and Sunken Military Craft Act (2005); and the Australian federal Historic Shipwrecks Act (1976).

Archaeological development control also frequently requires an understanding of related non-heritage-specific legislation. Many local as well as national government officials have responsibility for protecting and promoting biodiversity and ecology – often under more stringent laws than those protecting heritage. For example, in England alone, there is Section 40 of the Natural Environment and Rural Communities Act (2006) and the environmental and biodiversity requirements of the National Planning Policy Framework (2019). Local authorities have a duty to protect, manage, and enhance Sites of Special Scientific Interest (SSSIs) – a formal natural environment conservation designation in the United Kingdom that describes an area of special interest to science due to the presence of rare species of flora or fauna. Many nations around the world have similar area-specific nature designations, too many and too complicated to list and explain here. Working closely with natural environment colleagues is a growing component of many local government archaeological officers' roles, as more and more mutual interests are identified – not least in the preparation for and management and mitigation of

---

[3] Intangible Cultural Heritage is defined here using the terminology developed and used by UNESCO: 'traditions or living expressions inherited from our ancestors and passed on to our descendants, such as oral traditions, performing arts, social practices, rituals, festive events, knowledge and practices concerning nature and the universe or the knowledge and skills to produce traditional crafts. While fragile, intangible cultural heritage is an important factor in maintaining cultural diversity in the face of growing globalization. An understanding of the intangible cultural heritage of different communities helps with intercultural dialogue and encourages mutual respect for other ways of life. The importance of intangible cultural heritage is not the cultural manifestation itself but rather the wealth of knowledge and skills that is transmitted through it from one generation to the next. The social and economic value of this transmission of knowledge is relevant for minority groups and for mainstream social groups within a State, and is as important for developing States as for developed ones.' See https://ich.unesco.org/en/what-is-intangible-heritage-00003 for more information.

climate change on the landscape, including on historic landscapes, woodlands, parks, gardens, and coastlines. This includes working with colleagues in local and national government as well as in the voluntary/amenity sector – such as the Campaign to Protect Rural England (CPRE), Joint Nature Conservation Committee (JNCC), and Wildlife Trusts.

In addition to the formal planning review process under policies and laws such as those outlined above, county/state archaeologists are also usually responsible for the following:

- Coordinating archaeological research undertaken within their area of remit.
- Advising and assisting the various local and national agencies on cultural resource matters.
- Maintaining a preservation plan for their area of remit.
- Engaging in their region's public archaeology endeavours.
- Approving the licensing of professional archaeologists to undertake research on state land where applicable.

The primary role, and most of the daily life, of such officers is focused on providing reactive advice to, and the management of, archaeological consultations (see Figures 25 and 26). A site is being developed and the developers have hired an archaeological consultant and/or a CRM archaeology firm to lead them through the heritage-related stages of the planning/development process as laid out in various local and national heritage laws and ordinances. The development control officers receive a consultation pack – consisting of basic information such as the developers', consultants', and/or the CRM archaeology firm's details; the site's grid reference, extent, and current usage; and the project's proposed objectives and/or end products. Maps, plans, and other diagrams will also be included. Together, this package of information is used by the officers to advise on what work regarding the historic environment is required on the site. This may be no work at all, or it may entail a variety of processes on a sliding scale from a watching brief during development (observing construction work and seeing whether archaeological features appear, and, if so, intervening to record or preserve these remains), up to the total excavation of some or all of the site, and all the related post-excavation and publication commitments that follow from any work. The decision as to what scale of archaeological work to require is made by the development control officers in liaison with other professional colleagues (historic buildings officers, natural environment planning officers such as government ecologists, and the like). This decision-making process is informed by national and local planning policy and guidelines, meaning that the officers cannot, for example, require all and any projects in their area to undertake total area excavation, and attempting to ensure that approximately the same requirements are enforced nationally on all different sites. Most important, these decisions are guided by existing local heritage records – what are known in the United Kingdom as Historic Environment Records (HERs), a detailed record of all known heritage features (archaeological sites and monuments, historic buildings, parks, gardens, landscapes, wrecks, and so on) in the

Figure 25. Working in local government, part 1: Site visits play a major role in the work of local government archaeologists, in order to provide advice and check on standards and progress. Here, Tony Howe, one of the county archaeological officers of Surrey in South East England, undertakes a monitoring visit to a partially excavated Saxon burial at Fetcham, Surrey, in August 2010 (copyright Tony Howe 2010).

area, as well as details of the hypothesized archaeological potential of other areas on the basis of this existing knowledge (what are usually known in the United Kingdom as "areas of (high) archaeological potential" or the like). HERs are discussed in more detail later. Similar types of records are maintained in the United States and Australia by different offices of state archaeology (usually part of larger state historic preservation offices or similar entities).

The options open to archaeological officers in terms of archaeological consultations include requiring some or all of the entire remit of possible types of investigation outlined elsewhere in this book, from predetermination/early discussions and environmental impact assessments, by way of desk-based assessments, field-walking, field survey, and watching briefs to partial or full excavations, including, where required, specific types of work such as historic building surveys, human burials, remains assessments and excavations, and environmental sampling, as well as allied post-excavation work, mitigation and preservation of remains in situ, community archaeology, outreach, publication, and archiving. A management equation is achieved in this decision-making process, weighing the nature of the development proposed, its extent and physical impact on the landscape, other

Figure 26. Working in local government, part 2: Unexpected archaeological discoveries regularly occur, and local government archaeologists are at hand to advise under such circumstances. Here, a Roman tile kiln is under excavation in a residential garden near Reigate in Surrey. The structure was located less than 20 centimetres from the surface, yet missed detection during a prior evaluation carried out to inform a planning decision to redevelop the property (copyright Tony Howe 2010).

developments in the area that are undergoing or have undergone archaeological exploration, and the nature of the known archaeological record – in particular, its type, extent, and relative rarity – surrounding the proposed development. This process is inevitably imprecise because, despite popular perception otherwise, we still know shockingly little about the surviving archaeology of many areas, even those subject to massive and constant development. Consequently, although an estimate can be made of the likely archaeological *potential* of a site and thus a development's potential impact on the archaeology, surprise discoveries are still made regularly. For example, in 2001 an existing quarry site at North Park Farm, Bletchingley, in east Surrey, planned an extension to the quarry that was subject to a pre-development archaeological exploration. A range of prehistoric archaeological materials was found, as expected, but within these were a series of unexpected Mesolithic pits associated with buried soil (intact remnant landscape) containing only material of Mesolithic date within a topographic hollow, occupying an area of almost one hectare in extent. Here, in situ evidence was discovered for flint working at several of the sampled locations, alongside evidence of fires or cooking activities, showing that repeated visits were made to the area from around 8000 BCE to around 4500 BCE. This was a most unusual discovery, one of global significance[4].

Archaeological development control officers' work is not restricted to or completed by the provision of pre-application advice; they remain involved throughout the process, in the United Kingdom at least until the conditions they place with respect to work on the historic portions of the site have been completed (the technical term is "discharged") to their satisfaction. Site visits to monitor the type and quality of archaeological work and the precise nature of the features under exploration are common; so too are discussions by phone and email with developers about the nature and extent of the work required, the length of time, and thus ultimately the cost of the project. Some of these discussions are good-natured and mutually respectful and useful; a small number will be confrontational, as the development control officer argues for one thing and the consultant or CRM archaeologist for another.

Even when actual fieldwork, whatever this may comprise, is complete, the work of the officer is not over. Monitoring includes at least reviewing a final project report that must be submitted as part of the Historic Environment Record (HER) or equivalent, a report (commonly known as "grey literature") that must be of a sufficient standard and detail before the officer discharges the archaeological condition and that will have to show evidence of detailed reporting of both the site's exploration and any post-excavation work required on the site or in relation to it. Such officers will also advise on the final deposition of the archives and any excavated materials of the site in an appropriate, publicly accessible location, and upon any formal publication of data from it. Such officers may also write independent reports on the site for internal government as well as public consultation. In situations of legal dispute over the activities undertaken on a site, they may even be required to make a formal written or oral report to a planning inquiry or even, in extreme cases, in court.

Finally, unexpected discoveries of both archaeological and non-archaeological materials may also require officers' attention and even site visits. For instance, although not a terribly common occurrence, most officers who have been in their positions for any length of time will have had to advise the police at some point on the discovery of human (real or purported – many turn out to be animals) remains that may or may not be ancient/modern and so constitute either an archaeological site or a crime scene.

As can be imagined, it is necessary for such officers to possess a comprehensive understanding of local, national, and international planning law in relation to heritage, and a similarly high level of archaeological knowledge. Although this primary focus on planning development control is the main and most formal component of the development control officers' job, they may also undertake a host of other roles, depending on their workload, temperament, interest, and

---

[4] See https://archaeologydataservice.ac.uk/archives/view/northpark_he_2016/.

background. Some or all of this may be within their formal job remit, dependent on their seniority within local government and the structure of that local government authority. In the United Kingdom, at least, most of the senior archaeological officers (often referred to as county archaeologists – broadly equivalent to US state archaeologists) will, although sufficiently skilled to undertake development control work (and possibly having started off their careers as development control officers), handle some or all of this other, non-statutory work – which may take up all, or at least the majority, of their time. Such senior officers also usually have management responsibilities within local government, if only the management of their own team, representation on internal budgetary and planning meetings, and so on. These other roles include advising their government employer internally, and many different organizations as well as the media externally, on the archaeology of their area or specialty. Such work will usually be non-statutory – that is, accepted as important but not formally required under law.

All such officers, irrespective of their seniority, also need to keep up to date on the latest advances in archaeological method and theory, and new sites and discoveries of relevance to their work, to be able to provide the most up-to-date advice. In the United Kingdom, at least, they are also increasingly on the receiving end of more and more detailed legal and management advice from central government, both archaeological and non-archaeological, which requires detailed reading and then reporting on it to their managers, and are asked to advise central government on the content of such documents. The European Union also has various legal as well as management policies, conventions, and other statutory and non-statutory management instruments that some European nations have committed to enforce. Consultation and collaboration with a host of other colleagues and contacts is also very important – in some cases mandatory, as well as time-consuming – and may be with the following:

- Colleagues in other sections of their same local government: natural environment professionals such as ecologists, as well as planning officers and transport, minerals, waste, and other infrastructure colleagues.
- Officials in other sectors of local government: for example, in the United Kingdom, many county councils also have sub-county-level administration in the form of district and borough councils, and some towns, cities, and parishes have their own administrations (similarly also in the United States and Australia).
- Heritage colleagues from other areas/regions: for example, in the United Kingdom there is an organization called the Association of Local Government Archaeological Officers (ALGAO), which has regional, national (England, Wales, Scotland), and transnational (UK-wide) as well as thematic (e.g., marine or countryside) committees that meet regularly; the US equivalent is the National Association of State Archaeologists (NASA). Also included in this can be considered the CRM 'cousin' of ALGAO and NASA, the UK Federation of Archaeological Managers and Employers (FAME), nationally and regionally representing the CRM archaeology lobby (the US equivalent of FAME is the American Cultural Resources Association [ACRA]), and, alongside this,

165

organizations like the aforementioned Register of Professional Archaeologists (RPA) in the United States, Australian Association of Consulting Archaeologists (ACCAI) in Australia, and the Chartered Institute for Archaeologists (CIFA) in the UK – professional organizations that require membership on the basis of demonstrable experience and that enforce codes of conduct and ethical standards.

- Particular sectors of centralized government, most of which, in the United Kingdom at least, have both central and regional offices, and that include heritage-focused organizations such as English Heritage, as well as non-heritage but landscape- or resource-focused organizations such as the UK's Department for the Environment, Food and Rural Affairs (DEFRA), and specialized sectors of the government such as the National Park Service (NPS) and National Oceanographic and Atmospheric Administration (NOAA) in the United States and the various decentralized national parks of the United Kingdom (most of which, in fact, have their own dedicated heritage management teams). Included within this can also be all the different branches of the military, which remains a significant landowner in most nations of the world.

- Core service/utility and infrastructure organizations such as oil, gas, water, and electricity suppliers; telecommunications companies; road, rail, and airport authorities; strategic resource companies such as the aggregates industry; and representatives at the local and national level of farmers of every type and size.

- Other major heritage stakeholders such as national and local amenity societies (in the United Kingdom the National Trust (NT), a conservation charity and major landowner, in particular), local heritage societies, groups, museums, archives, and visitor attractions, and in the United Kingdom also the National Lottery Heritage Fund (NLHF), the management organization for heritage-related funding derived from the national lottery scheme.

- Local and national religious organizations, many of which own or care for historic sites, and not just Christian organizations looking after churches and cathedrals. Surrey, for example, is home to the oldest purpose-built mosque in the United Kingdom, an extremely important building that is at the heart of a thriving Islamic community as well as being a highly protected historic site by virtue of its age and cultural significance. Surrey also has a series of large historic cemeteries that are not associated with a single religious community and thus are managed communally.

Finally, such officers may also undertake, where time allows, archaeological research into their personal area or specialty, either primary fieldwork surveying or excavating sites or secondary data analysis, comparison, and theorizing.

## Career Structure: Historic Environment Records and Their Officers

The work of development control officers is only as good as the information to which they have access – from developers, on one hand, and from their own records, on the other. If a developer fails to fully advise the development control officers, whether accidentally or deliberately, of the nature or extent of the proposed development or the archaeological fieldwork related to it, then the advice the officers give will suffer for this; the result will be the same if the officers do not have access to the best possible data and sources that local government itself holds. These data and sources are known, in the United Kingdom at least, as Historic Environment Records (HERs). Similar types of records are maintained in the United States and Australia by different state and territory offices of state archaeology, usually part of larger state historic preservation offices or similar entities.

HERs are frequently misunderstood – in both their form and their use. This is because all HERs in existence vary in shape, form, and content, and so too do their uses. Their many different users worsen this misunderstanding. HERs began life in the United Kingdom as what were then known as Sites and Monuments Records (SMRs) in the 1960s and 1970s when local government (and, in some cases, local amenity organizations) first began to employ officers to try to regulate developer-led changes to regional heritage. Good management requires the understanding of what has gone before, in this case, the extent of the heritage resource, especially the location, date, format, and extent of sites and monuments, mainly archaeological sites. At first these were handwritten or typed lists and catalogues of appropriate data with associated paper maps (some simply marked up by hand) against which officers could check when providing advice. Various forms of indexing, card-record systems, and the like were used to manage more and more data, and after desktop computers came into widespread use in government in the late 1980s, SMRs were increasingly computerized. As computer technology, especially data processing and storage capacity, advanced, so too did these records (SMRs were early adopters of database, spreadsheet, and other similar systems, and of forms of computer-based mapping, the origins of today's GIS). Consequently, by the mid to late 1990s, SMRs had developed into complex electronic datasets comprising thousands of cross-referenced records. This was one of the reasons that SMRs began to be renamed in the early 2000s as HERs, to indicate their broader contents of historic data of all sorts, not just purely archaeological information. However, different types and standards of data, data acquisition, storage, and management were used by different organizations (even within different branches of government), and this situation has only worsened over the past decade. Although attempts have been made to nationally standardize HERs, these have not been comprehensive.

HERs, alas, remain an ambiguous part of government – essential for the smooth running of the planning system but not a statutory requirement for local government to maintain. The varied contents of HERs also often lead to confusion as to their extent; this is not helped by the varied roles that an HER serves. Although originally designed for, and still primarily used by, development control officers, CRM archaeologists and consultants also use HERs; so, too, do a variety of non-development-focused users, in particular, members of local heritage societies undertaking research in their area, and more unusually university-based academics or students undertaking research. HERs are best likened to a plant – organic, constantly growing, different to look at from different perspectives. They are not purely planning or development-related tools (no matter what some development control officers may imply), nor are these in any sense archives or libraries (HERs are far too current, too constantly evolving, for such a term to apply, and they do not hold original documents, but rather collate copies of useful records held elsewhere).

When first developed, SMR/HERs were generally managed and maintained by the development control officers who were their primary users; sometimes these were, in fact, managed by local archaeological organizations, many of which were the early employers of county archaeologists, who were then gradually absorbed into the formal structure of local government. As they grew ever larger and more complex, some local authorities began to employ individuals to work specifically on them, usually initially on a part-time basis. This situation has now developed into many dozens of full-time, permanent HER officers whose main responsibility is the management of these HERs, in all their forms. Such employment comprises many different tasks:

- Management, maintenance, and development of the HER, both its physical and electronic components, requiring a sound and diverse expertise in hard and soft data management.
- Assisting and working alongside development control officers in the provision of the best, most pertinent, and timely planning advice.
- Advising users of the HER on its use and undertaking paid research into its contents on behalf of consultants, CRM archaeologists, and any clients who would prefer not to visit and consult the HER in person.
- Liaising with the varied series of stakeholders identified earlier in relation to development control officers and undertaking the same types of continuing professional development in keeping up to date in advances in archaeological method and theory, new sites, and discoveries.
- Undertaking outreach, explaining the contents and uses of the HER to students, and recruiting volunteers willing to work on data input and refining.

As can be imagined, HER officers need a broad range of skills. On one hand, their job is deeply introspective, quiet, controlled, and desk-based – constantly keeping on top of ever more data in different formats and understanding how to best manage these data. On the other hand, their job can be incredibly public, requiring both enthusiasm and a calm professionalism when dealing with the many different types of individuals or organizations that wish to access the HER. Such officers also require as comprehensive an understanding of local, national, and international planning law in relation to heritage as their development control colleagues, as well as a similarly high level of archaeological knowledge. HER officers need to be optimistic pragmatists – turning their hand to many different tasks, happy to spend one day assisting a commercial client, the next day quietly refining data on their own, the third day working with a lively band of local volunteers to promote the HER as a resource. This is in some contrast to the more single-minded, as well as combative, average week of the development control officers with whom they work so closely – many HER officers would readily agree that they cannot imagine leading the life of a development control officer, and vice versa.

## Focus on: Sofie Vanhoutte (Belgium)

I am Sofie Vanhoutte, and I am an archaeological researcher at the Flanders Heritage Agency. This agency of the Flemish government is responsible for upholding laws and policies regarding inventories, studies, and the protection of historic buildings, landscapes, archaeological sites, and maritime heritage in the country. I am the responsible for coordinating research into chance archaeological discoveries made in West Flanders, of find locations brought to light during developments for which archaeological (commercial) fieldwork was not mandatory. The sites can be of all periods, but are mainly Roman, medieval, or post-medieval. As can be expected in West Flanders, an important share of these discoveries involves World War I sites and finds, amongst which are the remains of many casualties of the war. Besides my job at the Flanders Heritage Agency, I am also employed 20 per cent of my time as a teaching assistant in historical archaeology at Ghent University, a job that gives me a lot of satisfaction.

As a teenager, I was lucky that my parents took me on a cultural trip every year: to Greece, Egypt, Italy, and so on. I was very interested in all this history, and I was especially intrigued by the archaeological sites that we visited. A picture of me sitting on a statue on the Acropolis in Athens, reading out of the guidebook, says it all. As a seventeen-year-old, I joined an archaeology summer camp. My parents hoped it would change my mind, but after those two weeks, it was obvious for me: this is what I wanted to do for the rest of my life. I went to study archaeology at the KU Leuven, and I got my MA in 1998. As a job in archaeology at the time was something for the lucky few, I broadened my focus to the museum and exhibition sector through an extra MA in cultural studies. After my study, while I was looking for a job, I volunteered at excavations and in post-excavation works at the Flemish Heritage Institute. To cut a long story short, after ten months of volunteer work in 2000, the Institute gave me work on an excavation; it was the start of my career at what became the Flanders Heritage Agency.

As a young archaeologist, twenty-five years old and still rather a greenhorn, but fortunate to be in the right place at the right time, in 2001 I was asked to conduct the excavations of the south-west corner of the Oudenburg Roman fort, one of the most important mid to late Roman sites in Flanders. Working at such a well-known site, the pressure was high. Motivated by a passion for Roman archaeology and the promotion of our cultural heritage, I was determined to methodically retrieve as much information as possible on the occupation history of the fort before this archive was irrevocably destroyed. At the time, there was no digitization in the archaeological process; the excavation lasted until 2005. The post-excavation processing of the huge quantity of data and finds confirmed the high scientific potential of the site, which I strived to explore to the maximum on my own initiative. Working on other excavations – under my own direction or in collaboration – inside and outside the fort area and in the adjacent coastal plain enabled me to see the broader picture. The research of Roman Oudenburg became my life's work. As the agency gradually altered its course from research to heritage management, and I increasingly needed to focus on other tasks, I decided – encouraged by several experts – to start a PhD on the Oudenburg fort and its broader coastal military context, which I finalized in 2018. I believe it is my passion for archaeology in combination with my hard work that brought me the opportunities that I got and into the position that I have now.

As the person responsible for research into chance discoveries, I never know for sure what my week will look like or how it will evolve. At any moment, a notification of a new chance discovery can come in that I must rush to work at, as the time given to react to such finds is very restricted; regularly it is in an active building site where I must stop the construction earthworks, not always an easy message to bring to a developer or contractor. But it is very motivating when it leads to an excavation of an important site; for example, recently, part of a Roman harbour site and a late medieval leprosy site were rescued and excavated in this manner. And certainly, when a World War I soldier can be recovered and given a known grave, it is very emotional. The pressure is often high, negotiations are sometimes tough, and my job involves a lot of arranging, but I like the diversity (from excavating myself and following up outsourced excavations to organizing the whole trajectory, studying finds, doing research, and writing up reports). The job is too much for one person alone, but some excellent collaborations with local or regional services and the support of colleagues, and above all the knowledge that I can make a difference, albeit small, motivate me enormously.

My top tip for pursuing a career in archaeology is to realize that your own knowledge will always be only fragmentary, and so to collaborate! It is not an average job; be proud to be able to contribute to the knowledge of the past and be aware the whole time that archaeology is first of all a science, and not a routine job. Never stop learning and stay critical. Keep asking questions, keep questioning yourself. I believe strongly that in collaboration we can achieve so much more.

## Career Structure: Specialists

Several other heritage-related roles are nowadays fulfilled in local government, working alongside development control and historic environment record officers. All these career paths are applicable to individuals with a background in archaeology, although many require additional and/or alternative skills.

## *Specialists: Historic Buildings Officers*

Undoubtedly the most influential of these positions in the United Kingdom at least is that of historic buildings officers. Such individuals are effectively development control officers with similar responsibilities and broadly the same priorities and lifestyle as described earlier; the difference is that, first, historic buildings officers have expertise in historic buildings rather than in archaeological sites and monuments, and, second, that because under British law the protection of historic buildings is far more extensive (as well as draconian) compared with archaeological remains, historic buildings officers have considerably more 'on the ground' power and influence than their archaeological colleagues. Relatively few people ever end up in court for damaging archaeological sites; fewer still end up with any of the possible forms of sanction that can ultimately be applied, such as fines, a criminal record, and even a custodial sentence. But relatively more people (although still a tiny proportion of the population and the criminal justice system's workload) are pursued in such a manner for offenses related to the damage or destruction of historic buildings.

Beyond the difference in legal circumstances outlined previously, it should be clear from the outset that although a background in archaeology can be useful to a historic buildings officer, this is not essential. Such an officer needs, in addition, a considerable, and very different, alternative skill set. The study of historic buildings, although related to archaeology, is a discipline that requires years of study and experience if it is to be done well – and, ironically, there are few professional training courses in this. Most of the officers currently in post around the United Kingdom have learnt their skills on the job, usually in the company of the then-holder of their position; others have spent many years, often decades, getting to know their particular 'patch', quite often as district/borough/municipal conservation officers (this role is explained later). The dedication and commitment required, the lack of training courses, and, above all, the distinct lack of jobs mean that the United Kingdom at least is facing something of a skills crisis in this area in the next generation – many of the current post holders are now in their forties or fifties, and will retire within twenty-odd years, but there are relatively few new, younger officers in their twenties and thirties currently learning the ropes and getting ready to replace them. The full scope of skills and experience needed from historic buildings specialists is outside the scope of this book. An excellent starting point for those interested in this specialty, however, is various UK-based organizations, including the Institute of Historic Building Conservation (IHBC) and the Society for the Protection of Ancient Buildings (SPAB).

Historic buildings officers tend also to have a very different lifestyle from that of their archaeological development control colleagues. Although often based in the same teams and/or offices, they will tend to travel around their area of responsibility far more often than archaeological officers, undertaking site visits for advice, consultation, and, more occasionally, confrontation. The nature of developer-led archaeological work, in the United Kingdom at least, increasingly means that a relatively small number of industry clients are served by a similarly small number of CRM archaeology firms and that the impacts on and solutions for archaeological sites are relatively straightforward. Consequently, archaeological development control officers are, in general, spending more and more time these days working by phone and email rather than by on-site visits. In contrast, the nature of the impacts on the UK historic building stock is far more varied, requiring vastly more on-site work. Many different people are involved (often private owners of single properties rather than industrial developers, who are, consequently, far less familiar with the applicable laws, and who also tend to have far less money to spend on professional legal or management advice). Many different types of changes are also proposed to historic buildings, from small alterations that may still have dramatic consequences for a building's historic identity (replacement of traditional-style windows with modern wooden, plastic, or metal ones being the most common example of this) right up to the partial or even total demolition of a building, or the transformation of a building from one use to another.

The nature of the historic building stock also varies massively from county to county, even within individual counties, with variations in construction and roofing materials traditionally used, in internal layout and external appearance, and so on – and on which even apparently subtle changes can have great impacts. An officer may thus spend a morning advising on the proposed changes to a humble (but protected under law) nineteenth-century cottage, move on to a lunch meeting about the conversion of a rare seventeenth-century barn, and spend the afternoon at a grand manor house, before returning to the office to write up notes and download digital pictures. The meetings may have been with individual owners who care very much about, and deeply value, the historic nature of their property; with hard-nosed and unscrupulous property developers; or with public and private organizations responsible for large premises for which the proposed changes may cost hundreds of thousands, even millions, of pounds. And an officer will often need to spend many hours at a single location, not only discussing plans with the owner and the architect, builder, and other personnel, but also touring the property, even climbing up into the loft, roof space, basement, or outhouses, taking photos, writing notes, and so on. The visit may be in the middle of a town or at a muddy, rutted farmer's track, and the historic buildings officer may be wearing a fine suit for one visit only to have to pull on overalls and work boots for the next.

## Specialists: Finds Liaison Officers

A specialist role unique to the United Kingdom is that of the finds liaison officer (FLO) of the Portable Antiquities Scheme (PAS). The PAS is a voluntary program begun in 1997 to record the increasing numbers of 'small finds' of archaeological interest discovered by members of the public – in particular, objects found by metal detectorists (but not exclusively metal), although the scheme's officers take pains to make clear that they are there to help all members of the public to record finds of any type or period. Funded by the central government, the scheme is managed nationally at a central office in London, but it is most visible through the regional/ county-based FLOs, the majority of whom are based within local government or local museums, archives, or university archaeology departments. The scheme is particularly interested in recording materials that do not legally constitute 'treasure' (i.e., mainly precious metals) that must by law be reported and dealt with through the Treasure Act of 1996 – without the PAS, such materials would go largely unrecorded.

FLOs undertake a variety of roles in relation to their job. Most important, they examine finds and provide their finders with more information such as the likely material, age, and cultural significance of the materials discovered. With the finders' permission, the FLOs will record such information – including taking photos and/ or making detailed scaled drawings – together with the location of the discovery. These data are then stored on the national PAS database, offering professional and amateur archaeologists alike access to the data, helping to highlight previously undiscovered archaeological sites, producing distribution patterns of particular materials such as specific coins or find-types. As a consequence of this role, FLOs need to be extremely experienced and familiar with a wide range and age of different archaeological materials; they also tend to find themselves traveling widely across their region, often in evenings or on weekends, visiting metal detecting, archaeology, and other local clubs and societies to identify materials or give talks on the scheme, as well as being present at metal-detecting 'rallies', often held on weekends, at which metal detecting clubs will meet to systematically record the finds from a particular site.

The politics of work as an FLO are not to be underestimated. Many archaeologists and metal detectorists alike remain dubious of the scheme, and some on both sides are outright hostile to it. Some archaeologists consider the PAS to be anti-archaeology, pandering to an archaeologically destructive hobby that ought to be banned. Similarly, some metal detectorists consider the PAS to be the thin end of the wedge of government control, the first steps to monitor or even to ban all metal detecting, which is the case in many nations around the world. Passions concerning the PAS run high, so FLOs often encounter individuals who are hostile to the scheme and to their role. Individuals opposed to the scheme for whatever reason do not tend to hold back on their opinions. Consequently, FLOs must have a thick skin. The working conditions and hours of FLOs can also be quite varied: many clubs and societies to be visited meet in the evenings in village halls, libraries, and community centres, so there can be a lot of travel involved. On the other hand, the upside of the job is that it can be tremendously good fun, working with many enthusiastic people and seeing an extraordinary range of archaeological materials.

## Specialists: Project-Based Officers

Most local government heritage teams regularly employ project-based specialists. Some of these individuals may be permanent, full-time employees; unfortunately, though, the majority are usually fixed-term workers hired for the duration of a specific project, and are often paid for by third-party grants, such as the UK's

National Lottery Heritage Fund (NLHF), as well as by funding partnerships, such as those between the local government and a local heritage amenity society. Such officers and their jobs tend, broadly, to fall into one of two groups:

- *Data-based positions*: These are projects that have been commissioned to fill gaps in existing data, to expand on specific research themes/topics, or to coordinate wider research; examples in South East England, where the author used to work, include officers employed on the South East Historic Research Framework (SEHRF), a project that has funded both regional resource assessments and research agendas across the country to better understand the extent of the historic resource of England as well as gaps in knowledge of this. At the county level, the county of Surrey has been undertaking a somewhat similar project collating data on areas of high archaeological potential (AHAPs) – detailed analyses of specific regions, towns, and villages of the county with particular high historic significance and remains – building on a series of projects previously completed, the extensive urban survey and historic landscape characterization of the county that gave broader-brush analyses of the county's historic sites (and for which similar surveys have been undertaken in many other counties).
- *Outreach-based positions*: These are projects designed to promote access to and engagement in the historic environment of a county. For example, Surrey has the Exploring Surrey's Past project,[5] which has placed a modified version of the HER onto a user-friendly website, in addition to undertaking outreach activities within the community to both encourage use of the website and, perhaps more important, find volunteers to contribute new data to the website on their own area of interest or location.

## Career Structure: Conservation Officers and Other Planning Officers

Several other local government employees also influence the management of archaeological sites and historic buildings and landscapes. Some of these individuals have extensive training and an educational background in heritage; others have come into contact with heritage through very different routes. Briefly and broadly, the three most important of these groups are the following:

- *Conservation officers*: Part of local planning departments, usually at the district/borough (US county) level, such officers help to protect and enhance historic buildings, reporting and advising on buildings and areas of special historic or architectural interest and securing the improvement of such places for the benefit of communities. Conservation officers work with heritage specialists and planning officers to guide new developments to maintain the distinctive character of an area – up to a third of planning applications submitted in the United

---

[5] See www.exploringsurreyspast.org.uk/.

Kingdom involve conservation issues. They may also be involved in regeneration projects that have community, economic, and environmental benefits.

- *Planning officers*: Based at both the UK county (Canadian/US state) and UK borough/district (US county) level, such officers make both long- and short-term decisions about the management and development of towns and the countryside, balancing the conflicting demands of housing, industrial development, agriculture, recreation, transport, and the environment to allow appropriate development to take place. It is up to them to ensure that permission has been obtained for any development and that planning requirements are adhered to. Ultimately, when planning permission is breached, they will then negotiate a solution, and in extreme cases gather evidence to present to a formal planning committee, which can include councillors and magistrates. This means, for example, that if the laws applying to the management of an archaeological site discovered before or during a development have not been adhered to, the planning officer will liaise with the heritage specialists to guide the process of mitigation of the damage to the heritage features and either protect these or map out what is left.
- *Landscape architects*: Again, like planners, based at both the UK county (Canadian/US state) and UK borough/district (Canadian/US county) level, such officers help to create landscapes – planning, designing, and managing open spaces, including both natural and built environments. They work to provide innovative and aesthetically pleasing environments for people to enjoy, while ensuring that changes to this environment are appropriate, sensitive, and sustainable. Landscape architects work closely with heritage specialists to guide the development of historic landscapes, finding ways to make the best use of distinctive historic features while modifying landscapes for new uses – for instance, finding the most sympathetic means of inserting new homes into an existing historic parkland landscape. Some landscape architects are also specialists in historic parks and gardens, a particularly noteworthy specialty that requires highly specialized skills and knowledge, overlapping historic and natural environment knowledge in the understanding, protection, and management of living historic designed landscapes that may be hundreds of years old. Organizations in the United Kingdom such as the Association of Gardens Trusts (AGT) and the Garden History Society (GHS) provide specialist support on such matters.

Such types of local government employees enjoy all the same benefits and career structure of the other dedicated heritage professionals discussed elsewhere in this section. The major difference is that they tend to come from a wider range of backgrounds, many having studied planning policy, law, and wider conservation (including both historic and natural conservation) at university rather than solely heritage issues.

## Lifestyle

The lifestyle of the local government archaeologist is not for everyone. Above all else, although such people get to spend a lot of time reading, advising, and thinking about archaeology, they spend very little time *doing* archaeology in terms of its physical practice – surveying, excavating, and so on. Opportunities to go out, to participate in, or at least to physically monitor archaeology as it happens need largely to be generated by the archaeologists in question. Such opportunities do not naturally arise during their jobs. This is increasingly so as workloads get heavier and heavier, and developers grow ever warier of the legal problems and health and safety risks of having visitors on site.

In a positive light, though, all this can be a good thing. If most of such an archaeologist's time is spent reactively advising developers and their hired archaeologists on their responsibilities and practices, collecting and collating data from many different sites, and promoting this new knowledge to all who are interested in it, this time is not wasted. Archaeologists in local government who do their job well get to see, understand, and directly influence the future protection and understanding of the heritage of their region. No one should feel bad about having such an inherently positive role. Even if most of their time is spent reactively, some of such archaeologists' time can still be spent proactively doing a small but extremely worthwhile amount of field archaeology. Perhaps they may choose to follow up on a commercial excavation by undertaking a detailed keyhole excavation at the edge of a larger site to clarify a key point of a site's dating or morphology or to survey an area that is unlikely to ever see commercial development but that is surrounded by such developments, clarifying the heritage of that blank space on the map. Alternatively, such archaeologists may choose to focus on public archaeology, organizing and leading projects that can involve their local community. Many distinguished British archaeologists first were introduced to archaeology by participating on such projects in their youth, so such projects can have both immediate and long-term positive impacts on archaeology at the local, national, and even international scale. Finally, such archaeologists may choose to publish on specific subjects or locations with which their role has given them long-term familiarity and expertise.

Every desk job, no matter the sector, has its pros and cons, and archaeology is no different; to this can then be added the undoubtedly peculiar circumstances of local government civil service. Civil servants of all specialties, grades, and experience will admit that the benefits of such employment are, generally, (relative) job security, the generosity of pension schemes, and the more relaxed pace of work compared with work in industry. Compared with an academic archaeologist, however, a local government archaeologist has relatively less personal freedom to decide their daily work schedule. On the other hand, the local government archaeologist is also likely to work shorter hours than the academic, and when compared with a CRM archaeologist, a local government archaeologist is likely to be very much better paid and treated and will enjoy vastly superior job security. The downside is that, as noted, the local government archaeologist will not get to do much practical archaeology.

The overall result is that jobs in local government archaeology are highly sought after, especially by the middle generation of professionals in their thirties, forties, and fifties. The scenario is obvious once laid out: a young and lively archaeology graduate fresh from college starts off in field archaeology; their early twenties are a blur of sites, places, and people – the person does and sees a lot. By the person's late twenties or early thirties, however, the lifestyle begins to pale a bit. The parties are still great and the archaeology even more so, but their knees are starting to hurt a bit more and being out in all different types of weather is starting to lose its appeal. The individual may also have a long-term partner, possibly a non-archaeologist, who, though sympathetic to the archaeologist's devotion to the subject, would also like to see them have better job security and ideally a larger monthly pay check. The result is that the government job suddenly begins to seem much more appealing – there will be less field archaeology, but a chance to still make a difference in archaeology, to still do some field archaeology, and also there will be the refuge of a comfortable chair in an office on a cold winter's day.

## Skills, Expertise, and Qualifications

Because jobs in local government archaeology tend to be highly sought after, employers' demands for skills and experience are correspondingly high. For a start, as noted previously, because many such archaeologists are drawn from the middle ranks of the CRM archaeology community, many will have considerable field experience, including not only pure archaeological skills such as in survey, excavation, planning, finds identification, and the like, but also related skills in project management, perhaps in budget management – as well as in time and people management. One of the things that many such people making the move from CRM to government archaeology note after their first few weeks in their new job is that although timelines are often still tight in government, they are not nearly as tight as in industry. Such archaeologists are also likely to have consider-able specialist knowledge of one or more periods or archaeological specialties, meaning that they offer their employer, and the consultants and others whom they will advise, particular skills. Such specialist knowledge may have been developed in a practical professional context but is also likely to have been honed through postgraduate study.

Cumulatively, many local government archaeologists have a formidable array of different skill sets; even thinking about entry into this field can seem wildly intimidating. Entry-level positions do exist, however, for this is local government, and one of the benefits of this sector of archaeology is that career progression and on-the-job training are common and usually encouraged. A significant number of local government archaeologists are not drawn from the CRM archaeology transfer route described earlier, but rather come in as young and often inexperienced graduate archaeology students on short-term, low-level contracts (say, working within an HER on a particular project) who eventually get longer or even permanent contracts and develop their skill sets.

Most university degree courses in archaeology place little emphasis on this aspect of archaeology. Although most students will have to take one or more courses on the principles of heritage law in their respective countries or regions, few will receive detailed (or any) training in the practice and implementation of such laws – how local government archaeologists implement them. Fewer students still will have seen first-hand the types of paperwork and administrative documents and reports handled by these archaeologists, visited an office, consulted an HER, or talked to local government heritage staff. What this means is that students who are proactive – who seek out local government archaeologists, volunteer for unpaid work in the offices, write a dissertation or thesis using the data held in such offices, and so on –not only will make themselves known to a small and often underappreciated sector of archaeologists, but also will gain experiences that make them stand out in an interview. Pick a hundred archaeology graduates applying for one entry-level post in local government archaeology, and the one who gets the coveted post will be not necessarily the student with the highest grades, but rather the student who demonstrated experience in and enthusiasm for work in this environment. People who go the extra mile, who volunteer, who stand out from their peers – these are the people who get ahead in this world, as in any other. Thus, a good BA in archaeology, matched with some volunteer experience in a local government archaeology office, form a very good start to a career in this sector; some experience of work in the real world of CRM archaeology, even if only a few months' worth, is very useful as well. An MA/MSc in a specialty is certainly very welcome but is not essential; such a degree that involves a dissertation focused on heritage law or that uses data from a local government office is a real plus, however. A PhD when entering the sector is frankly uncommon, although many such officials, once secure in their employment, choose to undertake such study on an aspect of their region or specialty.

## Focus on: Randy Sasaki (Japan)

I am Randy Sasaki, and I work for Fukuoka City's Cultural Property Office in Japan. I also have a position at Kyushu National Museum as a visiting scholar. Basically, I have two jobs. At Fukuoka City, I go to local elementary schools, town halls, and libraries to teach children (and sometime adults) about history and archaeology. I also undertake educational tasks such as maintaining exhibitions, managing web pages, and making educational videos. At the museum, I mainly work from home, and sometimes in the field. I am involved with the Underwater Archaeology Committee organized by the Agency for Cultural Affairs (a national organization within the Japanese government). This committee discusses how Japan manages its underwater cultural heritage, and my team at the museum provides information and advice to the committee. My task is to provide technical support during field projects such as underwater archaeological surveys. I also provide information about how other countries in the world manage their underwater cultural heritage, so that our work meets – and exceeds – international standards and best practice. The committee is currently working on a national standard and guidance manual for conducting research on underwater archaeological sites, and it is using my work to help write this manual.

I became interested in archaeology when I found Jomon pottery sherds in the woods where I used to play as a child; I was ten or eleven years old at the time. After graduating from high school in Japan, I went to college in the United States to study anthropology. After graduating, I worked at several contract archaeological firms in the United States while going to the Middle East (including Turkey, Oman, and the Yemen) to excavate. After a few years, I decided to become a maritime archaeologist, so I started my graduate career at Texas A&M University. I returned to Japan after finishing my MA and while still working on my PhD, which I have since completed. I was involved with the above-mentioned committee, and I learned about running underwater archaeological projects, relevant heritage laws and policy, and so on. I also worked for the National Museum for five years before moving to my current job as an educator.

I worked on various types of archaeological jobs – land excavations, mitigation work, and research. I also conducted my own research in Vietnam, undertaking surveys at sea using side-scan sonar and multi-beam, and, most recently, using an airborne drone to see underwater in shallow water, using a green-spectrum laser. I have organized exhibitions at the museum as well. Basically, I simultaneously undertake many different tasks, since I have two jobs. It is difficult to attribute what was the most useful skill that helped me get the current job. Perhaps, the phrase 'never give up, but be flexible and do the best you can'.

It is difficult to describe my 'average' week because of the stay-home rule during the coronavirus outbreak. Below is what I am *supposed* to do. In my job at Fukuoka City, I go to elementary schools and teach children about local history and archaeology. I prepare for this by studying the sites located within their community. We make bronze mirrors (in truth, replicas constructed using a safer, more malleable metal composite), make jade bracelets, start (controlled!) fires, and undertake other hands-on activities with the children. This usually ends around 2–3 p.m. At the National Museum, in the late afternoon, I undertake research in history and archaeology, heritage law, and international management systems for archaeological sites. I also translate texts (e.g., a recent UNESCO manual, and texts about the conservation of artifacts) into Japanese. These are made available to the committee as part of the project to produce a working manual for underwater archaeological sites in Japan. I also go out into the field to conduct surveys, to find archaeological sites underwater. I work with a marine survey company, using sonar and other equipment. Basically, the work I do is reflected in the manual that the committee is writing.

My top tip for pursuing a career in archaeology is to have an open mind. Also, archaeology is about teamwork. You must find what you are good at, or perhaps, it is better to find what others are good at and include them in your team. Do what you can do best for others' sake. It may not be an easy path, but with good people, it will be a great way to go.

If you are interested in learning more about my work, see www.kyuhaku.jp/ en/ (Kyushu National Museum), www.city.fukuoka.lg.jp/maibun/html/ (Fukuokan City Archaeology Center), and www.bunka.go.jp/seisaku/bunka zai/shokai/maizo.html (the Agency for Cultural Affairs (Buried Cultural Property) (in Japanese)). I also organize the official Fukuoka City Archaeology Center YouTube Channel (in Japanese) – see, for example, www.city.fukuoka .lg.jp/keizai/maibun-c/life/mybun–doga.html

# Chapter 6

# Federal and Central
# Government Archaeology

## Introduction

Variations in the national format of archaeological employment become most evident at the level of central government. In federal systems such as those of the United States, Australia, and Canada, organizations such as these nations' respective national park services (the US National Park Service, Parks Australia, and Parks Canada) are part of a distinct system with many responsibilities, a clear legal remit, central and regional hierarchy, and a large budget that includes archaeologists and related heritage specialists. A broadly similar centralized approach is also taken in countries such as China, where the National Cultural Heritage Administration is the key national body for heritage protection and promotion, including leadership of the museums sector. In comparison, centralized but not federalized nations such as the United Kingdom have broadly comparable organizations to the US National Park Service, but the responsibilities, legal remit, organizational structure, and budgets involved are much less clear. The situation in the United Kingdom is complicated by the decentralized nature of government there, particularly the varying devolved legal responsibilities of the Regional Assemblies of Scotland, Wales, and Northern Ireland. Some nations around the world go even further in this devolved management model: the crucial funders and decision-makers in the archaeology of Germany, for example, are those working for the sixteen federal states of the nation. Notwithstanding the above, central governments around the world employ archaeologists alongside allied heritage professionals, and employment in these organizations can be an extremely rewarding career path for those

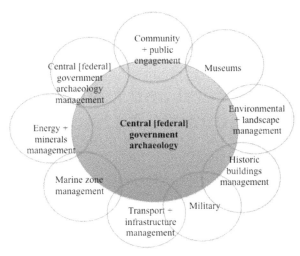

Figure 27. The structure and interrelationships of the central government archaeology sector.

who choose to pursue it, offering a unique vantage point at the intersection of commercial, academic, and local government archaeology (see Figures 27 and 28).

## Central Heritage Organizations in the United Kingdom

In Britain (i.e., the United Kingdom of England, Scotland, Wales, and Northern Ireland), working in central government archaeology primarily (but not exclusively) means working for one of five organizations, known in government parlance as *executive non-departmental public bodies* – part of (and primarily, but not exclusively, funded by) the government and operating on its behalf, but effectively run as independent organizations:

- *England*: Historic England (HE) (responsible for specialist heritage advice to government) and English Heritage (EH) (responsible for the care of state-owned historic sites).
- *Scotland*: Historic Environment Scotland (HES).
- *Wales*: Cadw (Welsh for 'to keep').
- *Northern Ireland*: the Northern Ireland Environment Agency (NIEA), which, unlike the other organizations listed here, is directly responsible for managing both the cultural and natural environment.

These organizations fulfil a broad remit of managing the historic built environment (including archaeological sites and monuments, historic buildings, parks, gardens, and landscapes, on land and at sea out to the twelve-nautical-mile limit of the territorial sea) of their respective nations. This includes the following:

Figure 28. Working in central government, part 1: Similar to local government, archaeologists and related specialists working in central government regularly undertake site visits and inspections to provide advice and check on standards and progress. Here, English Heritage officers visit the historic buildings at Battle Abbey in East Sussex, South East England (copyright Jeremy Ashbee/Historic England 2007).

- *Managing historic properties for public benefit and access*: English Heritage manages and promotes access to more than 400 sites and Historic Environment Scotland and Cadw more than 120 sites each (access to which is in some cases free, in other cases charged, either on a pay-per-visit basis or through payment of an annual membership fee that gives unlimited access to all sites, including a reciprocal agreement of visitation rights across the United Kingdom). This also includes a significant publication, education, and outreach program.
- *Managing sites of national and international importance that are formally protected by legislation*: This includes, in addition to the hundreds of sites noted previously, "scheduled monuments" (important buried and upstanding archaeological sites and monuments protected under the Ancient Monuments and Archaeological Areas Act of 1979), of which there are currently more than 30,000 in the United Kingdom, and "listed buildings" (important historic buildings protected under the Planning [Listed Buildings and Conservation Areas] Act of 1990), of which there are currently more than 380,000 in the United Kingdom.
- *Managing central heritage data resources*: In England, the National Monuments Record (NMR), in Scotland the Royal Commission on the Ancient and

183

Historical Monuments of Scotland (RCAHMS), in Wales the National Monuments Record of Wales (NMRW), and in Northern Ireland the NI Sites and Monuments Record (NISMR) and Monuments and Buildings Record (NIMBR). These are the national equivalents to local HERs.

- *Providing specialist services* such as dating and conservation and providing and promoting guidance and standards on best practice to the heritage profession. Historic England, for example, employs a range of specialists in the archaeological sciences, dating, environmental analysis, and related technical fields.

- *Advising the government* on new discoveries of historic sites of national historic significance, on matters of national importance such as attempting to control the international illicit antiquities trade, and advising the government on related matters such as the United Kingdom's responsibility to meet international heritage legislation/agreements to which it is a signatory (e.g., the 1992 Convention on the Protection of the Archaeological Heritage [known as the Valetta Convention]).

- *Liaison with other government departments* and comparable international heritage management organizations, especially promotion of the United Kingdom as a leader in best practice in heritage policy, as well as liaison with national amenity societies and stakeholder groups such as the Council for British Archaeology, the Institute of Historic Building Conservation, and the Chartered Institute for Archaeologists, and including also stakeholders of significant numbers of historic properties, such as the Church of England and the National Trust.

There is no directly comparable equivalent to HE/EH, HES, and Cadw in the United States or Australia – although the integrated environmental model used in Northern Ireland at the NIEA comes close. The remit, structure, and responsibilities of the nearest comparable organizations in these nations – in the United States, the federal National Park Service, and in Australia, the federal Department of Agriculture, Water, and the Environment (DAWE), including Parks Australia – are discussed later in this chapter.

Unlike most other nations, the United Kingdom divides its central and local government heritage management into distinct 'cultural' and 'natural' environment sectors. Consequently, a smaller number of archaeologists also work as part of the management of the latter, again through a series of executive non-departmental public bodies comparable to HE, HES, and Cadw:

- *The Environment Agency (EA)*: This organization has the primary 'natural environment' heritage remit in Britain, employing archaeologists for that purpose. Like HE, HES, and Cadw, the EA is responsible to a formal government department – in this case, the Department for the Environment, Food, and Rural Affairs (DEFRA) in England and to the Assembly Government in Wales. Scotland has a comparable organization based along similar lines, the Scottish Environment Protection Agency (SEPA), accountable to the Scottish Parliament. As noted previously, in Northern Ireland, the NIEA operates on a more collaborative system akin to that of the United States.

- *Natural England (NE)*: Established under the Natural Environment and Rural Communities Act of 2006 to 'ensure that the natural environment is conserved, enhanced and managed for the benefit of present and future generations, thereby contributing to sustainable development', this organization is similarly responsible to DEFRA in England only.
- *The Forestry Commission (FC)*: accountable in England to DEFRA once again and in Scotland and Wales to the Scottish Parliament and to the Welsh Assembly Government, respectively.

## Focus on: Hannah Fluck (UK)

I am Hannah Fluck, and I am Head of Environmental Strategy at Historic England. Historic England is the public body that looks after England's historic environment. Since we split from English Heritage in 2015, we do not manage historic sites ourselves, but we support others that do, and we advise government on matters relating to the historic environment (see Figures 27–29). My role involves looking at how the historic environment relates to the wider environment, in terms of policies, threats, and opportunities. A big part of my work is around how climate change is now affecting, and will continue to do so in the future, the historic environment, and how heritage can help us tackle the dual challenges of reducing the severity of the climate crisis and adapting to a changing climate. I work with colleagues across England and abroad to do this.

From a very young age I had always wanted to be an archaeologist, I joined the Young Archaeologists' Club, and as soon as I was old enough, I started going on excavations near my home on the south coast of England. I also took school placements with English Heritage and with the West Sussex County archaeologist, and I volunteered with Chichester Museum. By the time I went to university at Oxford to study archaeology and anthropology, I had already had a fair amount of fieldwork experience. After my undergraduate degree I travelled around the world joining local research excavations and worked for a time in commercial archaeology in England. I studied for an MA in archaeology of human origins, returned to work this time in planning archaeology, and then studied for a PhD in palaeolithic archaeology. My training has mostly been 'on the job' and I have been fortunate to work with some incredible archaeologists all around the world from whom I have learned an awful lot.

My first paid work in archaeology was as a field archaeologist in commercial archaeological units in England, but I spent several years with a mixture of short contracts, as well as working on research excavations and teaching on training excavations. My first permanent role was as a curatorial archaeologist at Oxfordshire County Council, and I returned to a similar role in Hampshire after I completed my PhD. These roles cover a very wide range of archaeological and heritage matters within a discrete local area, mostly related to mitigating the impacts of construction projects but also managing heritage sites and supporting community archaeology. My current role is very different.

I think it was the breadth of knowledge I had gained in my local government advisory roles and my research skills from my PhD that helped me gain my current job. I have always been interested in strategy and how research can help inform policy and practice. My current job is all about that.

I am writing this during the first Covid-19 lockdown in spring 2020, but prior to that I worked from home (just without the children being there all day!). I am not sure there is any such thing as a typical week in my job though. Sometimes I would travel to London, or other UK cities, perhaps one or two days per week for meetings, whether with other Historic England colleagues or with colleagues from government or other public bodies; since Covid-19 these meetings happen online. I also represent Historic England with some international climate change groups and research projects, so sometimes I am in meetings with people from all around the world. When I am not in meetings, I write reports and briefings for colleagues and government; write responses to policy consultations from government; review research proposals; write strategy documents, reports, and papers for publication; prepare and give presentations; attend and convene conferences and workshops; and supervise a PhD student with whom I have regular calls. As Historic England are an Independent Research Organization (IRO), I also undertake academic research with colleagues from other IROs and universities.

My top tip for pursuing a career in archaeology is to enjoy yourself, but to be prepared to work hard for it. The broader the range of experiences you can have, the better, but also remember that you never stop learning. Always be prepared to learn something new. I think a lot of people recognize that getting a job as an archaeologist can be tough; you might not always be able to work in archaeology, but that does not mean you are not an archaeologist, and it does not mean you cannot come back to it later in your life. There are so many paths through your career, and different routes that you can take, some through careful planning and choice, others through chance, but none is a dead end. Enjoy the adventure and the journey, don't be in a rush to 'progress'. Many of the archaeologists and colleagues I value the most are not necessarily the most senior, and expertise, knowledge, and experience are not always related to rank and position. Good archaeologists never stop learning, and they learn from each other.

There are several initiatives that I have found particularly inspiring recently. One in which I have had personal involvement is the international Climate Heritage Network. I was fortunate enough to be part of a small group of people from around the world that established this network and have served on the Steering Committee since its conception in 2018. The network maintains that 'to solve an anthropogenic problem we need human solutions' and aims to bring the power of the arts, culture, and heritage to climate action. Working with like-minded people around the world to find practical ways in which archaeology and heritage can contribute to helping address the climate crisis has been extremely rewarding. Another is the Mentoring Women in Archaeology and Heritage Group; this was set up initially on Facebook to provide a support network for anyone who identifies as a woman or as non-binary working in archaeology and heritage and is an amazing group of supportive people who are always happy to share knowledge advice and encouragement. There is also the related RESPECT group that has been working to address sexual harassment in archaeology, and the Seeing Red campaign that has been improving awareness and support on site work for those who menstruate. All these are making real and positive differences to the experiences of archaeologists.

Figure 29. Working in central government, part 2: A key part of the role of Historic England and similar central government archaeological organizations around the world is work with stakeholders in industry. Here, English Heritage officers talk to visitors to their display at 'Hillhead 2010', the United Kingdom's annual International Quarrying and Recycling Show (copyright Historic England 2010).

## Central Heritage Organizations in the United States

The United Kingdom is unusual in managing its heritage in the manner described previously, with its archaeological sites and monuments and historic buildings management being divorced from broader issues of the environment. It is far more common, as is the case in the United States, for different organizations to take responsibility for the combined management of natural and cultural environments.

187

The US National Environmental Policy Act (NEPA) (1969, amended 1975 and 1982) requires all federal agencies to implement procedures to make environmental consideration a necessary part of that agency's decision-making process. Federal agencies comply with NEPA by, for example, requiring commission licensees and applicants to review their proposed actions for environmental consequences – requiring licensees to consider potential environmental effects and disclose those effects in an environmental assessment that is filed for review. In particular, as regards archaeology and the broader historic environment, the National Historic Preservation Act (NHPA) (1966, most recently amended in 2016) is one of the federal environmental statutes implemented in the NEPA rules. Section 106 of the NHPA requires each federal agency to identify and assess the effects of its actions on historic resources. Section 106 applies when two thresholds are met:

- There is a federal or federally licensed action, including grants, licenses, and permits.
- That action has the potential to affect properties listed in or eligible for listing in the National Register of Historic Places.

The responsible federal agency must consult with appropriate state and local officials, Indian tribes, applicants for federal assistance, and members of the public and consider their views and concerns about historic preservation issues when making final project decisions. Effects are resolved by mutual agreement, usually among the affected state's State Historic Preservation Officer (SHPO) or the Tribal Historic Preservation Officer (THPO), the federal agency, and any other involved parties. The Advisory Council on Historic Preservation (ACHP) may participate in controversial or precedent-setting situations. The ACHP has also promulgated other regulations that define this process.

A broadly similar management model to that of the United States is also deployed at the federal level in Canada, where Parks Canada, the Historic Sites and Monuments Board of Canada, and the Canadian Environmental Assessment Agency have responsibility for heritage management at this level under a variety of laws, most prominently the Canadian Environmental Assessment Act (2003). See Denhez (2010) for more information (the organization Indian and Northern Affairs Canada also has some responsibility for First Nation cultural heritage management at the federal level in Canada).

## *Advisory Council on Historic Preservation*

The Advisory Council on Historic Preservation (ACHP) is an independent federal agency that promotes the preservation, enhancement, and productive use of historic resources, and advises the president and Congress on national historic preservation policy. As directed by the NHPA of 1966, the ACHP:

- Serves as the primary federal policy advisor to the President and Congress.
- Recommends administrative and legislative improvements for protecting the nation's heritage.

- Advocates full consideration of historic values in federal decision making.
- Reviews federal programs and policies to promote effectiveness, coordination, and consistency with national preservation policies.

The ACHP's three core program areas are (1) preservation initiatives (focusing on partnerships and program initiatives such as heritage tourism developments), (2) communications, education, and outreach (conveying the ACHP's vision and message to constituents and the general public through information and education programs), and, perhaps most crucially of all, (3) federal agency programs (administration of the NHPA's Section 106 review process, including working with federal agencies to help improve the ways in which they consider historic preservation values in their programmes).

Working in relation to the ACHP and the NPS under the terms of the NHPA are a variety of other federal organizations (including archaeologists) involved in historic and cultural preservation initiatives. In particular, the General Services Administration (GSA) Historic Preservation Program provides technical and strategic expertise to promote the viability, reuse, and integrity of historic buildings that GSA owns, leases, or has the opportunity to acquire. This includes the following:

- The Center for Historic Buildings, providing national leadership for compliance with the spirit and substance of the NHPA and other stewardship directives.
- Regional historic preservation officers and technical staff (based in each of the GSA's eleven regions), providing day-to-day consultant support to ensure that regional projects and actions comply with the NHPA and are consistent with GSA policy and national stewardship strategy.

The Historic Preservation Program collaborates with other federal agencies and programs, as well with non-profit organizations, on developing the following:

- Economical design solutions and building investment strategies to extend the useful life of historic structures and minimize the negative effects of changes needed to keep buildings safe, functional, and efficient.
- Stewardship initiatives to improve the impression buildings make on visitors, to accommodate tenant needs within a preservation framework, and to increase federal use of privately owned historic buildings.
- Strategies to make the most of available legal authorities and partnership opportunities to keep historic buildings occupied and viable – for example, by leasing underutilized federal historic buildings to private entities or transferring ownership of historic buildings no longer needed for federal use to other organizations that can provide better preservation and public access.

## The US National Park Service

The National Park Service (NPS) has a broad-based remit to study, enhance, and protect archaeological resources above, across, and under the water of the

Figure 30. Working in central government, part 3: A major part of the work of central government archaeologists is working with and promoting archaeology to the general public. Here, National Park Service underwater archaeologist Matt Russell demonstrates the use of a full-face communication mask to deaf children during outreach activities at Ellis Island, part of the Statue of Liberty National Monument, New York (copyright US National Park Service 2010, photograph by Brett Seymour).

United States (see Figures 30 and 31). The NPS also has a responsibility to enforce extensive laws regarding historic preservation of buildings and monuments, as well as a particular responsibility in relation to the rights and cultural property of Native American communities, primarily as laid out under the Native American Graves Protection and Repatriation Act (1990). The NPS also has a leadership and government advisory role in the management of the historic environment; this includes maintenance of the National Register of Historic Places (NRHP), the official list of historic places considered worthy of preservation in the United States,

Figure 31. Working in central government, part 4: Central government archaeologists undertake site visits in all different types of environment. Here, National Park Service underwater archaeologist Andres Diaz documents the bow of the sunken passenger steamer *America* at Isle Royal National Park, Michigan (copyright US National Park Service 2010, photograph by Brett Seymour).

as authorized by the NHPA. The NPS's activities in association with the NRHP are part of the much larger national program to coordinate and support public and private efforts to identify, evaluate, and protect America's historic and archaeological resources. There are currently more than 85,000 sites on the register, and more are added annually. Under the terms of the NHPA, the NPS (along with in some circumstances, particularly at sea, the US Bureau of Ocean Energy Management [BOEM], discussed later) also has a major archaeological responsibility in ensuring that these rules and regulations are followed on newly discovered historic sites. Just as on state lands (where these laws are enforced by state archaeologists), if a project such as road construction, mining, or property development takes place on federal land, uses federal money, or otherwise must comply with

191

federal regulations, then Section 106 of the NHPA comes into play, requiring identification of significant historic resources or sites (i.e., eligible for the NRHP), consideration of the potential effects of the project on those resources, and preparation of a memorandum of agreement (MOA) among all parties with prime interest in those historic resources.

## US National Oceanographic and Atmospheric Administration

The United States is distinctive in that the NPS is matched, so to speak, in the marine zone by the other significant federal government organization involved in archaeology and heritage management – the National Oceanic and Atmospheric Administration (NOAA), which has a similar command structure to the NPS with central, decentralized, and regional offices and operates under similar funding and legal structures. Thirteen national marine sanctuaries have been established under the National Marine Sanctuaries Act (1972) – these designate and protect areas of the marine environment with special national significance because of their conservation, recreational, ecological, historical, scientific, cultural, archaeological, educational, or aesthetic qualities as national marine sanctuaries.

The NOAA Maritime Heritage Program is responsible for the management of historic resources in relation to this act, working in partnership with other federal management organizations such as BOEM and NPS. Federal law requires proper care and preservation of items of significance to the nation's historical, educational, cultural, or artistic endeavours. NOAA's Maritime Heritage Program has been particularly successful in the development of its public archaeology remit, undertaking a wide range of high-profile expeditions across the United States, including those outside the formal national marine sanctuaries. Various other federal organizations have a passing role within the management of marine historic resources. Most notable of these is the Naval History and Heritage Command (formerly the Naval Historical Center), the official history program of the Department of the Navy, which includes an underwater archaeology branch operating under similar legislative frameworks to the NPS.

### Focus on: Marcy Rockman (US)

I am Marcy Rockman. I live in Washington, DC, and I am an independent consultant on two major climate change projects (see Figure 32). The first is with International Council on Monuments and Sites (ICOMOS), which is an international non-governmental organization founded in 1966 to preserve heritage places, and on a project to better integrate cultural heritage (including archaeology) into assessments and reports of the Intergovernmental Panel on Climate Change (IPCC). I serve as Scientific Coordinator for this project and my role is to work with partners such as UNESCO to determine the state of knowledge around culture, heritage, and climate; what the gaps are in this knowledge; and ultimately what will be needed to fill these gaps. I am also

Figure 32. Working in central government, part 5: Marcy Rockman presenting the ICOMOS proposal to hold an IPCC co-sponsored meeting on Culture, Heritage, and Climate Change at the 43rd session of the World Heritage Committee, Baku, Azerbaijan, July 2019 (copyright Andrew Potts/ICOMOS 2021).

working with the non-profit organization Co-Equal to connect members and committees of the US Congress with climate researchers and new climate research findings. While this work covers all aspects of climate change, my overarching role is to help assess what these findings mean for people and what appropriate policy responses might be.

I became an archaeologist because I wanted to save the planet through recycling. This may sound strange, but as I worked with a recycling program while an undergraduate, I realized I wanted and needed to know where our ideas and values for natural world had come from. To do this properly, I had to learn how to learn about the past. I did an MA and PhD looking at how humans learn new environments, because that is a starting point for understanding how the natural world has been viewed and used in any given place. I combined this with on-the-job training as a cultural resources management archaeologist for several years in the American West, and then a fellowship in science and technology policy that brought me to Washington, DC. The most useful training I have had in these travels is science communication, particularly, how to use narrative structure to tell scientifically sound stories.

The job that I most want to tell you about is the one that I held for seven years with the US National Park Service (NPS): the inaugural Climate Change

Adaptation Coordinator for Cultural Resources. My role in this position was to figure out what climate change does and will do for cultural heritage across the United States, and what the NPS needs to do in response. To the best of my knowledge, I would not have gotten that role without the vision I was able to draw from my research on how humans learn new environments, which is not only that cultural heritage will be affected by climate change but that information from cultural heritage – including archaeology – is essential to solving modern environmental problems. In turn, I expect I would not have been able to take on either of my current projects without my experience at the NPS and the capacity it helped me to build in moving back and forth between practical management issues, academic research, policy, and legislation, and how to tackle fundamental questions of place, meaning, value, and story.

There is almost no such thing as a typical week for me! Generally, as I am working on two major projects, I need to divide my time accordingly. As many of my ICOMOS and IPCC colleagues are in Europe (while I am in the eastern United States), I start my day with their emails and work on our proposals, project plans, and so on. Then by later morning or midday I switch over to working on my congressional work. This includes many emails, webinars, and a lot of reading of journals and climate news reports. I also try to keep track of major happenings in the US Congress, as all that effects attention available for climate policies and issues. The best part of both projects is getting to bring together ideas and people who were not previously connected. Bringing together multiple international partners to talk about heritage and climate change for the first time – how great is that?! Getting to connect a climate researcher with a congressional office that is trying to craft new policies – this is also a wonderful feeling. Sometimes it happens that my work on one project builds into work on the other project, which is basically bliss.

My top tip for pursuing a career in archaeology comes from my early experience with recycling: know what your question is. Have a sense of why you do or want to do archaeology and why it is important in our modern world – and then do not be shy about sharing that sense or story. Being able to explain my archaeological work about how humans learn new environments as a tool that helps us better understand ourselves and our world now has made it possible to for me to connect my skills and experience to projects and initiatives that otherwise likely would not have seen value in archaeology or an archaeologist. I also cannot emphasize enough the importance of being able to write well and speak easily in public settings – building those skills will make everything you want to do easier.

Governments have a voice, sometimes multiple voices, in making things happen, such as through policy and what they fund. What I did not realize until I was in government is how important professional societies and non-governmental organizations are in providing voices for individuals and civil society. I am currently working with ICOMOS on one of their projects, but want to shout out about one of their major reports: *Future of Our Pasts: Engaging Cultural Heritage in Climate Action*, which was released in 2019 with the ambitious but very needed goal of mobilizing everyone working with cultural heritage around the world to help work toward the goals of the Paris Agreement on climate change (report available at www.icomos.org/en/77-articles-en-francais/59522-icomos-releases-future-of-our-pasts-report-to-increase-engagement-of-cultural-heritage-in-climate-action).

## Central Heritage Organizations in Australia

In Australia, the national heritage management situation is complicated in comparison with those of the United States and United Kingdom by the variety of overlapping federal and state laws. Commonwealth (i.e., federal) legislation applies only when commonwealth decisions are required – for example, for matters of national environmental significance, Native Title, World Heritage, foreign investment, and uranium export. The commonwealth's Environment Protection and Biodiversity Conservation Act (1999) is particularly significant, defining the 'environment' in an admirably holistic fashion to include the following:

- Ecosystems and their constituent parts, including people and communities.
- Natural and physical resources.
- The qualities and characteristics of locations, places, and area.
- The social, economic, and cultural aspects of a thing mentioned in the preceding three bullet points – a broad-based definition and law that has no comparable model in current UK law (see Lennon et al. 2001: 8–9).

In addition, under the terms of the National Reserve System Program initiated by the Natural Heritage Trust in 1996 to improve the representation of the Interim Biogeographic Regionalization for Australia regions in the National Reserve System, there are 153 marine protected areas, including thirteen managed by the commonwealth government, some of which include historic/cultural remains (see Lennon et al. 2001: 27–29). Natural and cultural heritage are inherently and admirably intermeshed in Australia in a manner hard to ever imagine in the United Kingdom at either the national or local level, leading to an efficient and thoughtful management of these interlinked worlds.

A detailed guide to specific federal and state legislation in both the terrestrial and marine zone is provided in Smith and Burke (2007: 126–30 and 130–61); see also Lennon et al. (2001: 18–20, 148–51 and 160–62 [appendices 1 and 6]) for a review of such legislation and its operation. Table 26 of Lennon et al. (2001) provides a useful comparative review of funding provided for the protection and management of historic shipwrecks in Australia between 1995 and 2000. Many mining companies and other industries that have an impact on the historic environment of Australia have also established individual or communal codes of conduct for mineral exploration. This is particularly significant given the scale of extraction in some regions of Australia by major multinational organizations, such as Rio Tinto, which currently spends around US$10 million per year on its Australian exploration program, and which negotiated more than sixty-five Native Title agreements for access over the period 1995–2005 (Lenegan 2005).

The management situation is complicated in Australia through the requirements of native title and other Indigenous ownership/management rights (primarily those established by the Aboriginal and Torres Strait Islander Heritage Protection Act [1984], the Australian equivalent of the US Native American Graves Protection and Repatriation Act [1990]) (see Adams 2001; Greenfield 2003). However, such laws are, in many cases, the best – very often the only – protection of historic terrestrial resources on land that are directly or indirectly affected by industries such as aggregate extraction. For example, in the Australian state of Victoria, Indigenous heritage is protected via either a Cultural Heritage Management Plan (CHMP) or a permit. A CHMP considers the effects of an activity on the known and potential Indigenous sites in any area. It is mandatory if the activity area falls in an area of high cultural sensitivity (an area of known sites or high potential for sites based on predictive modelling) and it is considered a high-impact activity. If approved, a CHMP gives the proponent the go-ahead with the activity under the conditions proposed or outlined in the CHMP. Under the state of Victoria's Aboriginal Heritage Act (2006), mining is considered a high-impact activity, and hence always requires that a CHMP be undertaken. Furthermore, if a CHMP is not required, but a site is discovered inside the activity area during development, then a permit is required to disturb it.

## Heritage Organizations around the World

It is impossible in a book of this size and scope to discuss every heritage agency and management system in every country around the world. An excellent insight into many (but not all) different nations' heritage laws, policies and approaches can be gained from examining the documents held by the UNESCO on those nations that have ratified the 1972 World Heritage Convention.[1] The multi-volume *Encyclopedia of Global Archaeology* (Smith 2014) is a most helpful reference work; see also Kalman (2014) for an interesting partial global overview.

Beyond the main examples provided in this and the other chapters of this book on the heritage communities of Australia, Britain, and the United States, and the insights offered by different interviewees, I provide below a few examples, drawn from around the world, of various other nations' laws, management and organizational structures. The different nations discussed here were selected with the intention of providing a broad global perspective: the presence and/or absence of specific nations should not be interpreted in any way beyond that intention, and is not meant to promote nor to denigrate any nation or culture.

[1] See http://whc.unesco.org/en/statesparties/ and then search by nation; each has a tab entitled 'laws' that provides details of a specific nation's heritage laws.

## Argentina

Argentina is a federal republic, divided into twenty-three provinces and one autonomous city (Buenos Aires, the nation's capital). The provinces and the capital have their own constitutions, but exist under a federal system, making the management and protection of the nation's cultural heritage akin to that of the decentralized, federal system of countries such as Germany. There are both overarching national heritage laws as well as provincial legislation, and as such, many archaeological sites are managed by both national and provincial authorities. Local (municipality) governments can also enact their own rules to preserve archaeological sites that are situated within their territories. There is, however, no overarching law that protects both tangible and intangible cultural heritage, and natural and cultural heritage sites in Argentina are, as in countries such as the United Kingdom, managed by distinct and separate laws and institutions, meaning that archaeological sites may be under the jurisdiction of multiple authorities, for example, in national parks.

Article 41 of the National Constitution (1994) sets down the state's duty to care for and to preserve heritage, establishing that 'All citizens have the right to a healthy, balanced environment.... The authorities will provide for the protection of this right, the use of the natural resources, the preservation of the natural and cultural heritage and the biological diversity, as well as environmental education and information.' Various national laws then deal with certain aspects or categories of heritage. Among the oldest is Law No. 12.665, originally of 1940 and updated periodically since that time, which created the National Commission on Museums, Monuments and Historic Sites. This manages the preservation of national historic assets, monuments, and sites. Associated with this is Law No 25.197 (1999), which provides for a national register of cultural heritage, and Law No 25.568 (2002), which deals with the trade in illicit antiquities and artefacts.

The Dirección Nacional de Patrimonio y Museos (DNPM, National Directorate for Heritage and Museums), under the National Ministry of Culture, is the federal body charged with safeguarding cultural heritage. Many provinces have their own cultural heritage laws and departments, and thus employ their own archaeologists and other heritage workers. The DNPM implements ongoing actions aimed at government institutions and public servants in the provinces, promoting the development of specific protection measures at the local level. These measures aim to help spread an understanding of the importance of cultural heritage in society. See the UNESCO World Heritage Centre for additional information.[2]

## Brazil

Brazil is a federation, and as such both the central government and the regional governments – states and municipalities – have their own preservation councils. The lead national heritage organization is the Instituto do Patrimônio Histórico e

---

[2] See https://whc.unesco.org/en/statesparties/ar/laws/.

Artístico Nacional (IPHAN, National Historic and Artistic Heritage Institute), a federal agency subordinated to the Ministry of Culture, which also maintains the National Inventory of Cultural References. Some state and municipal governments also keep their own inventories. High-level constitutional principles (enshrined in a decree law of 1937 and a federal law of 1961) protect all archaeological sites and consider all such sites (including Indian/Indigenous ones) to belong to the state. Cultural heritage is widely defined under these laws, with historic and artistic heritage protected on both archaeological and ethnographic grounds and including many elements of intangible cultural heritage[3] (see Fridman et al. 2019; Funari 2004; Funari and Bezerra 2012; Funari and Menezes Ferreira, 2006). Specifically regarding Indigenous communities, the Fundação Nacional do Indio (FUNAI, Indian National Foundation) is the official Indigenist organization of the country. FUNAI is subordinated to the Ministry of Justice, and it is the coordinator and main executor of the federal government's Indigenous policy, its mission being to protect and promote the rights of Indigenous peoples in Brazil.

## Canada

The lead federal (e.g., national) heritage agency in the country is Parks Canada, the custodian of the nation's parks, historic sites, and marine conservation areas. As noted in Chapter 5, most heritage protection and preservation in Canada is enacted by the ten provincial and three territorial governments, each of which has its own legislation and policies to protect and preserve cultural heritage, including that of Canada's Indigenous communities (often referred to as First Nations)[4] (see examples in Budhwa 2005; Ferris 2003, and Lee 2002). Parks Canada provides detailed online advice about such federal and national laws and regulations[5] (see also Parks Canada 2005).

Parks Canada are a major employer of archaeologists in the country, certainly the largest government agency. As their website comments, 'Parks Canada employs more archaeologists than any other federal department or agency because of its involvement in the vast system of National Parks, National Historic Sites and National Marine Conservation Areas and other heritage areas and heritage protection programs.' Many more archaeologists are employed in CRM archaeological roles along the lines outlined elsewhere in the book in Australia and the United States, which are its closest comparators in terms of the federal/state balance of management responsibilities for heritage; in academia; and in museum-based and public-heritage roles. The lead non-governmental organization is the Canadian Archaeological Association[6].

---

[3] See www.loc.gov/law/help/indigenous-heritage/brazil.php.
[4] See www.loc.gov/law/help/indigenous-heritage/canada.php.
[5] See www.pc.gc.ca/en/docs/pc/poli/grc-crm and 'Archaeological Legislation on Lands in Canada', available at www.pc.gc.ca/en/docs/r/pfa-fap/index.
[6] See https://canadianarchaeology.com/caa/.

# China

China's management of its cultural heritage is a centralized system, its focus being the Law on the Protection of Cultural Relics (1982, most recently amended in 2002) (see Underhill 2013). The types of commercial CRM archaeology seen in nations like Australia, Britain, and the United States do not have any comparators in China. Almost all archaeological functions are fulfilled by one organization, the National Administration of Cultural Heritage (NCHA), a governmental agency subordinate to the Ministry of Culture and Tourism. The NCHA is responsible for the development and management of museums as well as the protection of cultural relics of national importance on land and under water. For some English-language publications on archaeological work in China, see Agnew and Demas (2004), Gruber (2007), Guo et al. (2008), Shen and Chen (2010), Su and Teo (2009), and Zan and Bonini Baraldi (2012). See also Yingying Jing (2019) on steps taken in China at the national level to protect its diverse underwater cultural heritage.

## Focus on: Haiming Yan (China)

I am Haiming Yan, and I am an Associate Research Fellow at the Chinese Academy of Cultural Heritage (CACH) in Beijing, China. I currently serve as the Deputy Director of China's World Cultural Heritage Center, a sub-unit of CACH, mainly involved in developing projects for World Cultural Heritage nomination, management, and monitoring in China. I also work as the Director of Secretariat of ICOMOS China, the Chinese National Committee of the International Council of Monuments and Sites.

I attended Peking University for college, where I majored in sociology. Although I was personally interested in learning culture and history in my childhood, I was not engaged in the field until I was twenty-two years old, when I joined ECHO Publishing, a press company famous for its magazines and books about cultural heritage. I worked as a text editor for a year, during which time I became more aware of the importance of, as well as my passion for, heritage. Then, I went to the University of Virginia for my doctoral degree, culminating in a dissertation about China's world heritage. It was sociologically oriented research, and it gave me a chance to be confident about my career path focused upon the conservation of cultural heritage.

I am currently working on the drafting of nomination dossiers for UNESCO World Heritage sites, mainly architecture and archaeological sites. My main projects are to create the World Heritage documents to demonstrate the heritage properties' Outstanding Universal Values, their authenticity and integrity, and the criteria they fulfil based on World Heritage standards. It is not a job of archaeological excavation or research, but to reuse the archaeological and architectural information to tell a 'heritage story'. I used to be a policy researcher at CACH, but in 2016, I joined the current sub-unit for heritage nomination. I think my most important merit for the current position is the sociological expertise. For World Heritage nomination, a lot of issues related to community and stakeholders will be handled, for which I could navigate between the requirement of nomination and the well-being of heritage communities.

Because I have two roles, researcher at CACH, and director for the secretariat of ICOMOS China, I need to split my time into two categories. For CACH, I am usually in charge of four or five ongoing projects, most of which are nomination and planning for heritage sites. We have a team of about twenty people working on these projects. I am usually the director and facilitator for them. For ICOMOS China, there are a lot of bureaucratic affairs, such as organizing workshops for heritage conservation and management, evaluating qualifications for conservation and restoration institutions, and membership service. Out of all tasks, my favourite time is when a conservation or nomination project is finally completed and implemented into practice. We could see our knowledge be realized on sites and be beneficial for the stakeholders.

My top tip for pursuing a career in archaeology stems from my background in sociology, which gave me a wide perspective in understanding complex issues. Heritage is not only a thing about the past, but it is more and more about the present and future. Factors for heritage conservation and management involve both human and non-human aspects. This requires us to understand the issues objectively and to understand humans' needs and relationship from both outsider and insider perspectives. The ability of academic research should be enhanced by the in-depth observation and treatment of human-related affairs.

Although I am currently working as a heritage conservationist, I would be more than happy to go back to my role as sociologist. I keep writing journal articles, reflecting on the daily work I am involved with. I published articles on world heritage sites, such as Hani Terraces Cultural Landscape, Maritime Silk Road, and China's industrial sites. My task is to create a conservation plan and nomination file, and my academic reflection is more oriented towards the projects' academic meanings. My current lifestyle gives me plenty of time to be focused on work, both daily work and night-time academic writing. I enjoy the situation very much. I also have my personal website, www .haimingyan.com.

## India

In India, the overriding heritage legislation is that enacted and enforced at the national level, with the Ancient Monuments and Archaeological Sites and Remains Act (1958, most recently amended in 2012) protecting sites and monuments of national importance and regulating archaeological excavations (see Paddayya 1996; Selvakumar 2006). This act also regulates the functions of the lead heritage agency for the nation, the Archaeological Survey of India[7] (see Chadra 2010). This is the government agency, based within the Ministry of Culture, that is responsible for archaeological research and the conservation and preservation of cultural monuments in the country, including work in the marine zone (see Gaur and Vora 2011). An important organization is also the Indian National Trust for Art and Cultural Heritage (INTACH).[8] Founded in 1984 to promote awareness of heritage and conservation in the country, it pioneered the preservation of natural and built heritage and also intangible cultural heritage.

## Mexico

Mexico's Federal Law on Monuments and Archaeological, Historic and Artistic Zones mandates that historic artifacts and human remains are to be managed exclusively by the Mexican state. The law states that human remains of individuals that belonged to civilizations that existed prior to the establishment of the Spanish civilization in national territory are the property of the nation, as are movable and immovable goods produced by those civilizations, as well as fossil remains of native species of palaeontological interest. The Instituto Nacional de Antropología e Historia (INAH, National Institute of Anthropology and History) is the official agency in charge of the protection, research, conservation, and dissemination of the national cultural heritage, including underwater archaeology. All projects aimed at discovering or researching archaeological monuments must be conducted either directly by the National Institute or by scientific institutions formally authorized by it. INAH has the authority to suspend projects that do not have proper authorization, to occupy the sites of unauthorized operations, and, where considered necessary, to impose penalties[9] (see Carballal Staedtler and Moguel Cos 2007; Charlton et al. 2009; García Bárcena 2007; Luna Erreguerena 2008; Robles García 2010).

## New Zealand

Heritage New Zealand Pouhere Taonga (HNZPT) (known until 2014 as the New Zealand Historic Places Trust) is the lead national heritage agency in the country.[10] They are empowered under the Heritage New Zealand Pouhere Taonga Act (2014), which replaced the Historic Places Act (1993), streamlining many procedures of the former act. In the particular context of this book, the archaeological provisions of the 2014 act improve alignment with the Resource Management Act (1991). The 2014 act makes it unlawful for any person to modify or destroy, or cause to be modified or destroyed, the whole or any part of an archaeological site without the prior authority of Heritage New Zealand. Such authority has to be obtained before the commencement of any works. The act defines an

[7] See https://asi.nic.in/.    [8] www.intach.org.
[9] See www.loc.gov/law/help/indigenous-heritage/mexico.php.    [10] See www.heritage.org.nz/.

archaeological site as a place associated with pre-1900 human activity, where there may be evidence relating to the history of New Zealand (a place associated with post-1900 human activity may be declared by gazettal as an archaeological site under the act but is not automatically protected). HNZPT also have responsibility for maintaining the New Zealand Heritage List/Rārangi Kōrero (formerly known as the Register), which is divided into five main areas: (1) historic places, (2) historic areas, (3) Wahi Tapu (Māori sacred sites), (4) Wahi Tapu areas, and (5) Wāhi Tūpuna, places important to Māori for ancestral significance and associated cultural and traditional values.

Specifically as regards Māori sacred areas and cultural artifacts, several New Zealand statutes also contains specific references to, and protections for, such sites and communities. In addition, the Protected Objects Act (1975) regulates the handling of Māori artifacts and provides a process for determining ownership of such items, including collective ownership.[11] The Māori Heritage Council (MHC) sits within HNZPT. The functions of the council include the protection and registration of Wahi Tapu and Wahi Tapu areas; assisting HNZPT in developing and reflecting a bicultural view in the exercise of its powers and functions; providing assistance to Whānau, Hapū, and Iwi in the preservation and management of their heritage resources; consideration of recommendations in relation to archaeological sites; and advocacy on Māori heritage in public and Māori forums.

## Norway

Norwegian cultural heritage sits within a centralized system managed by the state, universities, and county councils. Unlike many countries, natural and cultural heritage are protected under the same government body, the Ministry of Climate and Environment. Within this sits the Directorate for Cultural Heritage, responsible for the management of archaeological and historic sites and monuments, as well as wider cultural environments, including intangible cultural heritage. The Directorate plays a central role in public environmental management and engagement. Different branches of the national archaeological museum administer excavations and investigations of archaeological monuments and sites – for example, the National Maritime Museums are responsible for archaeological sites and monuments under water.[12]

The core legal instrument for the management of archaeological sites is the Cultural Heritage Act (last amended in 2015), which stipulates that it is a national responsibility to safeguard archaeological and architectural monuments and sites and cultural environments 'as part of our cultural heritage and identity and as an element in the overall environment and resource management'. Under the provisions of the act, the Directorate for Cultural Heritage can formally choose to

---

[11] See www.loc.gov/law/help/indigenous-heritage/newzealand.php.

[12] Excellent and detailed guidance is available online at the government's official English-language page 'Cultural Heritage Norway', available at www.norway.org.uk/culture/heritage/general/Cultural_Heritage/.

protect historic sites, buildings, and cultural landscapes, regulating activities on and developments of these sites, even those under private ownership.

At a local level, each county has a service responsible for cultural conservation in connection with the general administration of cultural affairs. The tasks of this service are to advise the county administration on cultural heritage management issues and to ensure that protected monuments and sites and cultural environments are taken into account in planning processes at the county and the municipal level. This is akin to the type of 'county archaeology' role that exists in the United Kingdom. The difference with the United Kingdom in this structure lies in Sami (Indigenous community) areas, where the Sámediggi (Sami Parliament) has the same tasks as the county cultural heritage service.

## Russian Federation

The official authority for cultural heritage protection is the national Ministry of Culture and its regional administrative offices. The Russian Federation is a multi-ethnic and multi-cultural country (although Russian legislation does not contain a general definition of Indigenous people or communities). National legislation to protect historic sites includes the Law on Objects of Cultural and Historic Heritage (Monuments of Culture and History). This law governs discoveries of human remains, sacred places, and artefacts; the process and policies for archaeological excavations, inventories, and the protection of finds; and provides a legal frame-work for land development in the context of the protection of objects of cultural and archaeological heritage. Notably, sacred places and places of worship of Indigenous Peoples are considered a part of their natural habitat. The Federal Law on Territories of Traditional Use of the Natural Habitat of Small-Numbered Indigenous Peoples of the North, Siberia, and Far East provides protection for these sites as parts of specially protected lands of traditional use of the natural habitat[13] (see Lbova and Sklyarevskyi 2006; Makarov 2004; Mazurov 2001; and Smirnov 2004).

## South Africa

The South African Heritage Resources Agency (SAHRA) is the lead national heritage agency, governed under the National Resources Heritage Act (1999) and its subsidiary legislation. The agency works in close alignment with a range of national, provincial, and local heritage authorities, all of which are empowered to formally declare any place, public or private, a national heritage. Citizens may also nominate places for such declaration. The 1999 act protects heritage resources, including archaeological objects and burial grounds and graves, in several ways: it bars unauthorized activities that may damage or alter known heritage places or objects, protects unidentified heritage resources or objects by subjecting certain

---

[13] See www.loc.gov/law/help/indigenous-heritage/russia.php.

types of development activities to independent impact assessments, and requires anyone who comes across a heritage resource during a development, or other activity, to report it. The act also regulates the export of heritage objects[14] (see Chirikure and Pwitti 2008; Hall 2005; and Scheermeyer 2005).

# Non-archaeological/Heritage Organizations

A variety of other organizations based within different nations' central governments have varied responsibility for archaeological as well as wider heritage matters. These include, most notably, the military (discussed later), as well as departments associated with specific industries (especially mining and energy production), transport and infrastructure, and, more broadly, various government-related funding bodies – particularly in the United Kingdom, where the National Lottery Heritage Fund is a major contributor to heritage protects in a way that the comparable lotteries of many US and Australian states are not.

## *Transport and Infrastructure*

An example of the types of other governmental organizations that employ at least a small number of archaeologists and related heritage professionals is the Canal and River Trust (covering England and Wales) and its counterpart, Scottish Canals (covering Scotland), which together manage 2,200 miles of canals and rivers with more than 11 million visitors per year. Their heritage responsibilities include the management of more than 2,700 listed buildings, more than 50 scheduled monuments, more than 400 miles (640 kilometres) of conservation area, and thousands of archaeological sites, including four World Heritage Sites, 14 historic battlefields, and 33 registered historic parks and gardens.

A very different and uniquely British example is the Crown Estate, which manages land and property owned by the British state (effectively the British equivalent of federal lands in the United States and Australia), and which fulfils most of the same management responsibilities shared by the NPS and the Department of the Interior's Bureau of Land Management in the United States. The organization was created under the Crown Estate Act (1961) to benefit the taxpayer by paying the revenue from its assets directly to the treasury, and to enhance the value of the estate and the income it generates. The estate's portfolio has a value of more than UK£8.5 billion and encompasses many of the United Kingdom's cityscapes, forests, farms, parkland, coastline, and communities, including hundreds of scheduled monuments, thousands of archaeological sites, and tens of thousands of listed and historic buildings. The Crown Estate also has a major role as employer, influencer, manager, guardian, facilitator, and revenue creator.

---

[14] See www.loc.gov/law/help/indigenous-heritage/southafrica.php.

In the United States, a variety of distinctive organizations exist that have a varied heritage and/or cultural resources remit. One example is the US Department of Agriculture's Natural Resources Conservation Service (NRCS) Cultural Resources Division. The NRCS considers cultural resources part of its broad-scale conservation planning remit. The stewardship of such non-renewable cultural and historic resources is an important link in the conservation ethic that underlies the NRCS mission, under the terms of various federal, state, and local laws enacted to preserve cultural resources, most importantly the NHPA.

Another example is the US Department of Transportation's Federal Highway Administration (FHWA) Historic Preservation and Archaeology Program. This program provides guidance and technical assistance to federal, state, and local government staff regarding these federal laws, as well as regulations, executive orders, policy, procedures, and training on topics related to historic preservation and cultural resources. This includes the provision of specific guidance on archaeological sites, historic bridges (particularly, encouraging states to incorporate the concepts of context-sensitive design in the rehabilitation and reuse of historic bridges), and historic roads.

In a similar context, the US Fish and Wildlife Service (FWS) has a historic preservation remit as part of the National Wildlife Refuge System. These refuges also protect many of important archaeological and historic sites dating from prehistory to the present day, ranging across all the National Wildlife Refuge System's 96 million acres spanning the diverse landscapes of North America, the Pacific Ocean, and the Caribbean Sea. Many of these cultural resources embody values important to communities and Indian tribes that are adjacent to refuges and national fish hatcheries. Alongside the FWS, the US Forest Service similarly undertakes various heritage programs to protect significant heritage resources, share their values, and contribute relevant information and perspectives to natural resource management. To put this in context, the Forest Service is responsible for the management of more than 350,000 recorded cultural resources on national forests and grasslands.

In a rather different context, the US Federal Emergency Management Agency (FEMA) also has an Environmental Planning and Historic Preservation (EHP) Program, as it is FEMA's policy to act with care to ensure that its disaster response and recovery, mitigation, and preparedness responsibilities are carried out in a manner that is consistent with all federal environmental and historic preservation policies and laws, including the NHPA. FEMA uses all practical means and measures to protect, restore, and enhance the quality of the environment and to avoid or minimize adverse impacts to the environment, including the cultural and historic environment. The entails the objectives of the following:

- Achieving use of the environment without degradation or undesirable and unintended consequences.
- Preserving historic, cultural, and natural aspects of national heritage and maintaining, wherever possible, an environment that supports diversity and variety of individual choice.

205

- Achieving a balance between resource use and development within the sustained carrying capacity of the ecosystem involved.
- Enhancing the quality of renewable resources and working towards the maximum attainable recycling of depletable resources.

Archaeologists and other heritage professionals working for these types of organizations have a broad professional remit and a highly varied working life, liaising with local and central government authorities (and local heritage volunteer groups) in advance of and during works to heritage features under their care, writing project designs, and influencing schemes of work, and in some cases leading or participating in fieldwork, analysis, and public archaeology promotion of sites. In this sense, their jobs are something of a blend of the responsibilities of local government heritage officers on one hand, and CRM archaeologists on the other. They spend most of their days in an office environment, but nonetheless will undertake a significant amount of on-site work, visiting sites in advance of and during development, meeting the CRM archaeologists employed, and speaking to the different groups involved. Archaeologists working for the Crown Estate are also responsible for large tracts of seabed within the United Kingdom's twelve-nautical-mile territorial sea zone, and so may have a specialized marine archaeological background and responsibilities, liaising, like their BOEM colleagues in the United States, with marine industry representatives and dealing with the distinctive types of survey data that result from seabed search and survey schemes.

## *Role of the Military*

The Ministry of Defence in the UK, Department of Defense in the United States, and Department of Defence in Australia all employ archaeologists working across all three branches of the services, and usually collaborating closely with other government, as well as industry, colleagues. The militaries of many other nations around the world have similar such structures in place, and there are also often various sub-departments and specialist archaeological branches of such militaries. For example, as noted earlier, the US Department of the Navy operates the Naval History and Heritage Command, including a dedicated Underwater Archaeology Branch. The United Kingdom's Ministry of Defence (MOD), for example, manages many hundreds of archaeological sites as well as historic buildings on its property through its Defence Infrastructure Organization. The MOD owns around 1 per cent in total of the UK mainland and is responsible for protecting and maintaining over 700 scheduled monuments, as well as elements of ten World Heritage Sites – including parts of the Stonehenge landscape, which is in an area historically used for military training dating back centuries, and which continues to this day. Of particular merit is an ongoing programme called 'Operation Nightingale'. This is an initiative to assist the recovery of wounded, injured, and sick military personnel and veterans by getting them involved in archaeological investigations. Running since 2011, it has undertaken fieldwork in the United Kingdom and overseas, with hundreds of military personnel having worked on

Figure 33. Working in central government, part 6: Two veterans on the Operation Nightingale Programme excavate postholes of a Late Bronze Age roundhouse at Dunch Hill on the Salisbury Plain Training Area, in September 2020 (copyright Harvey Mills, ARPS 2021).

projects (see Figure 33).[15] A different aspect of the MOD's involvement in archaeology then comes with the Cultural Property Protection Unit (CPPU). This unit was created in September 2018 so that the British government could fulfil its obligations after the United Kingdom signed the Hague Convention for the Protection of Cultural Property in the Event of Armed Conflict (with two Protocols of 1954 and 1999), enshrined in the Cultural Property (Armed Conflicts) Act (2017). The unit is staffed by military reservists from across the three services who are curators, art specialists, archaeologists, and others with similar types of expertise who advise military units on their cultural heritage responsibilities in conflict zones.

The United States similarly undertakes considerable work on military lands under the aegis of the US Army Corps of Engineers (USACE), as well as under the broader remit of the Department of Defense (DoD). In the United States, in particular, the DoD is the steward of the nation's largest inventory of federally owned or managed historic sites, including 73 national historic landmarks, 694 entries on the NRHP, and more than 19,000 individual historic properties, including more than 16,700 known archaeological sites and 3,200 historic buildings. Under the Environmental Management Directorate, of the Office of the Secretary of Defense (OSD), the Federal Preservation Office functions as the

---

[15] See www.gov.uk/guidance/operation-nightingale and www.wessexarch.co.uk/our-work/operation-nightingale.

historic preservation policy entity for all DoD historic properties. In addition, OSD's Legacy Resource Management Program has provided millions of dollars in financial assistance to protect and enhance cultural resources on DoD lands while supporting military readiness. In a related context, the US Department of Veterans Affairs (VA) Office of Construction and Facilities Management has a small Historic Preservation Office that keeps information about the VA's programs to comply with federal preservation requirements, as well as information about VA history, especially regarding historic building preservation issues (historical or genealogical research data, such as veterans' military service or patient residency records, are the responsibility of other organizations).

Even more so than the transport and infrastructure archaeologists and other heritage professionals discussed earlier, individuals working for the different branches of the military have an extremely broad professional remit and a highly varied working life, involving in some circumstances travel to locations anywhere in the world where military units are deployed and need guidance on the management of cultural heritage. This can involve extremely complex negotiations with local communities on one hand, and military authorities on the other, on how to manage historic sites while fitting into often much larger operational demands such as base security. For example, US and British archaeologists faced a tremendous challenge during and after the coalition invasion of Iraq in 2003, when they had to assist in local management of historic sites and museums – often in the face of armed looters – while simultaneously advising their own military authorities on how to avoid damaging historic sites. Some of these coalition bases were on extremely sensitive historic sites, most famously the historic city of Babylon, which suffered considerable damage when sections of the city were turned into a large military base in 2003. Because of such damage, a vociferous lobby within the wider archaeological community (especially in Europe) have argued that archaeologists fundamentally fail in their professional ethical responsibility if they work with, or for, military authorities either at home or abroad (see Rothfield 2009). Such debate, however, ignores the more common experiences of archaeologists working alongside the military at the domestic level, advising the authorities, for instance, on changes to the military bases that cover thousands of square miles in the United Kingdom and hundreds of thousands of square miles in the United States and Australia, as well as on training every rank of service personnel from all branches on basic good practice and the identification of heritage features.

## US Bureau of Ocean Energy Management

In the United States, the Bureau of Ocean Energy Management (BOEM), part of the US Department of the Interior, plays a significant role in mineral- and mining-related heritage management on land and under the sea. Akin to the NPS on land, the NHPA requires BOEM to take into account the effect of a proposed project on any historic property (including archaeological sites and monuments) under the terms of the Secretary of the Interior's standards for assessing 'historical significance' and to afford the Advisory Council on Historic Preservation (ACHP) an opportunity to comment, including on sites on the outer continental shelf leased by the federal government for oil, gas, and sulphur extraction and related pipelines and infrastructure. In the marine zone, BOEM, as a federal bureau, is required to ensure that activities it funds (e.g., environmental studies) and activities it permits, such as lease sales, the drilling of oil and gas wells, and the construction of pipelines, do not adversely affect significant archaeological sites on the federal outer continental shelf.

BOEM also undertakes proactive work on historic sites, under auspices of its own archaeological teams and commonly in collaboration with state heritage organizations, industry, and academia, both implicitly and explicitly aimed towards public archaeological agendas – and, in some cases, including the specific production of teaching resources. Such work is funded under the Environmental Studies Program, initiated in 1973 to gather and synthesize information to support decision making concerning the offshore oil and gas program under the terms of the Outer Continental Shelf Lands Act and Submerged Lands Act (both of 1953), which set the federal government's title and ownership of submerged lands at three miles from a state's coastline.

The following are examples of recently funded projects:

- Proactive, desk-based resource assessments of areas of high archaeological potential undertaken based on reactive report data submitted by industry.
- Non-invasive fieldwork using remote sensing and divers/remotely operated vehicles (ROVs) on specific identified single or multiple archaeological sites at risk.
- Invasive and non-invasive fieldwork on specific archaeological sites that allows methodological experimentation with new tools and techniques (especially deep-water investigation).
- Non-invasive analyses of the impact of specific invasive human activities on archaeological sites.
- Desk-based and remote-sensing modelling of site location probabilities.

## A Day in the Life

Although the organizations described earlier manage millions of square miles of land and seabed, and hundreds of thousands of archaeological sites, landscapes, and historic buildings, the reality of daily life for most of the people who work for such organizations is far more localized. Just as a soldier is one small part of the wider military community, so most of the archaeologists at work for central government (except for those who are very senior or involved in strategy) generally know or work alongside only a few colleagues, are based in localized offices, and have a focused remit and responsibility. Consequently, generalizing about a day in the life of a central government archaeologist can be very hard to do. A few generalizations are useful, however, as much as to define what such archaeologists do *not* do, and what in general their working conditions are. Although organizations such as Historic England and the National Park Service provide many opportunities, there are no organizations that will suit all comers (Table 8).

TABLE 8. The pros and cons of working in central government archaeology

| Pros | Cons |
| --- | --- |
| Job security: often permanent, relatively well paid (central governments do not generally go bankrupt) | It can be frustrating to watch decisions being made by other sections of government that contradict what you feel is best for archaeology. |
| Pensions and other benefits provided by the government sector, such as sports and family facilities, private health care, discounted rates at specific shops and services | Higher-level political decisions can affect your sector and security: a change in central administration can see funding priorities change and jobs placed under threat. |
| The right post can be very varied, a mix of site-specific issues and broader objectives. | Can be dull, in both types of sites analysed and types of decisions made. |
| Stability: usually based out of one office and doing day site visits. This makes it easier if you have personal commitments that tie you to one location. | Limited opportunity to do any 'dirt' field archaeology and/or research. |
| Can make a real impact on preservation and analysis of sites. | Opportunities for travel outside your area can be few. |
| Prestige: you are part of local government, so other people see it as reputable; some jobs also involve a uniform and clear role of service to your country akin to that of the military. | You must put up with corporate, management-heavy structure common in central government. |
| | Other archaeologists may resent you as being part of the power structure. |
| You can make good contacts for future jobs, and it looks good on a CV. | The right opportunity can take a long time to appear; people often stay in the same job for many years. |
| Good career structure within the archaeological community and government sector itself (regular pay progression based on performance is common in the first few years of such a job). | There are not many posts. |
| There are usually good opportunities for internal and external training and professional development; this can include negotiating paid/unpaid leave for further study. | |

Most important of all, it must be made clear that although central government organizations such as those described in this chapter do employ a significant number of archaeologists, extremely few of those archaeologists undertake any regular or extensive archaeological fieldwork. If your desire is to work extensively on excavating actual archaeological sites, then organizations such as these should not be your target – it would be far better either to work for a CRM archaeology

firm or to become an academic. Although a significant proportion of such archaeologists will also get to undertake site visits, most central government archaeologists' work is desk- or at least office-based and includes the following:

- Managing a specific site or series of sites; liaising with owners, users, and other
  stakeholders; identifying impacts to these sites; and devising management
  regimes, especially to deal with current and future threats.
- Meeting with other heritage professionals and stakeholders to share best practice,
  policy, and guidance, or meeting with non-heritage communities (including
  members of government, civil servants, industry, and the like) to explain policy
  and management principles.
- Analysing new evidence collected by other archaeologists to inform the understanding of a specific site or series of sites, informing policy and management
  guidance on a site's local, regional, national, or even international scale.
- Writing reports and other publications and giving presentations on a specific site
  or series of sites, to promote the public understanding of these locations.

Alongside this, organizations such as Historic England employ a growing number
of individuals with highly specialized skills, for whom archaeological expertise is not
necessarily the most important skill required, such as the following specialists:

- *Antique and antiquities specialists and curators*: Many of the historic properties under
  the care of organizations such as HE and the NPS include hundreds of thousands
  of rare historic items, ranging in scope from clothes, ornaments, and other
  personal possessions through household goods, such as kitchen and cleaning ware,
  furniture, art, clocks, and other antiques, up to ancient vehicles such as carriages,
  cars, and even boats, as well as oddities such as garden furniture and statues.
- *Engineers*: On one hand, many historic buildings have a need for specialist
  maintenance and repair by structural engineers with experience in historic
  buildings; on the other hand, there are also various engineering features of
  historic properties – including actual historic engineering equipment and features – that need management.
- *Historic buildings and gardens officers*: Historic buildings need constant maintenance and management, often involving detailed documentary research as well
  as specialist work on different types of construction, such as roofing techniques. Similarly, many historic properties also include ancient parks, gardens,
  and other designed or managed landscapes that need specialist knowledge
  and management.
- *Librarians, archivists, and conservation specialists*: HE's National Monuments Record
  maintains more than 10 million historic documents of virtually every form of
  media it is possible to archive; many of the historic properties under the care of
  EH then include hundreds of thousands of such items. These materials need
  constant specialist maintenance and, in some cases, conservation; they also need
  interpretation and management through resources such as GIS and other
  computer applications.

- *Planners and lawyers*: Expertise in general planning and planning law is an increasingly necessary skill for a large section of local, as well as central, government heritage professionals.
- *Scientists*: HE's Ancient Monuments Laboratory is an international centre of expertise in archaeological science, especially in different dating techniques, but also includes specialist skills such as environmental analysis and sampling (including soil and water chemistry and the like), human and animal pathology, and osteology, most of which have a basis in different sectors of the hard sciences of chemistry, biology, or physics.
- *Surveyors*: Specialist skills in detailed surveying of buildings, landscapes, and sites is an important and highly transferable skill, as are related skills in mapping and planning (including digital work and the use of GIS), as well as familiarity with old and new types of data, including aerial photos and LiDAR survey data. In the marine zone, this can include expertise in hydrographic survey tools such as towed sonar, sub-bottom profilers, and magnetometers, and the data that are derived from such tools.
- *Teachers and actors*: English Heritage employ hundreds of staff to undertake different forms of community outreach and involvement, many of whom have some experience or a background in teaching, at every age group from pre-school to lifelong learning. Many of these officers may have additional expertise, for instance, in drama and historic re-enactment, arts and crafts, or simply in lively public presentation, or expertise in working with specific groups, such as people with mental or physical issues.

Some people simply want to work for the government – the desire to actively serve the country is a very real issue for many government heritage professionals in the United States where, for example, members of the NPS have a uniform and an array of insignia. Similarly, NOAA has a selective uniformed branch known as the Commissioned Corps Officers, with a uniform like that worn by commissioned officers of the US Navy; so too do heritage professionals employed by the USACE. These branches have the most visible evidence of service, but many other non-uniformed heritage professionals in central and local government share a desire to do something worthwhile in the service of their country. These all being a part of government, the pay, additional benefits, and conditions in such roles are acceptable if not exceptional – certainly comparable to, and in many cases slightly better than, many other sectors of the heritage profession. And best of all, because governments do not often go bankrupt, job security is historically much better than in the private sector. Government employees also usually benefit from extremely good insurance and pension schemes, again often in positive comparison with the private sector.

## Career Structure, Qualifications, and Experience

As with all the other heritage sectors, supply exceeds demand in central government heritage organizations. There are usually dozens, if not hundreds, of applicants for every post that arises, although this is often less so for specialist officers and/or those based at historic sites, for whom very defined skills and expertise may be required. Consequently, central government heritage organizations can, and tend to be, extremely choosy about whom they appoint, requiring a high level of demonstrable specialist skills, qualifications, and expertise. Most archaeologists working in this sector have at least an MA in archaeology or a related subject; a significant percentage of the staff also has a PhD or equivalent. Alongside this usually comes extensive practical experience – there are extremely few entry-level positions for specialists at least, most of whom are recruited from the ranks of existing heritage professionals already working in the CRM archaeology industry or local government, who tend to be lured by better job security, on one hand, and new opportunities, on the other.

Career structure and progression can also be relatively problematic in this sector; progression, especially so. It is extremely easy to get trapped as a specialist in central government heritage, as much as anything because with so few jobs and so many highly qualified people, the only obvious career path is not sideways but directly up – into the shoes of the existing manager (also normally the manager of many dozens or more colleagues) who may either be perfectly happy where they are or else is stymied, at a higher level, by the same problem – the next-level manager will not or cannot move up, and so on.

The above being said, all is not lost for someone who wants to be a central government heritage professional. Two other methods exist:

- *Volunteers*: Many historic sites managed by central government happily accept unpaid volunteers. This may be as low-level as selling entry tickets, but can include, or rapidly lead to promotion to, more interesting roles such as acting as a guide to the site or working on education and outreach programs. Volunteers are well placed to get the jump on those few entry-level job opportunities that arise, and if nothing else, gain a new network of contacts and potential referees.
- *Interns*: Central government offices regularly have opportunities for interns, both paid and unpaid. This is particularly so for archaeology and other heritage profession students already enrolled in related university courses, especially postgraduate courses. These are no different from mainstream industry and government internships – the employer gets to see what the current crop of students is like, work them hard, and potentially cherry-pick the best for jobs; the interns get insider experience, contacts, and, if they work hard and are lucky, the inside track on jobs.

# Chapter 7

# Public and Community Archaeology

## Introduction

Until relatively recently, archaeologists were usually anonymous individuals unknown to the general population. Even on the rare occasions that someone knew an archaeologist, they probably would not know much about that archaeologist's daily life, and they would be even less likely to read about that archaeologist's work in the media or to visit their fieldwork or office. After a tentative beginning in the 1920s and 1930s, an expansion in the 1950s, and an explosion since the 1990s, public archaeology has become a major component of any archaeologist's life. There are entire careers to be forged in the business of this final chapter – of telling people about archaeology, of getting them involved in it, and of working for and alongside them (see Figure 34). The recent book (available for free online) *Public Archaeology: Arts of Engagement* (Williams et al. 2019) offers an excellent international insight into this aspect of the archaeological community. There is also a fascinating array of social media available online about this subject, including some wonderful archive footage of 'historic' archaeology media dating back to the earliest days of print, radio, and television production.

The most distinctive aspect of this sector is undoubtedly the TV archaeologists whose work regularly attracts millions of viewers. Some archaeologists have become household names in this process, and the popularity of such shows is a recognized cause of a rise in university applications for archaeology courses. Such shows, airing around the world, have had a significant impact on popular culture – so much so that one of the most common questions an archaeologist is likely to be

214

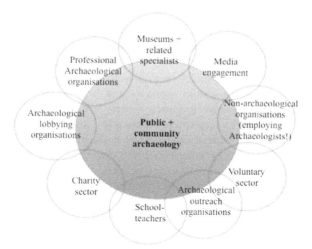

Figure 34. The structure and interrelationships of the public and community archaeology sector.

asked these days upon meeting someone new is, 'Would I have seen you on TV?' This is a strong indication of how deeply enmeshed into popular culture archaeology has become.

Despite these observations, 'public' archaeology remains the most difficult part of the discipline to define, not least in terms of pathways into a career. Crucially, all the career paths outlined in the previous chapters include within them aspects of public and community archaeology – ways of intermeshing archaeology into the daily lives of people around the world, whether they are aware of this or not. There is a massive public archaeology industry constantly at work, embedded within all aspects of the wider profession. Indeed, the only reason that this aspect of the archaeological career path is discussed in a separate chapter rather than blended into the previous chapters is the sheer extent of different opportunities to be involved in public archaeology, and the cross-fertilization of skills not only across archaeology, but also with related industries. The key thing to bear in mind on reading this chapter is that *all* archaeologists are public archaeologists. The broad-ranging skill sets of archaeologists should always include working with and alongside communities, communicating the value of archaeology to society. Archaeology is not ethically, and should not culturally be, a 'closed shop'. We work on behalf of all people and all communities, and we have a moral responsibility to involve, inform, and, crucially, to gain consent from our communities for such work.

## Public Archaeology Organizations

It is useful to begin by outlining the different types of activity discussed in this chapter. Often these activities overlap, but some priorities and skills can be identified that help to make sense of the situation.

- *Teaching archaeology at the school level*: A small and sadly declining number of schoolteachers have archaeological qualifications and teach archaeology, usually (but not exclusively) to students in the fourteen- to eighteen-year-old age range. In the United Kingdom, the tightening of the national curriculum has made this harder and harder to do, as archaeology is not a core subject, and so it must be integrated into other curriculum topics such as history and geography. Those who remain should not be forgotten – they are often the first people to introduce students to the concept of archaeology, and they are often the cause of a lifelong fascination with or even a career in the subject. A rather larger range of individuals employed by educational and outreach organizations, however, are happily involved in the creation and delivery of archaeology-themed teaching materials to schoolchildren of all ages, from primary school onwards.

- *Archaeological outreach and membership organizations*: There are numerous archaeology outreach and lobbying organizations. Three of the best-known in the United Kingdom are the Council for British Archaeology, Rescue: The British Archaeological Trust, and the Nautical Archaeology Society. Such organizations usually have a small membership fee for dedicated supporters, but they also gain financial support from public and private sources to make archaeology more visible in, and accessible to, communities. They provide archaeological training and fieldwork courses, publications, talks, and other events, and they lobby central and local governments to invest more in archaeology. Such organizations are joined by thousands of peer groups around the world, some of whose membership mainly comprises professional archaeologists with thousands of members, and others whose membership is more commonly comprised of avocational archaeologists, and whose membership numbers may be smaller and more regionally or locally focused. The latter are one of the best and most effective ways for people to first become involved in archaeology, as the thousands of such organizations that exist around the world have an enthusiastic local membership offering regular events close to almost everyone's home. There are also 'umbrella' organizations in this mould, which act on behalf of networks of smaller member organizations. In the United Kingdom, for example, the Heritage Alliance represents the independent heritage movement, acting on behalf of everyone from large organizations such as the National Trust to smaller specialist community organizations spanning the breadth of the sector, from museums to science and construction organizations.

- *Professional archaeological organizations*: Organizations such as the Chartered Institute for Archaeologists in the United Kingdom, the Register of Professional Archaeologists in the United States, and the Australian Association of Consulting Archaeologists in Australia promote professionalism in archaeology through regulation of their membership and creation of and adherence to codes of conduct and standards. Members must demonstrate, through submission of a portfolio and CV, that they have appropriate skills, training, and experience, although 'non-corporate' grades of membership are usually available for supporters of the precepts of these organizations who do not have formal qualifications or experience, or who are just starting out in their careers as professional archaeologists. Such organizations also undertake outreach and advocacy, and lobby government and industry for better standards and laws. An allied type of organization to these is then what are known as 'learned societies', organizations that exist to promote an academic discipline, profession, or a group of related disciplines such as the arts and sciences. Membership of such societies may be open to all, may require possession of some qualification, or may be an honour conferred by election. For example, the Society of Antiquaries of London was founded in 1707, and today its 3,000 Fellows include many distinguished archaeologists and art and architectural historians holding positions of responsibility across the cultural heritage community. The Fellowship is international in its reach and its interests are inclusive of all aspects of the material past. Members of the Society are known as Fellows of the Society of Antiquaries (FSA); to be elected, persons shall be 'excelling in the knowledge of the antiquities and history of this and other nations' and be 'desirous to promote the honour, business and emoluments of the Society'. There are similar such 'antiquarian' organizations, with allied objectives, in existence around the world.

- *Community and social enterprise organizations*: A new type of organization that has emerged between the first and second editions of this book are what that author has chosen to describe as 'community and social enterprises'. These organizations provide archaeological services, especially fieldwork and related practical activities (both physical and digital), on a community-led, usually crowdsourced, basis. They are not membership organizations in the conventional mould described above, since they do not aspire to replicate the often organizationally heavy structures of these types of group. Nor are they 'professional' organizations focused on the regulation of their membership (although the work that they undertake always meets the highest of standards). Rather, these are a new breed of agile, hybrid organization that brings together 'communities of action' to undertake a particular task such as the excavation of a site, usually in partnership with other heritage organizations. DigVentures in the United Kingdom is an exemplar of all that is best about such organizations, who have shed much of the historic baggage of the traditional archaeological sector to focus on the essentials of doing truly great participatory archaeology, communicating this activity widely and innovatively, and engaging with local communities as well as new, often global, audiences (see Figure 35). Organizations such as DigVentures have brought the best of archaeology (in terms of the pleasures of fieldwork and camaraderie of a community with the highest of professional standards) together with the flexibility and panache of the modern-day crowdsourcing models that have transformed how people proactively engage in events, publications, and product development.
- *Heritage organizations*: Organizations such as the National Trust and National Trust for Scotland in the United Kingdom, the National Trust of Australia, and the National Trust for Historic Preservation in the United States are private,

Figure 35. Public archaeology in action, part 1: DigVentures is a not-for-profit social business pioneering a collaborative, tech-enabled model with people at the very heart of their activities, both in the trenches and online (copyright DigVentures 2021).

non-profit charitable organizations that manage (and, in many cases, own) hundreds of historic sites and thousands of square miles of land. Consequently, these organizations also manage and maintain many archaeological sites and employ archaeologists and related heritage professionals to look after these sites and properties and engage with and involve the community in their understanding and curation.

- *Archaeology and the media*: A very small number of archaeologists make some of their living from the media, primarily presenting TV shows on the subject. As discussed later, the truth is that almost without exception, such individuals also have other jobs, based within CRM archaeology organizations or university archaeology departments, as there is simply not enough constant work in TV alone to generate a regular or reliable income. A much larger number of archaeologists are far more regularly involved in, and in some cases make an entire living from, work in either print or online media, writing and editing for popular archaeology magazines such as *British Archaeology* and *Current Archaeology* in the United Kingdom and *Archaeology Magazine* in the United States. Some of these individuals also regularly contribute to other mainstream scientific journals such as *Smithsonian Magazine*, *Popular Science*, *Discover Magazine*, and *New*

*Scientist*. Others work wholly in online media, such as the Archaeology Channel or About.com: Archaeology.

- *Museum archaeologists*: As discussed later, a wide variety of museums around the world employ archaeologists alongside numerous other related heritage and conservation professionals in a complex career path that is too detailed to explore here, one that could and should be the subject of another book entirely. Museum-based archaeologists often undertake research and lead fieldwork projects in a manner similar or identical to their colleagues in university archaeology departments, and many museums are either part of, or affiliated with, such universities. Such archaeologists design and curate displays, give talks and lectures, produce online and media content, and write guides to displays and their specialist subject fields and collections.

- *Non-archaeological organizations*: A small number of non-archaeological community organizations also employ archaeologists. Most notably in the United Kingdom this means the Church of England, Church of Ireland, Church of Scotland and the Church of Wales, all of which have small teams of archaeologists and other heritage professionals (especially buildings historians, architects, and the like) advising a much wider voluntary community involved in the upkeep of tens of thousands of historic properties (ranging from cathedrals to tiny chapels by way of thousands of other properties of all types), including advising on archaeological work within the grounds of such properties. A different but no less important example are the small number of professional archaeologists who work full- or part-time for different unions that represent archaeologists, and the much larger number of individuals who volunteer as union representatives within heritage organizations. Membership of a union is not required for anyone to be an archaeologist, and many professional archaeologists are not members of a union. Indeed, there is no dedicated 'archaeologists' union – archaeologists are members of many different wider unions, usually linked to their employer type: local and central government archaeologists usually join civil service unions, for example, academic archaeologists, university unions, and so on. Joining a union is an entirely voluntary decision, usually made as part of a wider, personal social perspective. For example, in the United Kingdom, the author is a member of the union Prospect, which represents many different professional communities. I joined them because I believe in the collective vision of unions for a fairer and more equitable society, embedded in the history of such organizations dating back to their origins in the industrial revolution. To me, membership is part of my personal code of ethics, and is much more to do with me as an individual than it is to do with me as a heritage professional. I like to think that I would be a member of a union no matter what job I did, who my employer was, or where I worked. There are, therefore, some like-minded individuals who were or still are professional archaeologists, but who have chosen on similar ethical grounds to work directly for a union. They are employed not as heritage professionals, but rather as leaders, managers, and in other roles by the union, on behalf of the union's members, and to the union's objectives.

Figure 36. Public archaeology in action, part 2: Remote sensing survey at the USS *Somers* shipwreck site (1846), off Veracruz, Mexico, August 2018, onboard the *Justo Sierra* oceanographic vessel. Left to right: geophysicist Francisco Ponce (UNAM), maritime archaeologist Nicolás Ciarlo (University of Buenos Aires), maritime archaeologist Jorge Herrera (UNAM) (copyright Eduardo Castillo 2021).

## Focus on: Jorge Herrera (Mexico)

I am Jorge Herrera, and I am a maritime archaeologist at the Instituto de Investigaciones Antropológicas (IIA, Institute for Anthropological Research), one of several research institutes at the Universidad Nacional Autónoma de México (UNAM, National Autonomous University of Mexico). I am based at UNAM's main campus in Mexico City, although my fieldwork takes place in the states of Veracruz and Tabasco, both looking towards the Gulf of Mexico (see Figure 36). I work out at sea, be this offshore or near to the coast, as well as in rivers, riverine and ocean waterfronts, coastal areas, and ports. UNAM is not only the largest university in the country, but it is also the main research institution in Mexico. Therefore, my duties encompass both research and teaching, which I certainly enjoy.

When I was a child, I knew that I was going to be either a writer or a scientist. Although at that age I was not sure what kind of a scientist, I had astronomy and archaeology as my main options. Despite starting to publish creative writing at a young age, in the long-term archaeology took pre-eminence in my life. I studied BA degrees both in archaeology and in Hispanic literature and languages in Mexico City, but I graduated first in archaeology, which since then has taken up most of my time and effort, so literature needed to take a sidestep as a priority. I gained a PhD at Southampton University and two post-doctorate qualifications, one at IIA-UNAM in Mexico, and another one at Paris 1 Panthéon-Sorbonne in France. Both were focused on maritime archaeology research.

I have passed most of my professional career as a researcher and in different countries, although it has been a rough and difficult road. Finding a permanent job in any science in Mexico is extremely hard, as positions are scarce. That situation is even worse if one tries to open new research avenues, such as scientific maritime archaeology. If I were doing some more traditional Pre-Hispanic or Mesoamerican archaeology, then there are at least some positions to be filled. But when I started in the field and when I obtained a specialized PhD on the subject, there were no such jobs in the country. It took me about ten years after my PhD to find an academic niche in which to develop proper maritime archaeology in Mexico, at UNAM. Perhaps the most helpful aspect for me to finally find an academic space was the wide field experience acquired through my years of practice outside the country.

On a city week I might be at my university, analysing historical maps and documents, studying the distribution of archaeological sites over a maritime landscape, reading old ship's navigational logs, or studying different aspects of epistemology as applied to archaeology. I devote regular time to teaching at the university, an activity I find quite enjoyable. On a fieldwork week, I am either offshore or at a coastal location, running geophysical surveys, looking for or recording archaeological coastal battlefields or shipwreck sites. The most enjoyable aspects of my job are the intellectual challenges that it entails and the richness involved in cultural interaction with the members of the coastal communities near the places I work at. As well, the intense contact with coastal and marine environments is exhilarating. Although from time to time one faces rough weather, the contact with nature at sea is soothing, particularly for one who lives in a big city.

My top tip for pursuing a career in archaeology is that discipline, patience, and perseverance have been instrumental to me, as well as engaging in other fields of knowledge different to archaeology. The ability to pursue archaeological knowledge (or any scientific knowledge) needs to be sustained by a strong dose of discipline, to learn how to perform the craft and to self-criticize our own results. Patience and perseverance are vital, as archaeological research often takes a long time before offering strong results. Archaeology is better served by avoiding the temptation of collecting fast and shallow results, good for the newspapers and self-promotion but weak for understanding the complexities of past societies. Finally, by engaging with other fields of knowledge related to the human condition, such as wider anthropological perspectives, history, painting, other arts, and literature, archaeological research can benefit from the added cultural value or significance. On the other hand, skills coming from different scientific disciplines, such as physics, geology, or chemistry, will strengthen how we study the material remains of past cultures, widening our understanding on their use by people from other times.

I embrace the role that my current project has in relation to training young archaeologists and students in the highly specialized field of maritime archaeology. As well, the project works with the idea that knowledge must always reach the general audiences, so we make a sustained effort in engaging public forums and keeping contact with the local communities where we run our fieldwork. The Maritime Aspects of the Mexican-American War (1846–48) Archaeological Project (Proyecto Arqueología Marítima de la Guerra de Intervención [1846–1848]) has a Facebook page on which we share details of our work. Most of the content has been written by students participating in the research. See www.facebook.com/arqueologiamaritimaunamiia.

## Lifestyle, Career Structures, and Qualifications

Generalizing about lifestyles and careers in public archaeology is even harder than for other sectors of the discipline; careers in this sector are not common and follow no regular pattern in terms of lifestyle or structure – most of the practitioners have ended up in their post through a mixture of chance and experience. Perhaps the only generalities that can be made come down to attitude and experience (Table 9).

### *Attitude*

More than anything else, those working in public archaeology must have a tremendously positive attitude. When it comes down to it, public archaeology is about sales – about selling archaeology through making it accessible, interesting, and fun (see Figure 37). When challenged with meeting many different people, day after day, and explaining archaeology to them in an accessible manner, only the most upbeat and enthusiastic of individuals will cope. There are precious few chances to relax or take downtime under such circumstances – if a school party of sixty excited eight-year-olds turns up at your museum on a rainy day, you must still be cheery, approachable, and enthusiastic, or you will fail in your job at the

TABLE 9. The pros and cons of working in public archaeology

| Pros | Cons |
|---|---|
| Stimulation of meeting/working with people from all walks of life who are excited by archaeology | Pay is often low, and almost all contracts are fixed-term, with few benefits but long hours. |
| Ideal if you like meeting people and are enthusiastic; you can get very life-affirming responses of people, especially kids, who catch on to your enthusiasm. | Employers may be unable to offer leave for training opportunities because they do not have the spare capacity or money. |
| Teaching can be rewarding and exciting. | Can become frustrating after a while to always present entry-level archaeology, not much in-depth work. |
| Can involve opportunities for travel | There are rarely opportunities to undertake any higher-level writing/research, or even to get really involved in an excavation or other project – you may always be only scratching the surface all the time to help others progress their skills. |
| Can help sites to become better protected/managed/understood, and you can get to meet and influence a wide range of people – from the public to government officials, even, occasionally, celebrities. | |
| Sense of community: people involved in public archaeology are usually very friendly and social; they like people and want to communicate. | Money is almost always tight, so projects usually run on a shoestring, costs are cut, and so on. You might end up living pretty rough for weeks on end to keep the project on budget. |
| | Projects are often relatively short-term, so you may not get to see the long-term development of a site and its analysis. |
| | Can be dull and have quite a lot of repetitive office/administration work |
| | Can feel like an uphill struggle to get things done or make major changes in the face of public and government disinterest. |
| | Limited career structure: the right opportunity can take a long time to appear. |
| | Most people advance by leaving one job and trading up to another post with a different employer based on their CV – which often works but can be risky. |

Figure 37. Public archaeology in action, part 3: Public engagement is one of the most enjoyable parts of any archaeological project. Here, archaeologists from the Thames Discovery Programme and the Portable Antiquities Scheme talk to visitors about their display at the Tower of London, during the Festival of British Archaeology in July 2010 (copyright Nathalie Cohen/Thames Discovery Programme 2010).

most fundamental level. You also need to be willing to make a fool of yourself in public and to be ruthless in the pursuit of your organization's ends. Most public archaeology organizations are charities of one form or another and they have the tightest of finances; as a result, they must be shameless in pursuing funding and support from the public, industry, and government alike.

## Experience

Without exception, those working in public archaeology have previous experience in other types of archaeological work itself, and quite commonly other transferable skills, especially formal teaching qualifications or extensive teaching experience (especially among particular age or skill groups of children). Archaeology is an experience-based profession, so it is very hard to tell others about archaeological sites, finds, or working practices without good personal knowledge and experience of the discipline. There are virtually no entry-level jobs in this sector; most people working full-time have either moved sideways within it from a related archaeological specialty (e.g., working as an archaeologist for a CRM archaeology firm that also has an outreach team, helping out that team at first on odd jobs and moving fully into it when a position opens up), or they get hired directly as public archaeologists on the basis of their previous experience.

As noted earlier, such relevant experience might be in archaeological work itself, or in teaching techniques that enhance the experience of participants in a project. Other useful transferable skills common among this community are those of professional communicators. This includes formal skills such as knowing different languages, being a good artist, or having handiwork or craft skills, and more informal skills linked to the previous point about attitude, such as a personable manner; an ability to explain things in a clear, concise, and unpatronizing way; and, above all, confidence in public speaking.

Given this information, the career path for a budding public archaeologist is relatively clear: first, get a degree (or multiple degrees) in archaeology; second, get experience working as an archaeologist; and third, if having achieved the first two steps you still feel that you have the right attitude to do well in the business of communicating archaeology, explore the possibilities that present themselves to you – perhaps first volunteering to do site tours for a project on which you are working, getting a placement to work with an existing outreach team of your current employer (or even volunteering to create a new such team if one does not exist), or approaching existing public archaeology organizations to see what opportunities might be available.

## Teaching Archaeology at the School Level

The lifestyle and career of those teaching archaeology at the school level are ultimately determined by how such people are employed. Those lucky enough to be formally employed by a school as a teacher (a minority) will benefit from the conditions and salaries of the teaching sector; the downside will be that they will have to teach far more than just archaeology, will be tied to the school calendar cycle, and will have to undertake additional management/administrative duties – all of which means that the actual amount of time doing or thinking about archaeology can be small.

Alternatively, several organizations (dedicated outreach organizations such as those discussed in more detail later, and a growing number of museums, CRM archaeology firms, and even national and local government heritage departments) have teams dedicated to producing school-based archaeological outreach materials such as lesson plans and teaching packs. Such teams also undertake formal teaching – either going into schools to lead a class or event or providing on-site and evening/ out-of-term activities. The upside of this second group is that its members get to think about and do much more archaeology, have a more varied and flexible working day, and do not need to do the kinds of administration and management with which the teaching sector is bedevilled; the downside is that they do not enjoy the same benefits – particularly in terms of length of contract, pay, and conditions – that are fairly standard for teachers. Meanwhile, because of the constraints of the curriculum, there are virtually no jobs for teachers solely specializing in archaeology – all teach other subjects (primarily, but not exclusively, history, as discussed later), and must find their own ways of integrating archaeology into the curriculum.

As already noted, members of the latter group are undoubtedly the more populous school-sector archaeologists and have a more distinctive and different 'day in the life'; that of the former, the full-time schoolteachers, in all honesty does not vary dramatically from that of any other schoolteacher of any other subject. A day in the life of school-sector archaeologists will generally depend on whether they are preparing materials for outreach or presenting these materials: during the former period, they will be office-based, researching the materials and stories behind their lesson plans and teaching materials and developing these materials, as well as doing administration – contacting partner schools and teachers, and very important, usually chasing new sources of funding or sponsorship. During presentations, such individuals will be even busier and may be anywhere from inside a classroom to at a beach to in the middle of a field. Despite the health and safety issues and time demands on the busy modern teaching schedule, parents and teachers alike remain keen on the types of hands-on activities that archaeology-related teaching can provide. Archaeology, being the study of the material remains of the human past, offers room for teaching across the curriculum – if people do something in the present there is usually some analogy for similar activity in the past, so archaeology relates to much more than just history. As discussed in Chapter 2, archaeology relates to all subject areas usually taught in schools and colleges around the world. Archaeology's special value lies in its interconnection of the humanities, social, and 'pure' sciences in a uniquely appealing combination of transferable skills:

- *Art*: the study of ancient art recovered from archaeological sites that date back to the dawn of humanity,[1] including the scientific dating of such sites and the analyses of the dyes, pigments, and tools recovered; and the consideration, and emulation, of their artistic styles, genres, and meanings.
- *Biology*: the study of human evolution, the uses and domestication of different plants and animals as resources by humans, and the spread of such plants and animals around the world.

---

[1] The date of the earliest human artefacts showing evidence of workmanship with an artistic purpose are the subject of intense debate. Such workmanship clearly existed 40,000 years ago in the Upper Paleolithic era, and it may extend back much further – the oldest currently known site dates back 73,000 years.

- *Chemistry*: the analysis of the composition of different historical materials, such as ancient metals and ceramics, recovered from archaeological sites and structures.
- *Computing*: the application of computers, particularly GIS, to archaeological data, and the linked sub-discipline of digital archaeology – the application of information technologies and digital media to archaeological questions.
- *Design and technology*: the undertaking of technological analyses of ancient approaches to engineering, including experimental archaeology in the reconstruction and use of such technologies; and the study of climate adaptation strategies in ancient technology, learning from ancient building techniques on how to improve modern-day resilience to climate change.
- *Drama*: the use of archaeological sites as performative spaces and inspiration for drama, including the performance of historic plays at historic and archaeological sites; the analysis of ancient theatres in terms of performance styles and acoustics.
- *English*: research into the development of language and communication skills, and the use of the past as a source of inspiration of creative writing exercises.
- *Geography*: analyses of the development of the landscape, of long- and short-term changes in the relative levels of sea and land, and of human responses to climate change.
- *History*: the comparison of documentary and iconographic materials with the physical evidence derived from archaeology; the study of the history of archaeology as a discipline.
- *Languages*: the study of linguistic evidence derived from archaeological sites and finds, and the involvement of historic and modern-day languages in research through anthropology and ethnography.
- *Mathematics*: the consideration of ancient counting systems, the use of forms of absolute and relative dating, and the development and spread of different forms of currency (relating more tangentially to economics and the history of banking).
- *Music*: the study of ancient musical instruments recovered from archaeological sites, the analysis of the acoustics of prehistoric and historic sites and monuments, and the use of the past as a source of inspiration for the composition of new music.
- *Physics*: the science behind ancient engineering tools and projects, for instance, how ancient societies constructed locations such as the pyramids without modern machines; the use of physics in scientific dating techniques.
- *Physical education*: the consideration of ancient sports and related practices (including evidence such as that derived from osteoarchaeology in terms of wear patterns on joints and bones associated with activities such as athletics and archery); the consideration of ancient societies' views on mental and physical health and well-being.
- *Religious studies*: the study of ancient religious sites and of ritual objects recovered from archaeological sites, and the analysis of sacred prehistoric and historic sites and monuments, including their reuse/adaptation by modern communities.

## Archaeological Outreach Organizations

Lifestyles and careers of individuals employed by archaeological outreach and wider heritage organizations depend on a series of factors outlined in this section. These two related sectors are dealt with in one section here because, at least in terms of public archaeology job opportunities and conditions, they have much in common. Most such organizations that fall into this grouping have a wide range of commitments that mean their staff almost inevitably multitask. For example, the United Kingdom's national amenity archaeological society, the Council for British Archaeology, is a non-profit educational charity, founded in 1943, with thousands of members spread across the United Kingdom, including many younger members through its subsidiary the Young Archaeologists' Club. Its membership is from all sectors of society, including professional and avocational archaeologists of all ages and backgrounds, and it has regional groups across the United Kingdom so that its members really can engage, meet likeminded people in their immediate area, and get out and about on archaeological sites. The organization has three strategic objectives:

- Participation: creating new opportunities for participation in and the popular audience of archaeology, promoting the development of skills and learning opportunities at a local level, especially for people under 25.
- Discovery: enabling and supporting research to advance knowledge of archaeology, providing a platform for the archaeological community to communicate and engage with others, and making new thinking in archaeological research accessible to non-specialist audiences.
- Advocacy: championing the role of the voluntary sector in archaeological research, campaigning to ensure that archaeology has a place in education and lifelong learning, and promoting care of the historic environment through key partnerships with the private sector, industry, and government (the organization also publishes the popular magazine *British Archaeology*).

Sadly, the opportunities to work for organizations such as the CBA are slim; with tight operating budgets in the best of times, the global recession of 2007 onwards seriously hurt this sector, and the ongoing geopolitical impacts of the coronavirus pandemic of 2020 onwards have exasperated such economic turmoil. Membership of such organizations always drops in such straitened times, as people choose to save money by not renewing their memberships of such organizations. In addition, the support of government and industry similarly declines in such circumstances, as investment income diminishes and spare capital for supporting community engagement dries up. Consequently, organizations such as these are, if anything, cutting rather than expanding the number of positions they offer, and increasingly are relying on either part-time or volunteer staff. This is especially so among local archaeological societies, the size of which has meant that they traditionally have extremely small budgets, too small to ever justify or employ full-time staff.

Figure 38. Public archaeology in action, part 4: Knole's volunteer archaeology team at work in the South Barracks in 2016, during the 'Inspired by Knole' Project (copyright National Trust/Nathalie Cohen 2021).

As noted earlier in this section, lifestyles and careers of individuals employed by archaeological outreach and wider heritage organizations are very similar in terms of public archaeology job opportunities and conditions. Organizations such as the National Trust and the National Trust for Scotland in the United Kingdom, the National Trust of Australia, and the National Trust for Historic Preservation in the United States all employ archaeologists alongside a range of other heritage professionals – often people with a first degree in archaeology who went on to specialize in these areas later on (see Figures 38 and 39). Perhaps the only significant difference is in the scale of these organizations and thus their relative impact on the job market. For example, the National Trust in Australia owns or manages more than 300 heritage places, has a volunteer workforce of 7,000, and employs about 350 people nationwide. It has more than 50,000 members and more than 1 million annual visitors to its properties. In comparison, the National Trust in the United Kingdom owns or manages more than 350 heritage places and more than 623,000 acres (970 square miles) of land, manages a volunteer workforce of more than 60,000, and employs about 10,000 people nationwide. It has nearly 6 million members. Consequently, the National Trust is both a major employer of heritage professionals (archaeological and otherwise) and a major training ground for

Figure 39. Public archaeology in action, part 5: Archaeologist Maggie Henderson during excavations in the Delos Garden, Sissinghurst, in 2019 (copyright National Trust/Nathalie Cohen 2021).

future such professionals. Many people begin their careers as National Trust volunteers before moving on into the professional sector – both within and beyond the organization – when they have formal qualifications to back up their experience. The author is now what is termed a 'Consultancy Manager' for the National Trust, leading an interdisciplinary team of heritage specialists working on sites and structures, places, and landscapes, across South East England. The sites range in date from prehistory to the late twentieth century (one site on the Isle of Wight literally includes everything from Bronze Age barrows to a former Cold War rocket-testing facility, all within a few minutes' walk of one another). The team includes archaeologists, building surveyors, conservators, curators, ecologists, planners, project managers, and woodlands specialists, to name but a few – a full range of all the skills required to care for environments both cultural and natural across the generations.

Archaeologists and other heritage professionals working for organizations such as the National Trust have a broad professional remit and a highly varied working life, liaising with local and central government authorities (as well as local heritage volunteer groups) in advance of and during works to heritage features under their care, writing project designs and influencing schemes of work, and in many cases leading or participating in fieldwork, analysis, and public archaeology promotion of sites. The organization also maintains for its own estate a version of the Historic Environment Records managed by local authorities, so there is a place also for specialists in this type of data management. Furthermore, akin to the archaeologists working for the Crown Estate, those working for the organization are also responsible for large stretches of coastline owned or managed by the organization, bringing with it the need for specialist survey skills and knowledge. In this sense, their jobs are something of a blend of the responsibilities of local government heritage officers, on one hand, and CRM archaeologists, on the other. They spend most of their days in an office environment, but nonetheless will undertake a significant amount of on-site work, doing visits to sites in advance of and during development, meeting CRM archaeologists employed, and speaking to different groups involved. However, archaeologists working for organizations such as the organization will also tend to work extremely closely with natural environment specialists such as biodiversity officers and ecologists, in the holistic management of all aspects of an environment, both historic and natural.

## Focus on: Shanti Pappu and Kumar Akhilesh (India)

We are Shanti Pappu [SP], the founder/secretary of the Sharma Centre for Heritage Education, India (SCHE, a non-profit organization established in 1999), and Kumar Akhilesh [KA], the director of the SCHE. Our centre undertakes research in archaeology and for public outreach in the field of Indian heritage. Since then, we have focused on research in areas of prehistory, palaeo-environments, experimental studies, and ethnoarchaeology in South India. We have been directing research projects, with a team of colleagues from India and abroad, at important sites such as Attirampakkam and Sendrayanpalayam in South India. KA is an expert lithic knapper, and we run experiments to investigate questions regarding lithic technologies at our sites. In addition, we have developed a children's museum, and we run regular outreach programs on archaeology for children, university students, teachers, and the community. These are delivered both in-house and as traveling modules that we have run in India, Sri Lanka, and South Korea. Our motto is to create, connect, and communicate, bridging gaps in terms of research knowledge and communicating the same to children and teachers.

[SP] My grandfather, Dr V. N. Sharma, and aunt, Gita Sharma, were educationists, and both were very interested in archaeology and brought it alive for me, right from my childhood. I was brought up in Kolkata, where a general interest in the past in books, music, and films was also a powerful influence. [KA] My influence stemmed from my studies at the Benaras Hindu University, where my teachers inspired me to study archaeology, shifting as I did from a science background. Overall, there were few opportunities other than museum or site visits as children, and that was a reason we developed our hands-on workshops in archaeology for children. Our MA and PhD degrees at the Deccan College were wonderful, with inspirations from great teachers, a marvellous library, and many interactions with archaeologists and other scientists from all over the world. Subsequently, we developed our own skills (e.g., KA in lithics, experimental knapping, and GIS) through attending workshops and practice, while learning a lot through interacting with people from diverse backgrounds.

[SP] I founded the SCHE soon after I completed my PhD, and although I recently served as Professor of Prehistory at the Deccan College, I resigned that position to focus on building our centre. I cannot say that I ever had a formal long-term university or other government job, the traditional areas of employment in India. [KA] I joined the SCHE as an intern, working with Prof. Pappu, and I have risen to become its director. I have never looked elsewhere for a job, as here I have the freedom and creativity needed for research, teaching, and public outreach. Being outside the traditional set-up of such organizations has its positive and negative sides. We have, however, always received licences to work from government bodies. Our colleagues have done their utmost to help build our collaborative research projects, with our results published in journals such as *Nature* and *Science*. We have always received grants (National Geographic, Leakey Foundation, Palarq, Earthwatch Institute, ISRO-GBP, etc.). Above all, our individual families have stood behind us throughout.

The best part of our job is the freedom and creative energy to develop our own research projects, shape the way we wish to plan, and execute the same in the field and lab. We spend at least four months of the year in the field (either surveying or in excavations), and the rest in the lab analysing our finds, primarily lithics. Of course, writing is essential, and we are currently working on a series of books based on our research in northern Tamil Nadu, South India. We like to constantly interact with our collaborators for various projects, and we seek new networks to improve our research output. We also devote a sizeable amount of time to public outreach through our workshops for children, teachers, and other students. This involves a lot of preparation and constant upgradation of our pedagogical approaches. We are currently upgrading our children's museum on prehistory, and we hope to complete that over the next few years. The rest of our time is spent in writing projects for the eternal task of raising grants to sustain our Institute and projects. Now, with the COVID-19 lockdown, we have moved some of this outreach online through our online *Down Ancient Trails* archaeology forum.

Our top tip for pursuing a career in archaeology is to persevere. In India, archaeology is a difficult profession to get into. Although it has a long and exciting history, jobs and funding are few, and we urgently require the expansion of these options for the future growth of the subject and for conservation. As in any discipline, one requires perseverance and a willingness to constantly grow and develop. A willingness to adopt an interdisciplinary perspective is also essential for knowledge growth. On our part, we have never sought high positions or recognition, or even traditional jobs, but took an alternate path, often traveling alone and in difficult circumstances. We have always emphasized the need to address research questions that interest us, and we try to resolve these to the best of our abilities and within our circumstances. We have tried to balance research with public outreach as this adds an additional meaning to our work, which would otherwise be trapped in 'ivory towers' of scientific journals.

We are committed to our research projects on prehistory in Southern India, where our excavations at several sites such as Attirampakkam and Sendrayanpalayam are changing our views on prehistoric adaptations, migrations, and palaeo-environments in this region. Our team of collaborating scientists are equally engaged in solving numerous questions in our study region that have importance for global debates in prehistory. We are really excited about these projects and our forthcoming books on this work. In addition, the need for creative outreach, especially in the field of prehistory, is, in our view, essential for long-term sustainable conservation of this rapidly vanishing heritage. That is also an area of great interest for us, and we hope to develop new hybrid programs (online and offline) in the coming years. We started our forum *Down Ancient Trails* to address this. We also look forward to developing more collaborations and internships at our centre, and of course to generate greater resources for research and public outreach. See www .sharmaheritage.com.

## Professional Archaeological Organizations

A small number of organizations around the world promote professionalism in archaeology through regulation of a corporate membership and creation of and adherence to codes of conduct and standards, with their members having to demonstrate, through submission of a portfolio and CV, that they possess appropriate skills, training, and experience.

Such organizations also undertake outreach and advocacy, and lobby government and industry for better standards and laws. In this light, they can be seen as public archaeology organizations. There are, however, few job opportunities in this subsector, as outreach in pure terms is not their main aim. The major UK organization, for example, the Chartered Institute for Archaeologists, employs a small core team assisting its 3,000 members. Most of these individuals' time is spent assisting current and potential new members rather than in outreach public archaeology. The closest most such officers come is in their liaison with existing heritage stakeholders, such as government, industry, and the avocational archaeological community, rather than the public, although organizations such as the CIfA are involved in archaeological advocacy alongside organizations such as the CBA.

## Archaeology and the Media

The starting point for this section is the following observation: no one goes into professional archaeology with the intention of becoming a media star. Although there are full-time TV presenters who regularly host archaeologically themed shows, none of these presenters is a professional archaeologist – in other words, they could not work as archaeologists for a CRM firm, university, or government department. Such individuals are professional TV presenters, not professional archaeologists – an important distinction. The follow-up to this is the point made earlier in this chapter: although a small number of archaeologists make some of their career in the media, without exception such individuals also have other – archaeological – jobs, as there is not enough constant work in TV alone to generate a regular or reliable income (see Figure 40). Indeed, such individuals' cachet to the audience comes from this authenticity – these are *understood* to be professional archaeologists with a wealth of experience to share with the viewers, and their value as presenters lies in that accumulated experience. This background experience is cited time and time again on the shows themselves and on associated websites and media. Thus, the only distinctive thing that differentiates these individuals from other archaeologists who are not on TV is their good luck to

Figure 40. Public archaeology in action, part 6: Archaeology makes good TV! Here, a journalist interviews project directors Andy Gardner and Peter Guest at the Priory Field excavation at Caerleon, south Wales, in mid 2010 (copyright Chris Waite/UCL Institute of Archaeology 2010, courtesy of Andrew Gardner).

get noticed by a TV producer/director, and their ability to be TV-friendly – a combination of charm and charisma, also possibly an appealing distinctive sartorial or personality trait or quirk. Above all else, such individuals must have a genuine ability to explain archaeology in a clear and accessible manner. Those working in TV archaeology generally found their way there by chance: they were either working on a site/project that an existing TV show decided to feature and ended up in that initial show – where if they did well, they often got invited to appear on other subsequent shows – or were approached by TV production companies on the basis of either a colleague's recommendation or their biography when the company went talent-hunting. Very occasionally such companies do put out a general call for new talent, but this is rare.

As noted earlier in this chapter, a much larger number of archaeologists are far more regularly involved in, and in some cases make an entire living from, work in either print or online media. Here there are both many more opportunities for individuals to become involved and clearer transferable skills that can be discussed. Above all, good written communication is a skill that *all* archaeologists should have and should constantly seek to improve. Good written skills make the reports, publications, and other documents that go out to not only the public but also policy makers, government officials, and funding organizations both effective and appealing. Badly written, dull reports do no one a favour and can even harm a site or project – they can lead to a decline public support or even a cessation of funding. Good writing also helps to sell individual archaeologists when they come to apply for new jobs with well-written packages of covering letter, CV, and supporting publications.

An ongoing – and expanding – success story in archaeological publishing is that of the popular magazine *Current Archaeology*. This was modestly begun by its founders (who are both still active in the business) Andrew and Wendy Selkirk literally from their kitchen table in 1967 as a 'popular periodical' for the general reader on archaeology, and the early editions are slim and simple, hand-produced in black and white, but still demonstrably high quality. The Selkirks built up a loyal following and impressive social network in archaeology long before archaeology became fashionable. Fast-forward fifty years, and the modern-day magazine is an impressive full-colour production of sixty-plus pages produced every month, together with allied online content. Over the years, the original magazine has been joined in a stable of related magazines produced by what evolved into 'Current publishing': *Current Archaeology* (the original magazine, focused on UK archaeology), *Current World Archaeology* (which takes a global scope on archaeology), *Military History Matters* (focused on military history, from prehistory to the present day), and *Minerva* (focused more on ancient arts and archaeology). What brings these magazines together is their shared ethos, which is that of their founders: to tell good archaeological stories, briskly and clearly, with excellent text and images, ideally because of physically visiting a project and speaking to its team. Over the years, these magazines' editorial teams have travelled hundreds of thousands of miles around the globe, speaking to thousands of individuals. And many of the names now famous in archaeology first appear in earlier editions of the magazine as

Figure 41. Public archaeology in action, part 7: Carly Hilts, the editor of *Current Archaeology* magazine, on a site visit at East Chisenbury Midden on the army training estate in Salisbury Plain, Wiltshire. The midden was excavated by Operation Nightingale, an initiative using archaeological fieldwork to aid the recovery of wounded service personnel, which features frequently in the pages of *Current Archaeology* (copyright Markus Milligan 2021).

enthusiastic young fieldworkers or writers. For the budding public and community archaeologist, *Current Archaeology* and *Current World Archaeology* are especially good products to read to get a sense of both the content and style of successful and engaging 'popular' magazines in the field (see Figure 41).

Writing for the media in the broadest sense is a sector worth considering and a skill worth acquiring, for entry-level and experienced archaeologists alike. For those already working in the field and with a track record of publication, this is less of a problem: they may well be asked to write a piece of text for a popular publication or choose to write an entire book. They may also be asked to review other people's books in the press or be interviewed about their work. For entry-level practitioners, there are still opportunities. Many of the archaeological and heritage organizations mentioned in this chapter have their own newsletters, journals, periodicals, and the like, and these accept unsolicited submissions for consideration, especially reports of recent projects, book reviews, or reviews of recent events, conferences, or symposia. Such works are a good way to build up experience of writing the types of clear and succinct work in which the mainstream media are interested. Such organizations also inevitably maintain websites where similar such work can be published. In addition, many such organizations have annual essay or report contests – some with financial or other prizes. These are excellent routes for archaeology students to pursue, and they offer good things to mention in CVs and job application letters. Since I wrote the first edition of this book in 2010, the opportunities for online engagement have also significantly increased. Numerous social media platforms have excellent archaeological content, some of it written on behalf of organizations, but much from individuals spread across the archaeological community around the world. On platforms such as Twitter and Instagram, the most successful producers generate significant interest in some wonderful content. Such platforms can be an excellent place to learn about archaeology, to share your love of archaeology with others, and to network.

## Museum Archaeologists

Museum-based archaeologists are in many ways very similar to the types of university-based archaeological specialists discussed in Chapter 4. Indeed, because many museums are affiliated with academic organizations, in some cases these are effectively the same groups (see Figure 42). Archaeologists who work in such organizations enjoy the same benefits as those of their university colleagues in terms of pay and conditions (plus, in some cases, additional benefits, such as free entry to their own and other museums), struggle in the same ways to pursue the few and highly sought-after jobs available, and, once in their positions, need to juggle the same types of responsibilities: administration and the pursuit of funding in grants and awards versus the more enjoyable processes of research and teaching. Such individuals also tend to need the same high levels of qualification to get positions – most museum-based archaeologists have one, if not several, higher degrees in archaeology, with many having PhDs, alongside extensive experience backed up by a good publication record.

The only significant differences between museum and university archaeologists lie in the audiences and the working environment. In closing this chapter, these are explored here:

* *Audiences*: Such archaeologists help design and curate both temporary and permanent displays, give talks and lectures to visitors, and write guidebooks for displays and their specialist subject fields. In this sense, their audiences and teaching environments are much wider than those of purely academic archaeologists: the latter will generally only be teaching undergraduate and postgraduate archaeology or related students, and so can present their data and arguments

Figure 42. Museum archaeology: Archaeological science and conservation play a central role in putting finds on display in museums. Here, Vanessa Saiz Gomez (UCL MSc Conservation of Archaeology and Museums student 2007–9) conducts a conservation assessment of an archaeological collection in a temporary fieldwork laboratory. (copyright Dean Sully/UCL Institute of Archaeology 2008).

at the higher intellectual level that such students are expected to be able to comprehend through supporting reading and research of their own. Academic archaeologists also generally teach through only a relatively narrow range of forms, primarily lectures, seminars, and small practical sessions. In contrast, museum archaeologists must present their work to a much wider range of audiences whose age, experience, and familiarity with archaeology may vary widely. Such archaeologists also must present their work through many different media – through displays of objects and associated texts; talks, gallery guides, and lectures to visitors; and guidebooks.

- *Working conditions*: Many museum-based archaeologists undertake, along with their other duties, research-based fieldwork akin to that of academic archaeologists. However, the primary workplace of most museum archaeologists is, obviously, a museum, so their working environment varies more widely from that of most academic archaeologists, including work in both public and private spaces – from the public galleries and exhibition halls of the museum to its storage, laboratory, and office areas. Museum archaeologists' working schedules also tend to be more flexible than those of academic archaeologists, being less closely tied to the academic calendar. Peak times for museum visits – the school holidays, in particular, the summer holidays – can cause pressures on workload; these are often the periods when the greatest number of staff are needed in the museum but, paradoxically, are also often the best times to undertake fieldwork, especially in collaboration with university colleagues for whom the summer is the primary research period of each year.

Working alongside museum archaeologists (and often sharing similar backgrounds, training, and skill sets) is a wide array of other museum-based heritage professionals. This sector of the heritage profession is so distinctive, so extensive, and ultimately so different from archaeology that it cannot be addressed in detail here; this is the subject of an entirely different book by a professional with experience in that field, not this author – see Schlatter's (2008) *Museum Careers* for a start. However, to give an indication of some of the skills and so training involved, such jobs include the following issues:

- *Business and marketing*: Modern museums, even small ones, are run like businesses. This involves people with business management skills, including financial and personnel management experience, and also involves a people with varied marketing skills – including public relations experience promoting museums and experience with producing marketing materials, flyers, posters, websites, and the like.
- *Conservation*: The immediate-term stabilization of historic materials (especially newly excavated archaeological materials) and the long-term conservation of these materials are a highly specialized and technical concern requiring years of training at the postgraduate level, extensive practice, and constant professional development as new techniques emerge. Modern heritage conservation facilities include laboratories to match the best of those found in scientific research facilities around the world, and they use an incredible array of tools and techniques drawn from dozens of different industries. Equipment includes tools for scanning, monitoring, and analysing the make-up and stability of different objects (including medical-grade scanners); different chemicals and machinery for cleaning, stabilizing, and conserving materials (including special types of drying and freezing facilities); and much else. Such facilities can cost hundreds of thousands or even millions per year to run; some of the best facilities are world-renowned, with rare objects being flown in from across the globe to be conserved.
- *Curation and display*: Once materials have been conserved, they need to be displayed. Displays must meet the sometimes-conflicting needs of visibility, on one hand, and long-term object stability, on the other. Many objects, for example, are best stored in conditions of very low light and humidity, but those are not the best conditions for the public to view the materials, and these can be difficult and expensive environments to maintain. Display issues also involve questions of providing sufficient supporting information – be this as text or multimedia – to visitors without overwhelming them with data and also involve even more ostensibly simple issues such as the appropriate use of fonts, colour schemes, and design layout. In a small museum or display this is complex enough; in major international museums with millions of visitors viewing hundreds of thousands of objects, this becomes an industry in and of itself.

239

- *Interpretation*: Working in relation to the preceding display issues, interpretation issues mean both making decisions on the immediate text/media of a display and influencing wider issues of additional interpretation – providing additional information/educational facilities and opportunities for a range of visitors of different ages, backgrounds, experience, and nationalities. Interpretation issues vary widely, from dealing with how many directional signs to place in a building and in how many languages, or how many restroom facilities to provide, to how to introduce a complex series of archaeological finds simultaneously to everyone from age eight to eighty-eight.
- *Legal/ethical issues*: Many museums have materials drawn from around the world. In some cases, especially for long-established museums, some materials they hold may have been obtained hundreds of years ago under terms that would never be allowed in the modern world. The most famous example of this is the ongoing claim by Greece for the return of the Parthenon Marbles (sometimes referred to as the Elgin Marbles) taken from the Parthenon in Athens between 1801 and 1812, and on display in the British Museum in London. A less well-known but as emotive an issue is the example of the thousands of skeletal remains of Indigenous peoples held in museums around the world that were taken for scientific study in the nineteenth and twentieth centuries, which numerous communities are now lobbying to have returned. The legal and ethical issues surrounding the ownership and possible return of such materials are a major concern of many modern museum archaeologists. So too are questions of more recent acquisitions, including issues of proving authenticity and the ethical rights and wrongs of materials on sale on the international antiquities market. For example, the second Gulf War that commenced in 2003 has led to thousands of objects stolen from Iraqi museums or looted from archaeological sites in the country coming onto the international antiquities market. Work in this field is undertaken by a variety of specialists – not just archaeologists, but also lawyers and art historians and even scientists involved in the dating and identification of provenance and origin of materials.

## Focus on: Hsiao Mei Goh (Australia)

I am Hsiao Mei Goh, and I am a Post-Doctoral Researcher at the University of New South Wales, Sydney, Australia. My current research focuses on under-standing the early prehistoric peopling of the Asia Pacific, with a particular interest in prehistoric diet shifts and early human behavioural signatures in Mainland and Island Southeast Asia over the past 50,000 years.

I have been fascinated with ancient history and the prehistoric world since a young age. However, it was not until I was at university that I had a chance to be directly involved in archaeology, studying it as part of my undergraduate programme. Later, I pursued an MA and PhD in archaeology, and I began to work as an archaeological researcher after I graduated. My postgraduate studies were mainly focused on the prehistoric culture of the cave during the late

Pleistocene and Holocene, and I received a lot of training in different fields, including in field archaeology (e.g., excavation and survey), speleology, and karst hydrogeology.

I started my career as a full-time academic, teaching and researching in a university in Malaysia after I graduated from my PhD. After spending almost five years in Malaysia, I transitioned into my current role at the University of New South Wales, with a stronger focus on archaeological research and outreach. My previous working experience and collaboration network in Southeast Asia helped me get my current role, as my projects require me to work closely with the local stakeholders and communities across different parts of Southeast Asia.

My working routine can be broadly divided into three parts: running laboratory analyses, writing, and working in the field. Each year I will spend approximately three to four months working in the field for data collection, and a big chunk of my time will be used for data processing and writing. In terms of my average week, I will spend one day attending meetings and discussions with my supervisor, and the rest of the week will be distributed among laboratory work, writing, student supervision, and undertaking outreach work. I think the best thing about my current role is that my team members are very dynamic and each of them has different expertise that allows us to develop and collaborate on many exciting projects.

My top tip for pursuing a career in archaeology is to be resilient and possess an aptitude to learn new skills. These are the two fundamental skills/qualities for pursuing a career in archaeology. As many of you may be aware, the career prospects of an archaeologist are not great, and to keep myself employed in this field I have had to be self-motivated and persistent. The aptitude for learning new skills is essential. Given that archaeology is a dynamic field, I have picked up new skills to champion different research projects. Of course, excellent interpersonal communication skills are critical too, as it is essential to develop a good relationship with students, collaborators, stakeholders, and a community drawn from diverse backgrounds.

I am a strong advocate of community archaeology, as I believe that diversifying the voices in the interpretation of the past will result in a better archaeological understanding among society and, at the same time, make archaeology more integrated and socially relevant. Over the past five years, I have developed a few community heritage projects; more details can be accessed at www .youtube.com/watch?v=aosw8EWc9YU and www.youtube.com/watch?v= wU8HQagwnig.

# Conclusion
## Archaeology for All

Archaeology offers tremendous opportunities for involvement, alongside another career or a career in itself. It is never too late to become involved in archaeology, and children grasp the inherent pleasures of the subject as well as any adult – who does not like a pursuit that so uniquely combines both mental and physical exercise? Archaeology transcends borders and cultures, languages and dialects, social and economic divisions – anyone, anywhere can become involved in archaeology if they wish to, and the opportunities to become involved improve all the time. All that involvement requires is your own decision to become an active participant – and if you are reading this book, you have already taken that decision. Here, then, are some suggested second steps.

## Top Ten Tips for Budding Archaeologists

*Explore*: The best way to get involved in archaeology is to find out what opportunities for participation are available in your own neighbourhood, through your local archaeology or history society or club, national organizations or local government, schools or universities. There are talks, walks, guides, and events nearly every week around the world. There are also hundreds of opportunities every year to obtain more formal training in archaeological techniques and become involved in actual fieldwork. Many events are free, and even the ones that cost are rarely all that expensive. Archaeologists are well aware that people do not have that much money to spare, and they fight to keep costs of such events to a minimum. Membership in local or national archaeology organizations is similarly cheap and is an extremely good value – membership brings you into contact with like-minded people in your neighbourhood and provides access to information and resources such as newsletters and magazines, events, and even library facilities. Some useful Internet links to get you started in your explorations are listed in Appendix A of this book.

*Read*: There are many excellent archaeology magazines now available, often from high-street retailers rather than specialist vendors, or through online platforms. These are a quick and enjoyable way to find out more about archaeology. Imagine how much more interesting your daily commute could become if, rather than your local newspaper, you are reading a magazine about someone exploring a new archaeological site. There are also many excellent introductory books on the basics, origins, and practice of archaeology – mostly published in paperback, cheap to buy, and easily purchased.

*Watch*: The chances are that if you are interested in getting more involved in archaeology, you are already doing this – there are so many good TV shows on archaeology these days, as well as online videos, webcasts, and podcasts, that these have become the main entry point for budding archaeologists. But just in case you have not been watching these, then start! Not all archaeologists like all these shows, and as your knowledge of archaeology increases then you will rapidly begin to differentiate for yourself between the good and the bad programs in terms of the quality of the archaeology done and the validity of some of the claims. Nonetheless, many of these shows do a great job of introducing key concepts, ideas, and sites that are central to archaeology.

*Listen*: As noted previously, there are talks, walks, guides, and events about archaeology nearly every week around the world, and most of these events are free or very cheap. There are also countless podcasts and audiobooks on archaeology now available. A great place to look beyond your local archaeology society or club is your local university archaeology, anthropology, or history department: most have weekly talks scheduled by staff and visiting scholars. Although primarily designed for students and staff, visitors are normally welcome by prior arrangement, and such events are usually advertised on departmental home pages. Going to events such as these is a great way to meet real archaeologists and like-minded people.

*Talk*: Archaeologists are friendly people who love their subject. They want to tell other people about their work and to help them to get involved. Never be afraid to look up archaeologists who work in your neighbourhood and ask them for advice on how to participate. They may not be able to help you themselves, but they will know other people who can help you and be able to put you in contact with them. A good starting point is either your local archaeology society or your local government archaeologist – both can be searched for online. If these people cannot help you, then your local university archaeology department should be able to help.

For those of you interested in taking the next step, considering not only becoming involved in archaeology but possibly pursuing a career as an archaeologist, the next five steps are especially for you.

*Plan*: Start out by asking yourself what you want out of archaeology – do you really want a career as an archaeologist, to earn a living doing this? Or do you simply want to become more involved in fieldwork? Understand the implications of a career in archaeology from the outset – long years of training, limited job opportunities, low pay, and often short employment contracts – and place this against your other personal aspirations and commitments. Talk about your aspirations with your family and what this lifestyle might mean for them, and be realistic – if you have always wanted a big house and a luxury car in your driveway, then archaeology really is not the career for you. Once you have come to a decision, plan what you need to do to make a start in your career regarding training, experience, and contacts.

*Train*: Realistically, a professional career in archaeology begins at university. You might not like to hear this, but there it is. Without a university degree in archaeology or anthropology, you are seriously harming your chances of getting any job in the discipline, let alone advancing your career as a professional. So if you are serious about a career, find out what qualifications you need to get into such a university degree programme, find out what university you would like to attend, and apply for a place. Remember, in particular, that it is never too late to do this – universities have students with an incredibly diverse array of backgrounds, ages, nationalities, and experience.

*Develop skills*: Archaeologists who do well in their careers have multiple skills and fields of expertise. As Charles Darwin was alleged to have once stated: 'It is not the strongest of the species that survives, nor the most intelligent that survives. It is the one that is the most adaptable to change.' Multiple skills and specialties make you the most adaptable to change, the most able to apply for the largest number of jobs. This means both archaeological and non-archaeological skills, experience, and expertise. For those already at work who are considering a mid-career move into archaeology in particular, it is well worth making a list of what you do in your current job, what skills you have already, and seeing how these skills might apply to archaeology. Membership in professional organizations such as the CIfA, RPA, and AACAI in any case necessitates evidence of continuing professional development throughout a career, evidence of training of your own and as provided by your employer.

*Volunteer*: There are more archaeologists out there than available jobs – supply exceeds demand. Beyond expanding their training, skills, and expertise, successful archaeologists volunteer to do things that make them, and their CVs, stand out, that provide opportunities for networking, publication, and self-promotion. Early in any career this means volunteering to work, often unpaid (but hopefully with at least some costs covered) on projects – both the exciting fieldwork components of any project and the much less glamorous but equally important pre- and post-excavation phases; planning the project, cleaning, recording, investigating, and conserving finds; and writing up notes and reports. More experienced archaeologists who can get jobs that perhaps pay them to do these tasks still usually volunteer in other ways – serving on local or national archaeological organizations' committees, editing newsletters and journals, writing conference and book reviews, organizing events and symposia, and so forth. All these different volunteer activities can be seen on the CVs of successful archaeologists and distinguish them from their peers. By volunteering, such archaeologists have also been busy networking – making informal links and contacts with people, getting known as friendly, efficient, and trustworthy, being the people others want to work with and employ.

*Persevere*: Finally, do not be afraid or dismayed if at first you do not seem to be getting anywhere. Everyone who has ever ended up with a job in archaeology, from the lowliest digger to the most senior professor, has hit a low at some point, when they wonder if they will ever get work and whether so many struggles are worth it. Struggle and disappointment are part of this lifestyle. If you cannot handle rejection – for jobs, grant applications, or article and book proposals – then get out now. Similarly, learn to accept constructive criticism: archaeology is too big and complex a subject for any one person to know all the answers – there is always something new to learn and some other opinion that can be of significance. When they have a bad day, most archaeologists simply take a deep breath and then get a good night's rest. The next day they get back to work.

# Appendix A

# Useful Websites

## Chapter 1: What Is – and Isn't – Archaeology?

American Anthropological Association: www.aaanet.org/

American Archaeological Conservancy: www.americanarchaeology.com/

American Society for Amateur Archaeology: http://asaa-persimmonpress.com/

Archaeological Institute of America: www.archaeological.org/

Archaeology Scotland: www.archaeologyscotland.org.uk/

Australian Archaeological Association: www.australianarchaeologicalassociation .com.au/

Council for British Archaeology: www.britarch.ac.uk/

Council for Independent Archaeology: www.independents.org.uk/

Discovering the Archaeologists of Europe: http://discovering-archaeologists.eu/

International Council on Monuments and Sites: www.international.icomos.org/ home.htm

RESCUE: The British Archaeological Trust: www.rescue-archaeology.org.uk/

Save Britain's Heritage: www.savebritainsheritage.org/

Society for American Archaeology: www.saa.org/

Society for Historical Archaeology: www.sha.org/

UNESCO: www.unesco.org/new/en/unesco/

World Archaeological Congress: www.worldarchaeologicalcongress.org/

## Chapter 2: Skills and Training in Archaeology

Advisory Council on Underwater Archaeology: www.acuaonline.org/

American Anthropological Association student webpage: www.aaanet.org/resources/students/

American Cultural Resources Association: http://acra-crm.org/

Archaeological Institute of America Guide to Local Societies: www.archaeological.org/societies

Archaeology Abroad: www.britarch.ac.uk/archabroad/

Archaeology Training Forum: www.britarch.ac.uk/training/atf.html

Archaeology Volunteer Opportunities: www.archaeologyfieldwork.com/forums/viewforum.php?f=4

Australasian Institute of Maritime Archaeology: http://aima.iinet.net.au/

Australian Association of Consulting Archaeologists Inc.: www.aacai.com.au/

British Archaeological Jobs and Resources: www.bajr.org/

Institute for Archaeologists: www.archaeologists.net/

Nautical Archaeology Society: www.nasportsmouth.org.uk/

Register of Professional Archaeologists: www.rpanet.org/

Society for American Archaeology Careers Center: https://careers.saa.org/

Training Online Resource Centre for Archaeology: www.torc.org.uk/

Young Archaeologists' Club: www.yac-uk.org/

## Chapter 3: Cultural Resource Management

Archdiggers Portal: www.archdiggers.co.uk/

British Archaeological Jobs and Resources: www.bajr.org/

Federation of Archaeological Managers and Employers: www.famearchaeology.co.uk/

Shovelbums: www.shovelbums.org/

Tom King's CRM Plus blog: http://crmplus.blogspot.com/

## Chapter 4: Academic Archaeology

*The Chronicle of Higher Education*: http://chronicle.com/

*Times Higher Educational Supplement*: www.timeshighereducation.co.uk/

# Chapter 5: Local and State Government Archaeology

Association of Gardens Trusts: http://gardenstrusts.org.uk/new/index.asp

Association of Local Government Archaeological Officers: www.algao.org.uk/

Building Conservation Directory: www.buildingconservation.com/

Campaign to Protect Rural England: www.cpre.org.uk/home

Garden History Society: www.gardenhistorysociety.org/

Heritage Gateway (for HERs): www.heritage-gateway.org.uk/

Institute of Historic Building Conservation: www.ihbc.org.uk/

Jobs Go Public: www.jobsgopublic.com

National Association of State Archaeologists: www.uiowa.edu/~osa/nasa/

National Association of Tribal Historic Preservation Officers: www.nathpo.org/mainpage.html

National Conference of State Historic Preservation Officers: www.ncshpo.org/find/index.htm

Portable Antiquities Scheme: www.finds.org.uk/

Royal Town Planning Institute: www.rtpi.org.uk/

Society for the Protection of Ancient Buildings: www.spab.org.uk/

# Chapter 6: Central and Federal Government Archaeology

Advisory Council on Historic Preservation: www.achp.gov/

Archaeological Survey of India: www.india.gov.in/official-website-archaeological-survey-india

BOEM: www.boem.gov/

Cadw: www.cadw.wales.gov.uk/

Canadian Environmental Assessment Agency: www.ceaa.gc.ca/

Crown Estate: www.thecrownestate.co.uk/

Department of Agriculture, Water and the Environment (DAWE), Australia: www.awe.gov.au/

English Heritage: www.english-heritage.org.uk/

Fundação Nacional do Indio (Brazil): www.gov.br/funai/pt-br

Heritage New Zealand Pouhere Taonga: www.heritage.org.nz/

Historic England: https://historicengland.org.uk/

Historic Environment Scotland: www.historicenvironment.scot/

Historic Sites and Monuments Board of Canada: www.pc.gc.ca/clmhc-hsmbc/

Instituto Nacional de Antropología e Historia (Mexico): www.inah.gob.mx/

Instituto do Patrimônio Histórico e Artístico Nacional (Brazil): www.iphan.gov.br/
montarPaginaInicial.do;jsessionid=5F32513B5622FE28CB99B9FD1E3AFE9F

Ministry of Culture of Russia: http://government.ru/en/department/27/

National Administration of Cultural Heritage (China): www.sach.gov.cn/

National Oceanographic and Atmospheric Administration: www.noaa.gov/

National Park Service archaeology program: www.nps.gov/archeology/

Naval History and Heritage Command (formerly the Naval Historical Center):
www.history.navy.mil/

Northern Ireland Environment Agency: www.ni-environment.gov.uk/

Parks Australia: https://parksaustralia.gov.au/

Parks Canada: www.pc.gc.ca/

Royal Commission on the Ancient and Historical Monuments of Scotland:
www.rcahms.gov.uk/

South African Heritage Resources Agency: www.sahra.org.za/

UNESCO: http://portal.unesco.org

US Army Corps of Engineers: www.usace.army.mil

US Bureau of Indian Affairs: www.bia.gov

US Department of Agriculture, Natural Resources Conservation Service
Cultural Resources Division: www.nrcs.usda.gov/technical/cultural.html

US Department of Transportation Federal Highway Administration, Historic
Preservation Division: http://environment.fhwa.dot.gov/histpres/index.asp

US Department of Veterans Affairs, Historic Preservation Division: www.cfm.va
.gov/historic/

US Fish and Wildlife Service, Historic Preservation Division: www.fws.gov/
historicpreservation/

US Forest Service Heritage Programs: www.fs.fed.us/recreation/programs/
heritage/

US National NAGPRA Guidance: www.nps.gov/history/nagpra/

## Chapter 7: Public and Community Archaeology

American Anthropological Association: www.aaanet.org/

The Archaeology Channel: www.archaeologychannel.org/

*Archaeology Magazine*: www.archaeology.org/

Association of Preservation Trusts: www.ukapt.org.uk/

Australian Archaeological Association: www.australianarchaeologicalassociation
.com.au/

*British Archaeology* (magazine): www.britarch.ac.uk/ba/

Council for British Archaeology: www.britarch.ac.uk/

*Current Archaeology* (magazine): www.archaeology.co.uk/

Historic Houses Association: www.hha.org.uk/

International Council of Museums: http://icom.museum/

Museum Association: www.museumsassociation.org

Museum Jobs: www.museumjobs.com

*National Geographic* (magazine): www.nationalgeographic.com/

National Trust: www.nationaltrust.org.uk/

National Trust of Australia: www.nationaltrust.org.au/

National Trust for Historic Preservation: www.preservationnation.org/

Nautical Archaeology Society: www.nasportsmouth.org.uk/

*Past Horizons* (magazine): www.pasthorizons.com/

Portable Antiquities Scheme: www.finds.org.uk/

RESCUE: The British Archaeological Trust: www.rescue-archaeology.org.uk/

Save Britain's Heritage: www.savebritainsheritage.org/

Sierra Club: www.sierraclub.org/

*Smithsonian Magazine*: www.smithsonianmag.com/

Society for American Archaeology: www.saa.org/

Society for Historical Archaeology: www.sha.org/

University of Leicester Museum Jobs Desk: www.le.ac.uk/ms/jobs/jobs/htm

# Appendix B

# Suggested Equipment to Take on an Archaeological Project

Please exercise your own judgment in deciding what to take from the following. This is an exhaustive list of things that the author has used in extremely varied circumstances around the world – but if the project you are going on is a fifteen-minute drive from your home, much of this equipment is superfluous. Some of this equipment may also be provided by the project itself, so the golden rule is: *check first*. Do not be afraid to ask what equipment is appropriate to bring and what behaviours you will be expected to meet. Better to ask before you go than to get there and find that you should have brought some essential equipment, or the project is not what you expected.

## Things to Do before You Go on Fieldwork

- Speak to the project director and ensure that you have been given specific guidance on any equipment that you might need to bring and/or any special circumstances of the project. This should include details of any vaccinations that you need to get in advance of the project, as well as details of any personal health, equipment, or travel insurance that you might need to take out in relation to the project. Ensure, above all else, that any questions you might have about any aspect of the project are answered. This is also the time to be introduced to expected behaviours on site and the project's code of conduct. If such advice and guidance is not given, then ask for it – and if having asked for it, none is forthcoming, then this is a massive red flag that ought to cause you and all participants concern about being involved in such a project at all.

- Get from the project director details of the project's precise location and address (both of the fieldwork itself and any off-site accommodation), and ensure that you leave a copy with a family member/relative/close personal friend and that this includes emergency contact details such as the project director's mobile phone number, so that in an emergency a message can be delivered to you and/or someone can come and find you.
- Provide the project director with any medical or other personal information that might have an impact on your participation in the project – such as any underlying health issues that you experience or any allergies you have.
- Ensure that you have any vaccinations required for the location and duration of the project – and a record of these to take with you.
- Ensure that you have any personal insurance necessary in place – especially medical and/or travel insurance – and a record of this to take with you. This might include ensuring that your home building/contents insurance covers your prolonged absence if no one else will be living there while you are away (some insurers cover a property being vacant only for up to twenty-eight days at a time).
- Ensure that you receive from the project director precise instructions about travel arrangements and timing to and from the project, and your responsibilities in this. If it is your responsibility to arrange travel to and from the site, make sure that you have done so; if the project is taking care of this, be sure to know where you need to be at what times, and ideally also who some of your fellow travellers are in advance. Think especially about airport transfers – how you will transfer to and from the nearest airport to the site, especially if this is very remote.

## General Items

- *Identity information*: passport, driver's license, and other important documents. It is a good idea to take digital photos of all these documents in case you lose them.
- *Banking necessities*: credit and/or debit card and cash. When working beyond your home country, it is also well worth bringing a modest sum of cash both in the local currency and in an easily exchanged foreign currency such as US dollars.
- *Contact essentials*: mobile phone, charger, and charge adaptor, or an external power source like a solar charger (check that your service provider covers the area you are going to and the costs of calls in and out – some phone companies charge you for receiving a call overseas); also a list of key addresses and phone numbers written down elsewhere (so you have these even if your phone breaks or is stolen). This should include a clearly labelled emergency contacts section listing the contacts you would like notified in an emergency.
- *Guidebook and phrase book for the places you will be visiting/working in, and a map of the immediate area of the site*: a little politeness goes a long way, so memorize at least some basic polite phrases before you arrive and learn about local social conventions of behaviour and dress.

# Archaeological Equipment

At an absolute minimum, you should bring along the following personal equipment:

- Four-inch solid forged pointing trowel (WHS brand in the United Kingdom; Marshalltown in the United States).
- One-metre folding ruler.
- Ten-metre retracting tape measure.
- Notebook.
- Drawing kit: pens, pencils, eraser, paper, etc.
- Carry-bag, box, or other container in which to carry this material.

Your project director should advise you of any additional personal archaeological equipment that you would be expected to provide.

*When advised in advance*, you may also need to provide specific health and safety equipment, including:

- Protective boots (with steel or Kevlar toecaps).
- A protective hard hat.
- A high-visibility vest, jacket, and/or trousers.
- Protective eye and ear covers, also in some cases protective dust masks.
- Protective gloves.

# General Clothing

- Comfortable, flexible, hard-wearing clothes appropriate to the location and climate you will be working in. Jeans are fine in many places, but they can be uncomfortable when they get soaking wet and take a long time to dry, so these are to be avoided on some sites; low-cut or short-sleeved tops will cause offence in some countries, and are also not a good idea in very sunny places where you need to protect yourself from sunburn; military sourced or stylized clothing or equipment is also to be avoided in many counties because of political sensitivities; so too are clothes with political slogans or jokes on them. Common choices are simple, plain-coloured cotton shirts, T-shirts, and trousers. These are cheap, comfortable, easy to wash, and quick drying.
- Comfortable socks and simple underwear: bear in mind that you may have to wash these yourself in a public place: think twice about racy designs or cuts. Women may also wish to bring sports bras as a more comfortable alternative if the project is likely to involve a lot of walking around or very heavy work.
- Smarter casual clothes for the evenings/weekends/travel.
- Swimwear (if anywhere near a beach, pool, and the like).

# Footwear

- Boots for daily wear: steel toecap if advised by the site director, and/or weather-proof ankle boots for general use.

- Sneakers or athletic shoes for off-site wear.
- Sandals or flip-flops for evening/beach wear.

Some projects in very wet locations – pretty much anywhere in the United Kingdom, for one – may also mean that a pair of Wellington or rubber knee-high boots is a good addition.

## Outerwear (Situation Dependent)

- The best quality waterproof jacket, over-trousers, and hat you can buy – ideally again not in military colours such as camouflage. Good waterproof outerwear is particularly worth investing in – the quality stuff is tough, durable, and breathable and will last for years if you care for it.
- Sun hat, sunglasses, and sunscreen (of a high SPF factor).
- Scarf: warm for cold weather, thin and light for the sun and heat. The keffiyeh/ shemagh scarf is popular in many countries, as it can be tied in different configurations and used for many more things than as just a head covering, although it does have political connotations in many locations around the world, and so can be a culturally sensitive thing to wear.
- A light windproof jacket and/or pullover/sweater/jumper/sweatshirt for evenings – a good compromise are synthetic fleeces.
- Gloves and hat: warm and waterproof for the cold, suitably wide-brimmed and secure for the sun. On very rocky/stony/thorny sites, some people also choose to wear lightweight protective gloves of the type that can be purchased at hardware or gardening stores; similarly, wearable knee protectors bought from the same location can be useful on such sites.

## Health and Hygiene

All this should be capable of being packed down into a small, portable, waterproof bag, except for the towel.

- Towel (ideally, two: a larger bath towel and a smaller hand towel).
- Washing and grooming kit including nailbrush, soap, shampoo, deodorant, and so forth, plus a nail file and clippers – dirty and torn fingernails are an occupational hazard. A small mirror, ideally one of the unbreakable sort, is also a useful addition here. Many people – of any gender – also do not bother to shave on projects, but this is a personal choice. If you cannot imagine not shaving, then be sure to pack your standard shaving kit – and ensure if so that you take a mirror with you.
- Makeup (if that is your thing).
- Travel sickness medications (if necessary).
- Insect repellent (and in some circumstances, a personal mosquito net).
- No-water antibacterial gel hand wash and/or wet wipes.

- Spare/emergency toilet paper/tissue (pocket tissues are a handy and flexible compromise).
- Sanitary products for women; for excellent guidance on menstrual care in the field, see the 'Seeing Red' initiative at https://mentorwomxn.org/2020/06/05/seeing-red/.
- Spectacles, contact lenses, and spares of these if you need them, plus cleaning and storage materials (plus a copy of your current prescription that can be used to make you a new pair if your main and spares both get broken, lost, or stolen). If you are going somewhere very sunny and do not already own a pair, prescription sunglasses are a worthwhile investment.
- Contraceptive devices (if that is your thing; however, condoms can be used in an emergency, for example, to provide a waterproof cover for small pieces of electronic equipment).
- Personal first aid kit (containing disposable gloves and aprons, antibacterial swabs, various sizes of bandages/plasters, tweezers, safety pins, and so on). A useful addition to this pack is an emergency whistle (the no-ball ones that work anywhere, even in the water) and a foil emergency space blanket.
- Personal medications, such as allergy medicines, EpiPens, and insulin, as well as over-the-counter painkillers and throat/cough medications). *You must clearly label prescription medications as to what the products are, who prescribed them, to whom they belong, and how they are to be administered. You may also need to bring along a letter from the prescribing physician explaining their use, and/or have formal, written permission from the embassy of the nation you are visiting to carry medications into the country.*

## Miscellaneous Equipment

- Rucksack sufficiently big to carry everything in, but not too big that you cannot personally carry it.
- A tough, waterproof day pack – big enough for all your daily essentials, including for travel to and from the project, but as small as you can make it given what you need to carry.
- Plug adaptor for the location(s) you will be visiting.
- Spare AA and AAA batteries and batteries of other sizes for any electronic equipment you might be bringing.
- Different sizes of strong, reusable, zip-lock bags (useful for spare kit and to keep things dry).
- Disposable cigarette lighter: even if you do not smoke, lighters have many potential uses. If you are a smoker, ask the project director before you join about site rules for smoking and the local laws and social conventions in the community that is hosting you. If in doubt – don't smoke!
- A roll of heavy-duty trash/rubbish bags (useful for spare kit and to keep things dry).
- Waterproof watch with alarm setting.
- Compass (and the knowledge how to use it properly, both with and without the aid of a map), especially if you will be in a remote location.

- Camera plus spare batteries and memory cards.
- Unbreakable, lightweight water bottle; in some circumstances an unbreakable, lightweight mug, plate, bowl, and cutlery may also be required.
- Penknife/multitool (remember to pack this in your check-in luggage, not your carry-on, if you are flying).
- Flashlight plus spare batteries. Head lamps are a useful choice on badly lit sites or where there is no power/lighting, allowing you to keep your hands free.
- Ear plugs and eye mask (to enable sound sleeping).
- A ball of strong string (endless uses).
- Bungee cords (useful for tying things on to other things and tying things on to vehicles).
- A roll of duct tape: the strong, usually silver-coloured, reinforced tape (useful for mending nearly anything).
- Fun books to read, such as paperback novels that you do not care about and so can swap or throw in the trash.
- Snacks, sweets, chocolate, candy, etc. – fieldwork is tough and tiring, and while site catering is likely to be generous, most people will at some time want a favourite tasty snack or sweet, chocolate or candy bar. Not all sites are close to any facilities that sell such things, so bring along a decent stash of whatever you most imagine craving when you're starving hungry between meals.

Between the writing and editing of the first and second editions of this book, the availability and popularity of personal electronic devices has soared. This includes laptops, tablets, smart phones and e-books, as well as smart watches and similar wearable tech. Providing the best advice on whether to bring such valuables to a site is difficult. Most of us cannot imagine living without one or more of these devices for any length of time – but they are portable, valuable and as such, at risk of theft. The conditions experienced on many archaeological sites are also not ideal for sensitive electronics – copious mud, dust and dirt, cycles of wetting and drying, and extremes of heating and cooling are all things that can easily break them. Before any project commences, ask for advice from the project director about the safety and wisdom of bringing such kit to a particular site, whether there are secure places to store valuables, and if need be, either leave such equipment at home, or protect it with weather-resistant cases, bags and suchlike.

## Things Not to Do or Bring

There is no such thing as a stupid question, and no such thing as too obvious a warning. Please do not even think about bringing the following things onto a site:

- Drugs of any kind or alcohol, except when permission to bring the latter *has been explicitly given in advance by the project director.*
- Weapons of any kind.
- Pornography.

- Political and/or religious documents, magazines, books, and other media, including clothes with any related slogans on them, or any rude or crude statements or images on them. This includes copies of any sacred texts. These materials may well be precious to you, but they may cause offence to others, including the police, immigration, and other government officials with whom you may come into contact. Like all precious things, these items are thus best kept safely at home.
- Anything that you value too much to want to risk losing – a prized heirloom, piece of jewellery, and so on.

This is also a good place to reiterate Smith and Burke's (2007: 119) guide, "What Not to Do at a Site":

- Do not interfere with the site in any way.
- Do not collect souvenirs.
- Do not leave rubbish behind.
- Do not make details of the site public without obtaining the proper permissions first.

Above all else, think about the communities you are living and working among. Act with the utmost respect for all people, showing interest in and due regard to local customs, and adapting your own behaviours accordingly.

# References

Adams, R. (ed.). 2001. *Implementing the Native American Graves Protection and Repatriation Act*. American Association of Museums.

Agbe-Davies, A. 2002. Black Scholars, Black Pasts, *SAA Archaeological Record* 2(4): 24–28.

Agbe-Davies, A. 2003. Conversations: Archaeology and the Black Experience, *Archaeology* 56(1): 22.

Agnew, N., and Demas, M. 2004. *Principles for the Conservation of Heritage Sites in China*. Getty Conservation Institute.

Aitchison, K. 2012. *Breaking New Ground: How Professional Archaeology Works*. Landward Research.

Aitchison, K. (ed.). 2014. Special Issue: Discovering the Archaeologists of the World, *Archaeologies: The Journal of the World Archaeological Congress* 10(3). Springer, https://link .springer.com/journal/11759/10/3.

Aitchison, K. 2019. *State of the Archaeological Market 2018*, https://landward.eu/wp-content/ uploads/2019/03/Archaeological-Market-Survey-2017-18.pdf.

Aitchison, K., and Edwards, R. 2008. *Archaeology Labour Market Intelligence: Profiling the Profession 2007/08*. Chartered Institute for Archaeologists.

Aitchison, K., and Rocks-Macqueen, D. 2014. *Discovering the Archaeologists of the United Kingdom 2012–14*. European Commission, www.discovering-archaeologists.eu/national_ reports/2014/UK%20DISCO%202014%20UK%20national%20report%20english.pdf.

Aitchison, K., and Rocks-Macqueen, D. 2020. *State of the Archaeological Market 2019*, https:// famearchaeology.co.uk/wp-content/uploads/2020/07/State-of-the-Archaeological-Market-2019.pdf.

Altschul, J., and Patterson, T. 2008. Trends in Employment and Training in American Archaeology, in W. Ashmore, D. Lippert and B. J. Mills (eds), *Voices in American Archaeology*. Society for American Archaeology Press.

# References

American Anthropological Association. 2009. *Statements on Ethics: Principles of Professional Responsibility*, www.aaanet.org/committees/ethics/ethcode.htm.

Association Research Inc. (ARI). 2005. *Salary Survey Conducted for the Society for American Archaeology and Society for Historical Archaeology*. ARI, https://documents.saa.org/container/docs/default-source/doc-careerpractice/salary_survey2005.pdf?sfvrsn=44a76241_8.

ARI. 2006. *Needs Assessment Conducted for the Register of Professional Archaeologists*. ARI.

Atalay, S. 2006a. Decolonizing Archaeology, *American Indian Quarterly* 30(3–4): 269–79.

Atalay, S. 2006b. Indigenous Archaeology as Decolonizing Practice, *American Indian Quarterly* 30(3–4): 280–310.

Australian Archaeological Association. 2020. *Code of Ethics*, https://australianarchaeological?association.com.au/about/code-of-ethics/.

Barber, B., Carver, J., Hinton, P., and Nixon, T. 2008. *Archaeology and Development: A Good Practice Guide to Managing Risk and Maximising Benefit*. CIRIA.

Bass, G. 1966. *Archaeology under Water*. Thames and Hudson.

Baxter, J. 2002. Popular Images and Popular Stereotypes: Images of Archaeologists in Popular and Documentary Film, *SAA Archaeological Record* 2(4): 16–17, 40.

Beck, W. 1994. Women and Archaeology in Australia, in C. Claassen (ed.), *Women in Archaeology*. University of Pennsylvania Press. 210–18.

Benjamin, R. 2003. Black and Asian Representation in UK Archaeology, *The Archaeologist* 48: 7–8.

Benjamin, R. 2004. Building a Black British Identity through Archaeology, *Archaeological Review from Cambridge* 19(2): 73–83.

Bowens, A. (ed.). 2009. *Underwater Archaeology: The NAS Guide to Principles and Practice*. Blackwell.

Bruchac, M., Hart, S., and Wobst, H. (eds). 2010. *Indigenous Archaeologies*. Left Coast Press.

Budhwa, R. 2005. An Alternate Model for First Nations Involvement in Resource Management Archaeology, *Canadian Journal of Archaeology* 29: 20–45.

Byrne, D. 1991. Western Hegemony in Archaeological Heritage Management, *History and Anthropology* 5: 269–76.

Canadian Archaeological Association. 2020. *Statement of Principles for Ethical Conduct Pertaining to Aboriginal Peoples*, https://canadianarchaeology.com/caa/bout/ethics/statement-principles-ethical-conduct-pertaining-to-aboriginal-peoples.

Carballal Staedtler, M., and Moguel Cos, M. 2007. Salvage and Rescue Archaeology in Mexico, *The SAA Archaeological Record* 7: 23–25.

Chadra, A. 2010. The Archaeological Survey of India and the Science of Postcolonial Archaeology, in J. Lydon and U. Rizvi (eds), *Handbook of Postcolonial Archaeology*. Left Coast Press. 227–33.

Chari, S., and Lavallee, J. 2013. *Accomplishing NAGPRA: Perspectives on the Intent, Impact, and Future of the Native American Graves Protection and Repatriation Act*. Oregon State University Press.

Charlton, T., Fournier, P., and Otis Charlton, C. 2009. Historical Archaeology in Central and Northern Mesoamerica: Development and Current Status, in T. Majewski and D. Gaimster (eds), *International Handbook of Historical Archaeology*. Springer. 409–28.

Chartered Institute for Archaeologists. 2017. *Professional Practice Paper: An Introduction to Professional Ethics*, www.archaeologists.net/sites/default/files/03.%20CIfA%20Ethics%20Practice%20Paper%20digital.pdf.

Chartered Institute for Archaeologists. 2018. *Policy Statements: Equal Opportunities in Archaeology*, www.archaeologists.net/sites/default/files/Policy%20statements%20revised%20Aug%202018.pdf.

Chartered Institute for Archaeologists. 2019a. *Code of Conduct*, www.archaeologists.net/sites/default/files/Code%20of%20conduct%20revOct2019.pdf.

Chartered Institute for Archaeologists. 2019b. *Regulations for Professional Conduct*, www.archaeologists.net/sites/default/files/Regulations%20for%20professional%20conduct%20May%202019.pdf.

Chirikure, S., and Pwitti, G. 2008. Community Involvement in Archaeology and Heritage Management: Case Studies from Southern Africa and Elsewhere, *Current Anthropology* 49(3): 467–85.

Claassen, C. (ed.). 1994. *Women in Archaeology*. University of Pennsylvania Press.

Cleary, K., and McCullagh, N. 2014. *Discovering the Archaeologists of Ireland 2012–2014*. European Commission, www.discovering-archaeologists.eu/national_reports/2014/IE%20DISCO%202014%20Ireland%20national%20report%20english.pdf.

Cobb, H. 2015. A Diverse Profession? Challenging Inequalities and Diversifying Involvement in British Archaeology, in P. Everill and P. Irving (eds), *Rescue Archaeology @ 40*. RESCUE. 232–51.

Cobb, H., and Croucher. K. 2016. Personal, Political, Pedagogic: Challenging the Binary Bind in Archaeological Teaching, Learning and Fieldwork, *Journal of Archaeological Method and Theory* 23(3): 949–69.

Cobb, H., and Croucher. K. 2020. *Assembling Archaeology: Teaching, Practice, and Research*. Oxford University Press.

Colwell-Chanthaphonh, C., and Ferguson, T. (eds). 2008. *Collaboration in Archaeological Practice: Engaging Descendant Communities*. Left Coast Press.

Council for British Archaeology. 2012. *CBA Research Bulletin 2: Diversifying Participation in the Historic Environment Workforce*. UCL Centre for Applied Archaeology.

Darvill, T. 2008. *Concise Oxford Dictionary of Archaeology*. Oxford University Press.

Davis, M. 2005. *How Students Understand the Past: From Theory to Practice*. Left Coast Press.

DeBlasis, P. 2010. Twenty Years of Heritage Resource Management in Brazil: A Brief Evaluation (1986–2006), in P. M. Messenger and G. S. Smith (eds), *Cultural Heritage Management: A Global Perspective*. University Press of Florida. 38–47.

de Boer, T. 2004. *Shovel Bums: Comix of Archaeological Field Life*. Left Coast Press.

Delafons, J. 1997. *Politics and Preservation: Policy History of the Built Heritage, 1882–1996*. Spon.

Denhez, M. 2010. *Unearthing the Law: Archaeological Legislation on Lands in Canada*. SynParSys Consulting.

DigVentures. 2018. *Learning Agreement*, Digventures.com

Doeser, J. 2010. *Diversifying Participation in the Historic Environment Workforce*, www.ucl.ac.uk/caa/Projects/Projects/index.htm.

Dromgoole, S. (ed.). 1999. *Legal Protection of the Underwater Cultural Heritage: National and International Perspectives*. Kluwer.

Dromgoole, S. (ed.). 2013. *Underwater Cultural Heritage and International Law*. Cambridge University Press.

Dowson, T. 2000. Why Queer Archaeology? An Introduction, *World Archaeology* 32(2): 161–65.

Dowson, T. 2005. Que(e)rying Archaeology's Loss of Innocence, *The Debitage* 3(1): 7–11.

Everill, P. 2012. *The Invisible Diggers: A Study of British Commercial Archaeology*. Oxbow.

Fagan, G. 2006. *Archaeological Fantasies: How Pseudoarchaeology Misrepresents the Past and Misleads the Public*. Routledge.

Ferris, N. 2003. Between Colonial and Indigenous Archaeologies: Legal and Extra-Legal Ownership of the Archaeological Past in North America, *Canadian Journal of Archaeology* 27: 154–90.

# References

Flannery, K. 1982. The Golden Marshalltown: A Parable for the Archeology of the 1980s, *American Anthropologist* (New Series) 84(2): 265–78.

Fridman, F., de Araújo, A., and Daibert, A. 2019. Public Policies for the Preservation of Historical Heritage in Brazil. Three Case Studies (1973–2016), *Revista Brasileira de Estudos Urbanos e Regionais* 21(3): 621–38.

Fritz, J., and Plog, F. 1970. The Nature of Archaeological Explanation, *American Antiquity* 35(4): 405–12.

Funari, P. 2004. Public Archaeology in Brazil, in N. Merriman (ed.), *Public Archaeology*. Routledge. 202–10.

Funari, P., and Bezerra, M. 2012. Public Archaeology in Latin America, in R. Skeates, C. McDavid and J. Carman (eds), *The Oxford Handbook of Public Archaeology*. Oxford University Press. 100–115.

Funari, P., and de Carvalho, A. 2009. The Uses of Archaeology: A Plea for Diversity, *Archaeological Dialogues* 16(2): 179–81.

Funari, P., and Menezes Ferreira, L. 2006. A Social History of Brazilian Archaeology: A Case Study, *Bulletin for the History of Archaeology* 16: 18–27.

García Bárcena, J. 2007. Law and the Practice of Archaeology in Mexico, *The SAA Archaeological Record* 7: 14–15.

Garrow, B., Garrow, P., and Thomas, P. 1994. Women in Contract Archaeology, in C. Claassen (ed.), *Women in Archaeology*. University of Pennsylvania Press. 182–201.

Gaur, A., and Vora, K. 2011. Maritime Archaeological Studies in India, in A. Catsambis, B. Ford and D. Hamilton (eds), *The Oxford Handbook of Maritime Archaeology*. Oxford University Press. 513–34.

Gnecco, C., and Ayala, P. 2012. *Indigenous Peoples and Archaeology in Latin America*. Routledge.

Gorman, A. 2019. *Dr Spacejunk vs the Universe*. NewSouth.

Greenfield, J. 2003. *The Return of Cultural Treasures*. Cambridge University Press.

Gruber, S. 2007. Protecting China's Cultural Heritage Sites in Times of Rapid Change: Current Developments, Practice and Law, *Asia Pacific Journal of Environmental Law* 253: 253–301.

Gould, D. 2020. *Historical Archaeology and Indigenous Collaboration: Discovering Histories That Have Futures*. University Press of Florida.

Guo, Y., Zan, L., and Liu, S. 2008. *The Management of Cultural Heritage in China*. Egea.

Hall, M. 2005. Situational Ethics and Engaged Practice: The Case of Archaeology in Africa, in L. Meskell and P. Pels (eds), *Embedding Ethics: Shifting Boundaries of the Anthropological Profession*. Berg. 169–96.

Hawkins, K., and Rees, C. 2018. *RESPECT – Acting against Harassment in Archaeology*, BAJR Guide 44, www.bajr.org/BAJRGuides/44.%20Harrasment/Sexual-Harassment-in-Archaeology.pdf.

Heritage Alliance. 2020. *Heritage, Health and Wellbeing*, www.theheritagealliance.org.uk/wp-content/uploads/2020/10/Heritage-Alliance-AnnualReport_2020_Online.pdf.

Hicks, D. 2020. *The Brutish Museum: Tthe Benin Bronzes, Colonial Violence and Cultural Restitution*. Pluto.

Hinds, B. 2017. Twenty-Five Years Later: The Amendments to the National Historic Preservation Act and Tribal Consultation, *American Indian Law Review* 42(1): 141–71.

Historic England. 2019. *Heritage and the Economy 2019*, https://historicengland.org.uk/content/heritage-counts/pub/2019/heritage-and-the-economy-2019/.

Historic England. 2020. *Heritage and the Economy 2020*, https://historicengland.org.uk/content/heritage-counts/pub/2020/heritage-and-the-economy-2020/.

Holtorf, C. 2005. *From Stonehenge to Las Vegas: Archaeology as Popular Culture*. Left Coast Press.

Holtorf, C. 2007a. *Archaeology Is a Brand! The Meaning of Archaeology in Contemporary Popular Culture*. Archaeopress.

Holtorf, C. 2007b. An Archaeological Fashion Show: How Archaeologists Dress and How They Are Portrayed in the Media, in T. Clack and M. Brittain (eds), *Archaeology and the Media*. Left Coast Press. 69–88.

Hudson, K. 1981. *A Social History of Archaeology: The British Experience*. Macmillan.

Hunter, J., and Ralston, I. (eds). 2006. *Archaeological Resource Management in the UK: An Introduction*. Sutton.

ISGAP. 2012. *National Occupational Standards for Archaeology*, https://isgap.org.uk/.

Johnson, M. 2019. *Archaeological Theory: An Introduction*. Wiley-Blackwell.

Jones, B. 1984. *Past Imperfect: The Story of Rescue Archaeology*. Heinemann.

Jourdane, J. 2017. *Fieldwork Fail: The Messy Side of Science*. Makisapa Editions.

Kalman, H. 2014. *Heritage Planning: Principles and Process*. Routledge.

King, T. 2002. *Thinking about Cultural Resource Management: Essays from the Edge*. Left Coast Press.

King, T. 2009. *Our Unprotected Heritage: Whitewashing the Destruction of Our Cultural and Natural Environment*. Left Coast Press.

King, T. 2012. *Cultural Resource Laws and Practice*. Left Coast Press.

King, T. 2016a. *Saving Places That Matter: A Citizen's Guide to the National Historic Preservation Act*. Routledge.

King, T. 2016b. *Doing Archaeology: A Cultural Resource Management Perspective*. Left Coast Press.

Kohl, P., and Fawcett, C. (eds). 1995. *Nationalism, Politics and the Practice of Archaeology*. Cambridge University Press.

Lbova, L., and Sklyarevskyi, M. 2006. The Management of History, in V. Molodin (ed.), *State Protection in the Sphere of Archaeological Heritage*. NSU.

Lee, E. 2002. Archaeology and the Public Cultural Conscience in Canada: The Federal Story, *Journal of American Archaeology* 21: 45–51.

Lenegan, C. 2005. *Resourcing an Innovative Industry: Minerals Week 2005 Address on 'the Minerals Sector and Indigenous Relations'*. www.atns.net.au/papers/Lenegan.pdf.

Lennon, J., et al. 2001. *Natural and Cultural Heritage Theme Report: Australia State of the Environment Report 2001*, www.environment.gov.au/soe/2001/publications/theme-reports/heritage/pubs/heritage.pdf.

Lovata, T. 2007. *Inauthentic Archaeologies: Public Uses and Abuses of the Past*. Left Coast Press.

Luna Erreguerena, P. 2008. The Submerged Cultural Heritage in Mexico, in M. Leshikar-Denton and P. Luna Erreguerena (eds), *Underwater and Maritime Archaeology in Latin America and the Caribbean*. Left Coast Press. 55–65.

Makarov, N. 2004. *Predatory Excavations as a Factor in the Destruction of the Archaeological Heritage of Russia*. Russian Institute of Archaeology.

Mate, G., and Ulm, S. 2016. Another Snapshot for the Album: A Decade of Australian Archaeology in Profile Survey Data, *Australian Archaeology* 82(2): 168–83.

Mazurov, U. (ed.). 2001. *Methodical Recommendations for the Environmental Monitoring of Immovable Cultural Heritage*. Institute of Heritage.

McDermott, C., and La Piscopia, P. 2008. *Discovering the Archaeologists of Europe: Ireland*. Institute of Archaeologists of Ireland, www.discovering-archaeologists.eu/national reports/DISCO national Ireland Final Web.pdf.

McGhee, R. 2008. Aboriginalism and the Problems of Indigenous Archaeology, *American Antiquity* 73(4): 579–97.

# References

McGrail, S. 2001. *Boats of the World*. Oxford University Press.

Membury, S. 2002. The Celluloid Archaeologist: An X-Rated Exposé, in M. Russell (ed.), *Digging Holes in Popular Culture: Archaeology and Science Fiction*. Oxbow. 8–18.

Mickel, A. 2021. *Why Those Who Shovel Are Silent: A History of Local Archaeological Knowledge and Labor*. University of Colorado Press.

Moshenska, G. 2009. Second World War Archaeology in Schools: A Backdoor to the History Curriculum?, *Papers from the Institute of Archaeology* 19: 55–66.

Muckelroy, K. 1978. *Maritime Archaeology*. Cambridge University Press.

Nelson, M., Nelson, S., and Wylie, A. (eds). 1994. *Equity Issues for Women in Archaeology*. American Anthropological Association.

Neumann, T. W., and Sanford, R. M. 2001. *Practicing Archaeology: A Training Manual for Cultural Resources Archaeology*. Left Coast Press.

Nicholas, G. 2008. Native Peoples and Archaeology (Indigenous Archaeology), in D. Pearsall (ed.), *The Encyclopedia of Archaeology*. Elsevier. 1660–69.

Nicholas, G. 2010. *Being and Becoming Indigenous Archaeologists*. Left Coast Press.

O'Mahony, T. 2015. Enabled Archaeology: Working with Disability, *BAJR Guide*, www .bajr.org/BAJRGuides/41_Enabled_Archaeology/41EnabledArchaeology.pdf.

O'Mahony, T. 2018. Reflections in UK Archaeology: A Personal Journey in Academic Life, *Journal of Community Archaeology & Heritage* 5(3): 216–18.

Paddayya, K. 1996. Modern Impacts on Archaeological Sites in India: A Case Study from the Shorapur Doab, Karnataka, *Man and Environment* 21: 75–88.

Parks Canada. 2005. *Guidelines for the Management of Archaeological Resources*. Parks Canada.

Patterson, T. C. 1994. *Toward a Social History of Archaeology in the United States*. Harcourt Brace.

Perry, S. 2019. *Six Fieldwork Expectations: Code of Conduct for Teams on Field Projects*, https:// saraperry.wordpress.com/2018/05/04/fieldwork-code-of-conduct/.

Philips, J. E. (ed.). 2005. *Writing African History*. University of Rochester Press.

Phillips, T., and Creighton, J. 2012. *Disability and the Archaeological Profession, Employing People with Disabilities: Good Practice Guidance for Archaeologists*. CIfA Professional Practice Paper No. 9, www.archaeologists.net/sites/default/files/Disabilitypaper.pdf.

Phillips, T., and Gilchrist, R. 2005. *Inclusive, Accessible, Archaeology. Phase 1: Disability and Archaeological Fieldwork*. University of Reading and Bournemouth University, https:// archaeologydataservice.ac.uk/archiveDS/archiveDownload?t=arch-736-1/dissemination/ pdf/iaa_phase_1/iaa_phase_1_report.pdf.

Phillips, T., Gilchrist, R., Hewitt, I., Le Scouiller, S., Booy, D., and Cook, G. 2007. *Inclusive, Accessible, Archaeology: Good Practice Guidelines for Including Disabled Students and Self-Evaluation in Archaeological Fieldwork Training*. Higher Education Academy, www .heacademy.ac.uk/hca/archaeology/features.resources/guides.

Poirier, D., and Feder, K. (eds). 2001. *Dangerous Places: Heath, Safety and Archaeology*. Bergin and Garvey.

Praetzellis, A. 2000. *Death by Theory: A Tale of Mystery and Archaeological Theory*. Left Coast Press.

Praetzellis, A. 2003. *Dug to Death: A Tale of Archaeological Method and Mayhem*. Left Coast Press.

Procter, A. 2020. *The Whole Picture: The Colonial Story of the Art in Our Museums and Why We Need to Talk About It*. Cassell.

Quality Assurance Agency for Higher Education (QAA). 2014. *Subject Benchmark Statement: Archaeology*, www.qaa.ac.uk/docs/qaa/subject-benchmark-statements/sbs-archaeology-14.pdf.

266

Rahtz, P. 1974. *Rescue Archaeology*. Penguin.

Ramos, M., and Duganne, D. 2000. *Exploring Public Perceptions and Attitudes about Archaeology*. Society for American Archaeology, www.saa.org/Portals/0/SAA/pubedu/nrptdraft4.pdf

Reilly, S., Nolan, C., and Monckton, L. 2018. *Wellbeing and the Historic Environment*. Historic England, https://historicengland.org.uk/images-books/publications/wellbeing-and-the-historic-environment/wellbeing-and-historic-environment/.

Register of Professional Archaeologists. 2009. *Code of Conduct*, www.rpanet.org/displaycommon.cfm?an=1&subarticlenbr=3.

Robinson, W. 1998. *First Aid for Underwater Finds*. Archetype.

Robles García, N. 2010. Indigenous Archaeology in Mexico, Recognizing Distinctive Histories, in G. Nicholas (ed.), *Being and Becoming Indigenous Archaeologists*. Left Coast Press. 277–86.

Rocks-Macqueen, D. 2014a. Jobs in American Archaeology: Pay for CRM Archaeologists, *Archaeologies: Journal of the World Archaeological Congress* 10(3): 281–96.

Rocks-Macqueen, D. 2014b. Professional Archaeology: Disability Friendly? *Doug's Archaeology: Investigating the Profession and Research*, https://dougsarchaeology.wordpress.com/2014/08/11/professional-archaeology-disability-friendly.

Rocks-Macqueen, D., and Lewis, B. 2019. *Archaeology in Development Management: Its Contribution in England, Scotland and Wales*. Landward, www.algao.org.uk/sites/default/files/documents/Archaeology_in_Development_Management.pdf.

Rothfield, L. 2009. *The Rape of Mesopotamia: Behind the Looting of the Iraq Museum*. University of Chicago Press.

Russell, M. (ed.). 2002a. *Digging Holes in Popular Culture: Archaeology and Science Fiction*. Oxbow.

Russell, M. 2002b. 'No More Heroes Any More': The Dangerous World of the Pop Culture Archaeologist, in M. Russell (ed.), *Digging Holes in Popular Culture: Archaeology and Science Fiction*. Oxbow. 38–54.

Sabloff, J. 2008. *Archaeology Matters: Action Archaeology in the Modern World*. Left Coast Press.

Scheermeyer, C. 2005. A Changing and Challenging Landscape: Heritage Resources Management in South Africa, *The South African Archaeological Bulletin* 60: 121–23.

Schlanger, N., and Aitchison, K. (eds). 2010. *Archaeology and the Global Economic Crisis: Multiple Impacts, Possible Solutions*. Culture Lab Editions, https://landward.eu/wp-content/uploads/2010/10/2010_25Archaeology-and-the-crisis.pdf.

Schlatter, N. 2008. *Museum Careers: A Practical Guide for Students and Novices*. Left Coast Press.

Selvakumar, V. 2006. Public Archaeology in India: Perspectives from Kerala, *India Review* 5: 417–46.

Shen, C., and Chen, H. 2010. Cultural Heritage Management in China: Current Practices and Problems, in P. Messenger and G. Smith (eds), *Cultural Heritage Management: A Global Perspective*. University Press of Florida. 70–81.

Silliman, S. (ed). 2008. *Collaborating at the Trowel's Edge: Teaching and Learning in Indigenous Archaeology*. University of Arizona Press.

Smirnov, A. 2004. Protection of Archaeological Heritage in the Federal Law 'On Objects of Cultural Heritage (Monuments of History and Culture of the Peoples of the Russian Federation', in *Proceedings of the Round Table of the Federation Council Conservation of the Archaeological Heritage of Russia*. Russian Federation.

Smith, C. (ed.). 2014. *Encyclopedia of Global Archaeology*. Springer.

Smith, C., and Burke, H. 2007. *Digging It Up Down Under: A Practical Guide to Doing Archaeology in Australia*. Springer.

# References

Smith, C., and Jackson, G. 2006. Decolonizing Indigenous Archaeology: Developments from Down Under, *American Indian Quarterly* 30(3–4): 311–49.

Smith, C., and Wobst, H. (eds). 2005. *Indigenous Archaeologies: Decolonizing Theory and Practice*. Routledge.

Smith, L. 2001. *Archaeological Theory and the Politics of Cultural Heritage*. Routledge.

Smith, L. 2006. *Uses of Heritage*. Routledge.

Smith, L., and du Cros, H. 1991. *Equality and Gender in Australian Archaeology*, www.anthrosource.net.

Society for American Archaeology. 2009. *Principles of Archaeological Ethics*, www.saa.org/AbouttheSociety/PrinciplesofArchaeologicalEthics/tabid/203/Default.aspx.

Society for American Archaeology. 2018. *Ipsos American Perceptions of Archaeology Poll*, www.saa.org/education-outreach/public-outreach/public-perceptions-studies.

Society for Historical Archaeology. 2009. *Ethical Principles*, www.sha.org/about/ethics.cfm.

Stolte, G. 2020. *Aboriginal and Torres Strait Islander Art: An Anthropology of Identity Production in Far North Queensland*. Routledge.

Su, X. B., and Teo, P. 2009. *The Politics of Heritage in China: A View from Lijiang*. Routledge.

Talalay, L. 2004. The Past as Commodity: Archaeological Images in Modern Advertising, *Public Archaeology* 3: 205–16.

Trümpler, C. (ed.). 2001. *Agatha Christie and Archaeology*. British Museum.

Turnbull, P., and Pickering, M. (eds). 2010. *The Long Way Home: The Meaning and Values of Repatriation*. Berghahn.

Two Bears, D. 2006. Navajo Archaeologist Is Not an Oxymoron: A Tribal Archaeologist's Experience, *American Indian Quarterly* 30(3–4): 381–87.

Ucko, P., Ling, Q., and Hubert, J. (eds). 2007. *From Concepts of the Past to Practical Strategies: The Teaching of Archaeological Field Techniques*. Saffron.

Ulm, S., Nichols, S., and Dalley, C. 2005. Mapping the Shape of Contemporary Australian Archaeology, *Australian Archaeology* 61: 11–23.

Ulm, S., Mate, G., Dalley, C., and Nichols, S. 2013. A Working Profile: The Changing Face of Professional Archaeology in Australia, *Australian Archaeological Association, Australian Archaeology* 76: 34–43, https://researchonline.jcu.edu.au/23289/1/ulm_etal_2013b.pdf.

Underhill, A. 2013. *A Companion to Chinese Archaeology*. Wiley.

Vitelli, K., and Colwell-Chanthaphonh, C. (eds). 2006. *Archaeological Ethics*. Left Coast Press.

Walz, J. 2009. Archaeologies of Disenchantment, in P. R. Schmidt (ed.), *Postcolonial Archaeologies in Africa*. School for Advanced Research Press.

Watkins, J. 2000. *Indigenous Archaeology: American Indian Values and Scientific Practice*. Left Coast Press.

Watkins, J. 2002. Marginal Native, Marginal Archaeologist: Ethnic Disparity in American Archaeology, *SAA Archaeological Record* 2(4): 36–37.

Watkins, J. 2005. Artefacts, Archaeologists, and American Indians, *Public Archaeology* 4(2–3): 187–92.

Weiss, E., and Springer, J. W. 2020. *Repatriation and Erasing the Past*. University Press of Florida.

Wheeler, R. 1954 *Archaeology from the Earth*. Penguin.

White, W. 2016. *Becoming an Archaeologist: Crafting a Career in Cultural Resource Management*. Succinct Research.

Whittlesey, S. 1994. Academic Alternatives: Gender and CRM in Arizona, in C. Claassen (ed.), *Women in Archaeology*. University of Pennsylvania Press. 202–9.

Williams, H., Pudney, C., and Ezzeldi, A. (eds). 2019. *Public Archaeology: Arts of Engagement*. Archaeopress.

Wright, R. 2002. Gender Equity, Sexual Harassment and Professional Ethics, *SAA Archaeological Record* 2(4): 18–19.

Yingying Jing. 2019. Protection of Underwater Cultural Heritage in China: New Developments, *International Journal of Cultural Policy* 25(6): 756–64.

York Archaeological Trust. 2014. *Discovering the Archaeologists of Europe 2012–14: Transnational Report*. European Commission, www.discovering-archaeologists.eu/national_reports/2014/transnational_report.pdf.

Zan, L., and Bonini Baraldi, S. 2012. Managing Cultural Heritage in China: A View from the Outside, *China Quarterly* 210: 456–81.

Zarmati, L. 1995. Popular Archaeology and the Archaeologist as Hero, in J. Balme and W. Beck (eds), *Gendered Archaeology: The Second Australian Women in Archaeology Conference*. ANH Publications. 43–47.

Zeder, M. 2000. *The American Archaeologist: A Profile*. Left Coast Press.

Zorpidu, S. 2004. The Public Image of the Female Archaeologist: The Case of Lara Croft, in H. Bolin (ed.), *The Interplay of Past and Present*. Södertörns Högskola. 101–7.

# Index

271

# Index

# Index

Milton Keynes UK
Ingram Content Group UK Ltd.
UKHW022027300723
426060UK00033B/1153